COMICS

ROCKETS
Defying Gravity

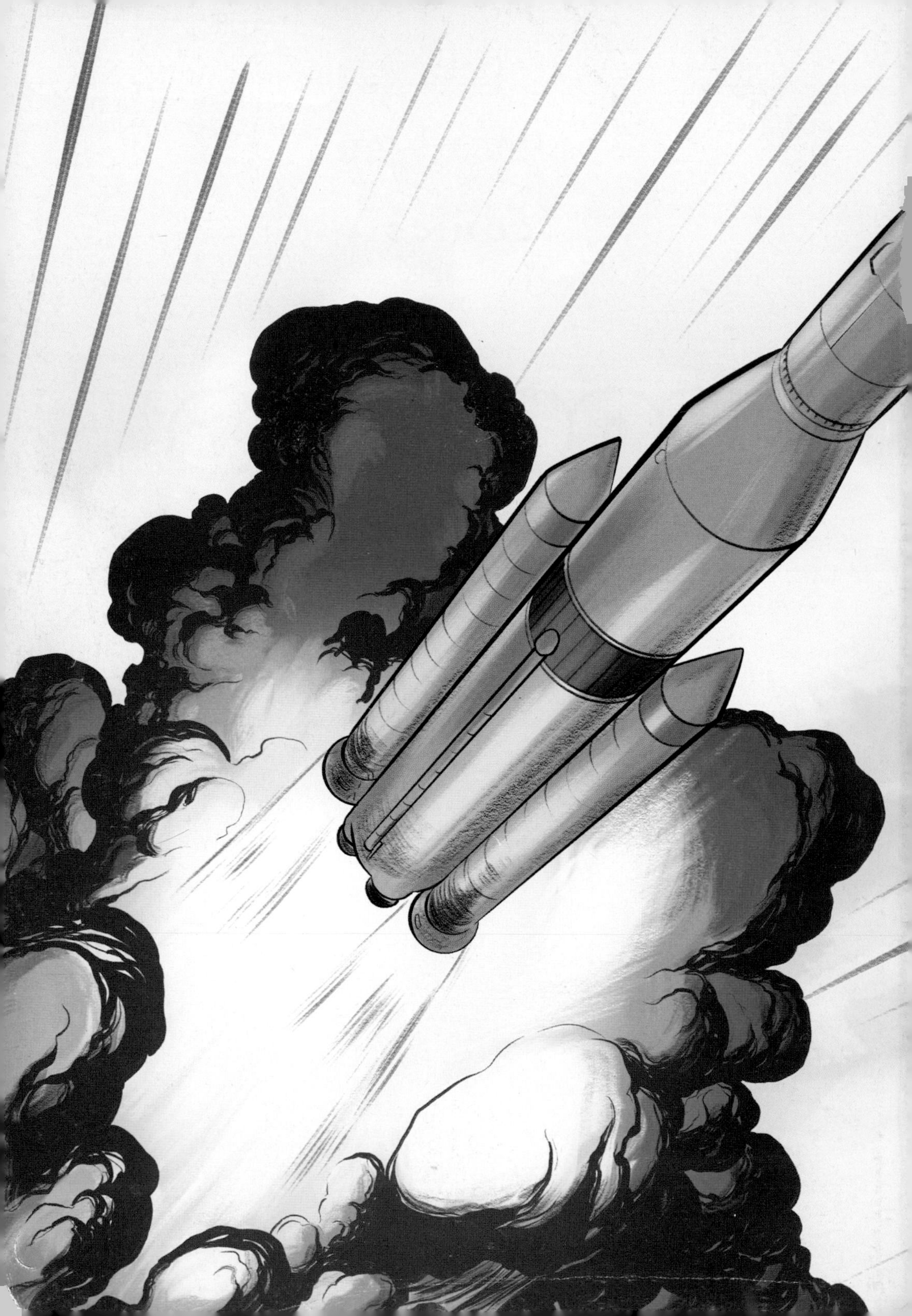

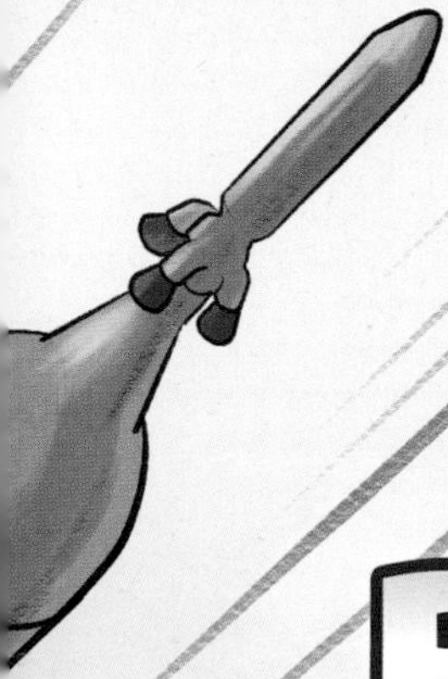

ROCKETS

Defying Gravity

Anne Drozd
Jerzy Drozd

First Second
New York

For all of the animals who helped humans
take rockets to the skies and beyond.

First Second

Penciled with a Pentel Twist-Erase pencil and Clip Studio Paint. Inked with a Kuretake G-Pen nib
on Strathmore 300 Series smooth Bristol, as well as self-made digital brushes in Clip Studio Paint.
Colored digitally in Clip Studio Paint and lettered in Adobe Illustrator.

Published by First Second
First Second is an imprint of Roaring Brook Press,
a division of Holtzbrinck Publishing Holdings Limited Partnership
175 Fifth Avenue, New York, NY 10010
All rights reserved

Library of Congress Congress Control Number: 2017946155

Paperback ISBN: 978-1-62672-825-7
Hardcover ISBN: 978-1-62672-826-4

Our books may be purchased in bulk for promotional, educational, or business use. Please
contact your local bookseller or the Macmillan Corporate and Premium Sales Department
at (800) 221-7945 ext. 5442 or by e-mail at MacmillanSpecialMarkets@macmillan.com.

First edition 2018
Edited by Dave Roman
Book design by John Green
Physics consultant: David Coupland

Printed in China by Toppan Leefung Printing Ltd., Dongguan City, Guangdong Province
Paperback: 10 9 8 7 6 5 4 3 2 1
Hardcover: 10 9 8 7 6 5 4 3 2 1

Ten. Nine. Eight. Seven . . .

Inside your head, you're already counting the rest of the way down, aren't you?

Three. Two. One. LIFTOFF!

A blinding flare of light. An intense roar. An enormous column of engineering slooooowwwwly begins to rise upward, speeding up, faster, faster. You crane your neck and try not to blink as the spacecraft disappears from sight, leaving an arc of white smoke behind. Maybe you wish you were on the rocket.

Rockets are scary. They contain huge amounts of incredibly explosive chemicals. On top of them, we put spacecraft that cost hundreds of millions of dollars. Sometimes we even put people up there. And then we light the rocket and hope for the best. Rocket scientists have a saying: a thousand things can happen during a rocket launch, and only one of them is good.

Despite how powerful and dangerous they are, rockets today are very reliable. Rockets have launched humans to the Moon, and could send people to Mars or asteroids soon. Robots have traveled farther. Inward to Venus and Mercury. Outward to Mars and the giant planets. Robots have landed on Mars and on Saturn's giant moon Titan and on

a comet named Churyumov-Gerasimenko. If you could launch a robot on a rocket, where would you explore?

Space explorers owe thanks to the pioneers of rocketry, and to the people who continue to make rockets lighter, more efficient, more reliable, more precise, and cheaper. You'll learn about some of them in this book.

When humans first started developing modern science and technology, scientists and engineers worked mostly alone, or in small groups. In a book like this one, we can name those original individuals—Isaac Newton, Claude Ruggieri, Qian Xuesen—but the more modern and complex science gets, the more people are involved; it's impossible to name all of them. That's a good thing, if you like space exploration, because there are more ways than ever to get involved.

When we send an astronaut or a robot into space, it's never just one astronaut or robot doing the exploring. It takes thousands of people working in all kinds of roles to make a space mission a success. And they're not all genius inventors.

Do you like math and physics? You can be a rocket designer or an astronomer. Do you like chemistry and making things? You could

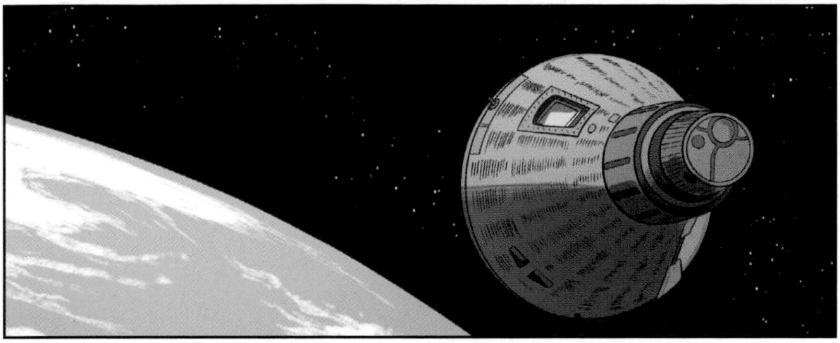

develop rocket fuel or study the minerals of other worlds. Do you like to code? You could write software for rockets or for driving robots on Mars. Are you the kind of person who worries about what will happen if something goes wrong on a rocket? There are jobs checking the work of the engineers to make sure they have made no mistakes. Do you like to take charge of group projects? All those scientists, engineers, and programmers work in teams that need to be coordinated to get big projects done. Do you like to write, tell stories, or create art? Space missions need educators, storytellers, technical writers, and press officers to explain to the world how all of this works.

When a robot sends pictures from Mars or Saturn and you look at them on your computer, you are part of that mission, exploring space through the robot's eyes. If you ask even one question, you're beginning to do science.

I hope you'll enjoy this introduction to rocketry, and that someday—whether you do it through a robot's eyes, or atop your own rocket—you get to explore space.

—Emily Lakdawalla,
planetary geologist, science writer,
and senior editor at the Planetary Society

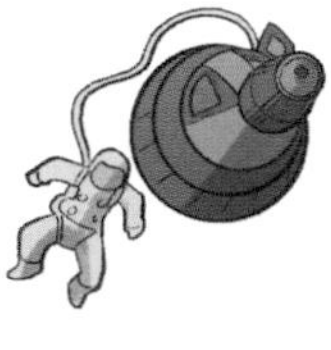

CHAPTER 1: WHAT MAKES ROCKETS GO

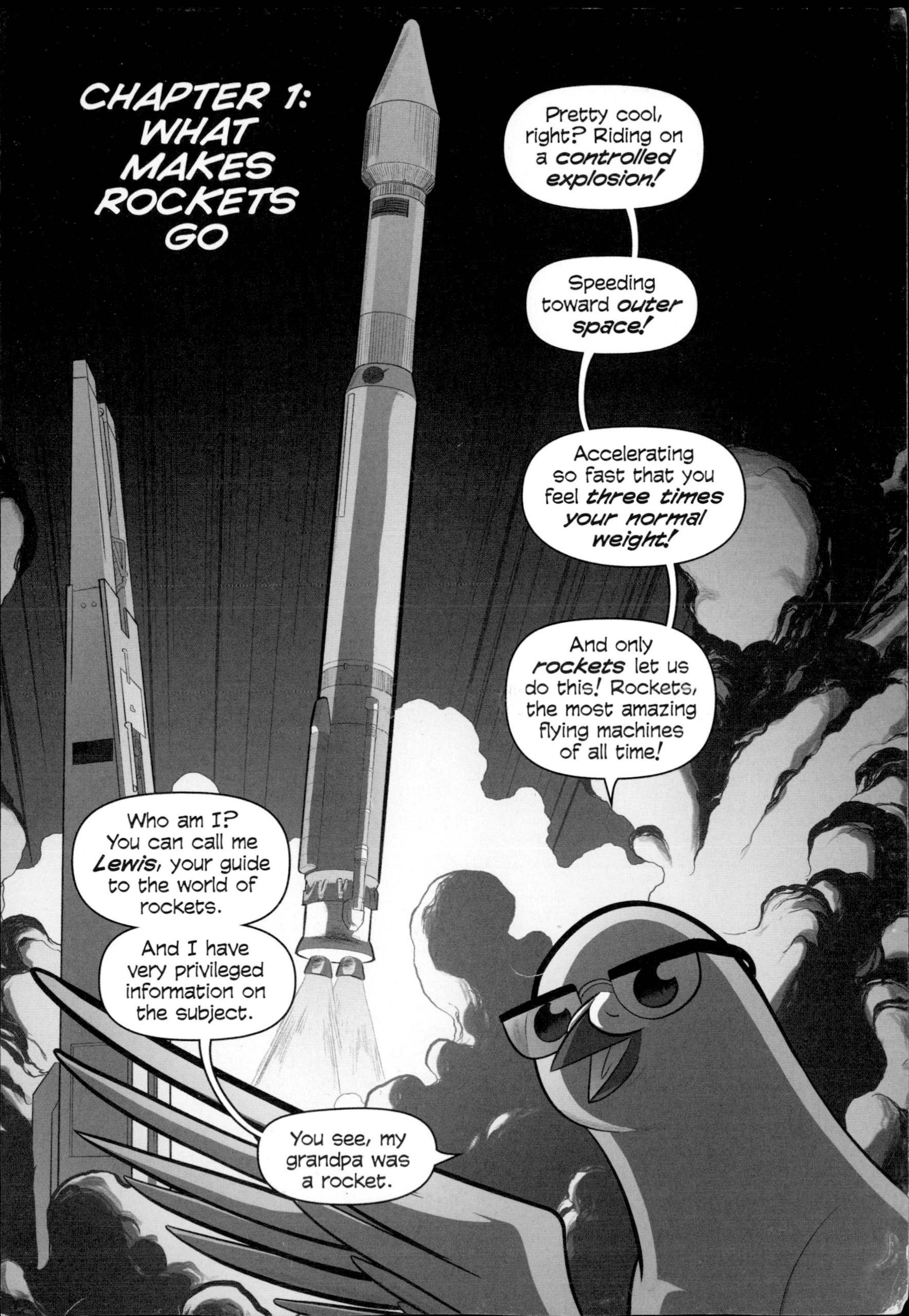

Pretty cool, right? Riding on a *controlled explosion!*
Speeding toward *outer space!*
Accelerating so fast that you feel *three times your normal weight!*
And only ***rockets*** let us do this! Rockets, the most amazing flying machines of all time!
Who am I? You can call me *Lewis*, your guide to the world of rockets.
And I have very privileged information on the subject.
You see, my grandpa was a rocket.

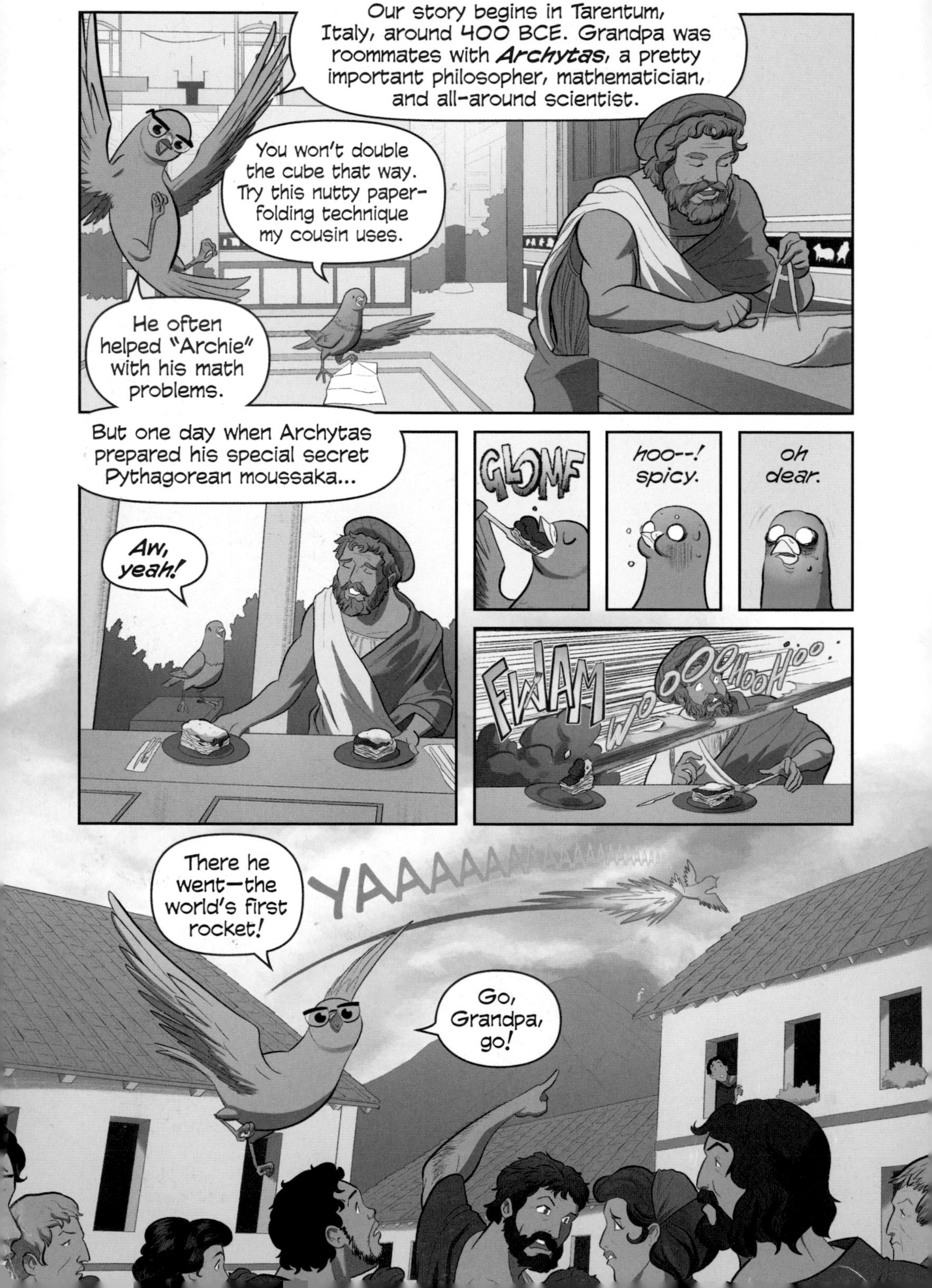
Our story begins in Tarentum, Italy, around 400 BCE. Grandpa was roommates with *Archytas*, a pretty important philosopher, mathematician, and all-around scientist.
You won't double the cube that way. Try this nutty paper-folding technique my cousin uses.
He often helped "Archie" with his math problems.
But one day when Archytas prepared his special secret Pythagorean moussaka...
Aw, yeah!
GLOMF
hoo--! spicy.
oh dear.
FWAM
WOOOOOHOOHOO
There he went—the world's first rocket!
YAAAAAAAAAAA
Go, Grandpa, go!

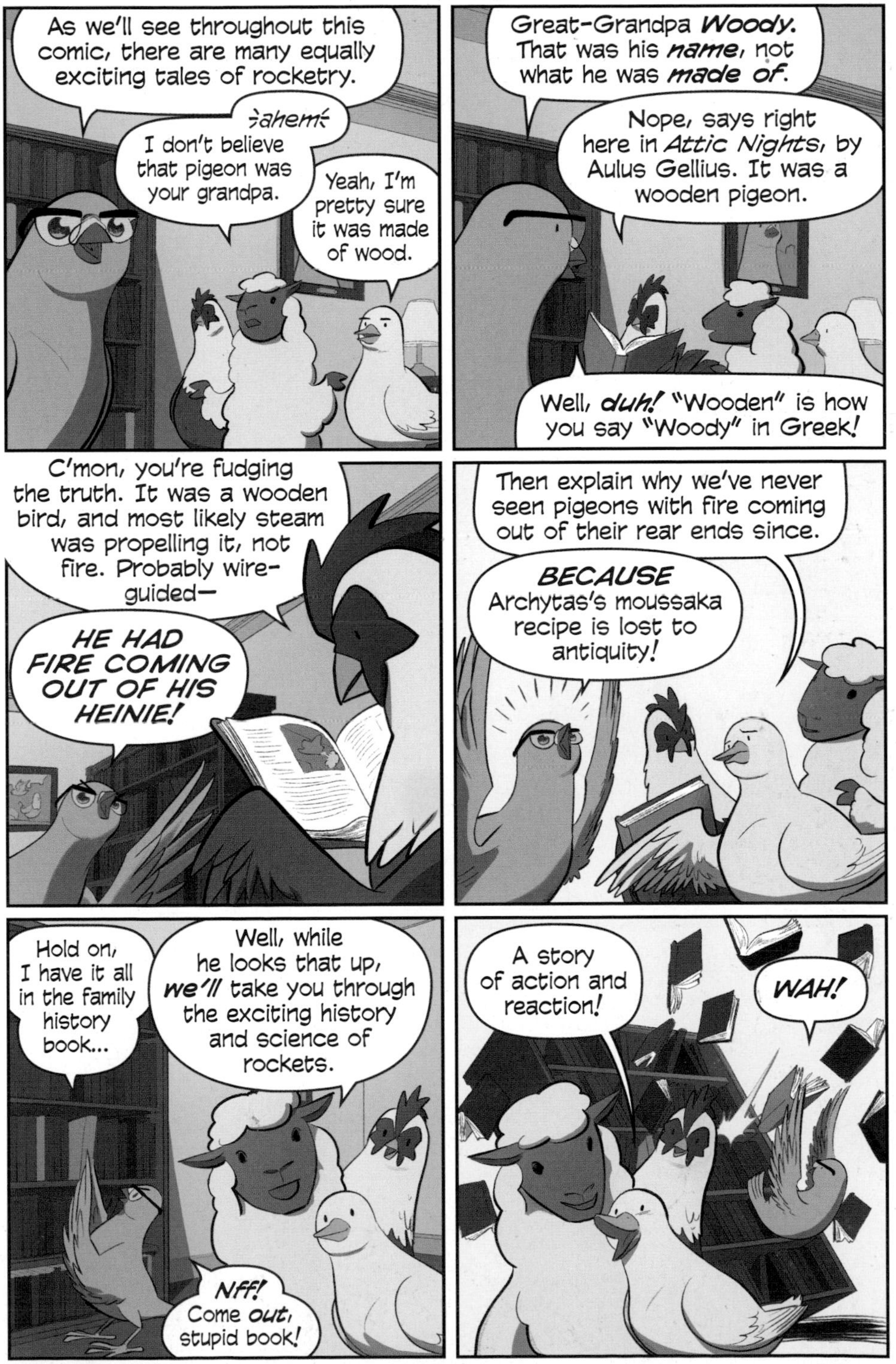
As we'll see throughout this comic, there are many equally exciting tales of rocketry.
ahem
I don't believe that pigeon was your grandpa.
Yeah, I'm pretty sure it was made of wood.
Great-Grandpa Woody. That was his name, not what he was made of.
Nope, says right here in Attic Nights, by Aulus Gellius. It was a wooden pigeon.
Well, duh! "Wooden" is how you say "Woody" in Greek!
C'mon, you're fudging the truth. It was a wooden bird, and most likely steam was propelling it, not fire. Probably wire-guided—
HE HAD FIRE COMING OUT OF HIS HEINIE!
Then explain why we've never seen pigeons with fire coming out of their rear ends since.
BECAUSE Archytas's moussaka recipe is lost to antiquity!
Hold on, I have it all in the family history book...
Well, while he looks that up, we'll take you through the exciting history and science of rockets.
Nff! Come out, stupid book!
A story of action and reaction!
WAH!

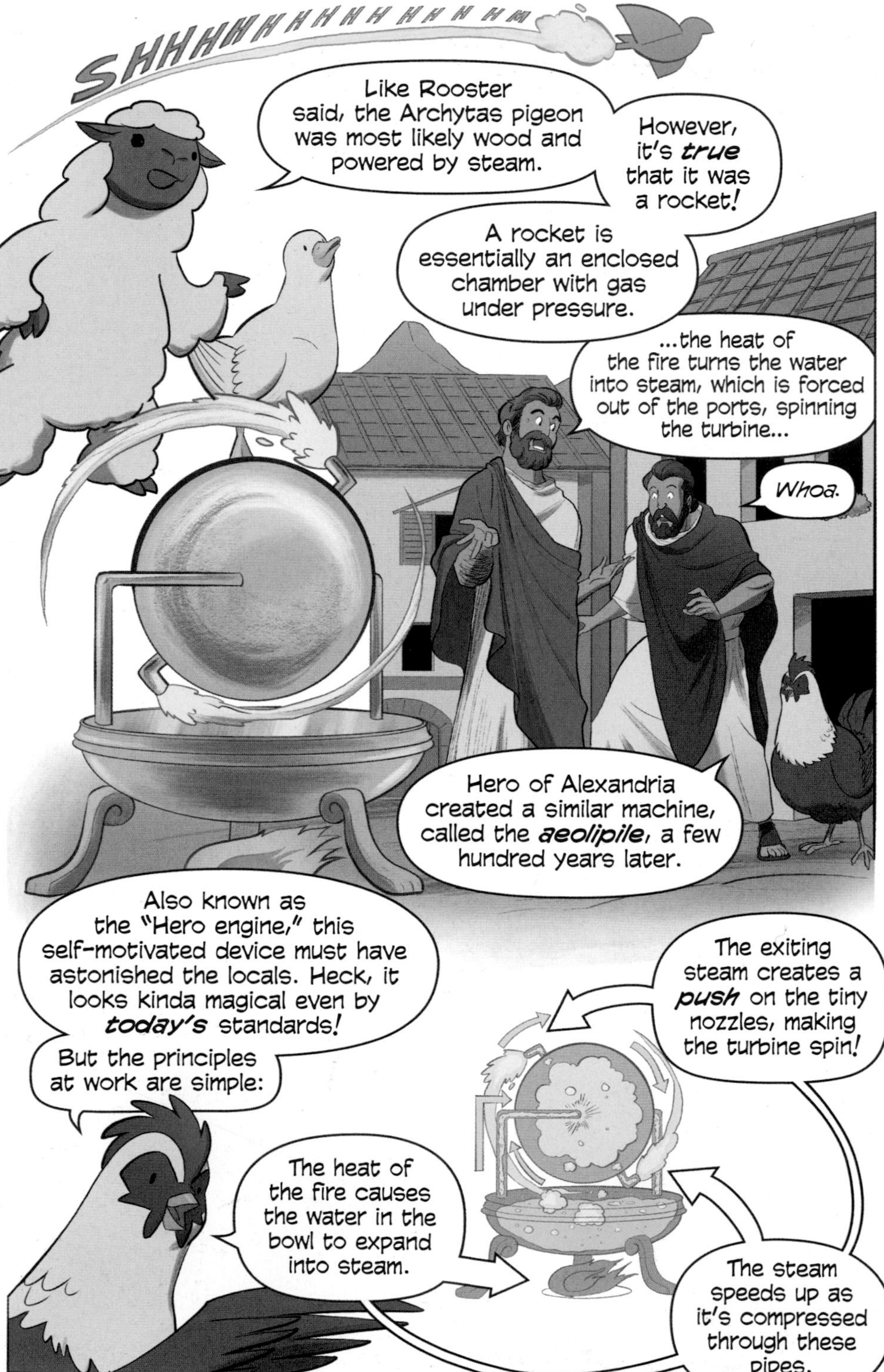
SHHHHHHHHHHHHHHM
Like Rooster said, the Archytas pigeon was most likely wood and powered by steam.
However, it's *true* that it was a rocket!
A rocket is essentially an enclosed chamber with gas under pressure.
...the heat of the fire turns the water into steam, which is forced out of the ports, spinning the turbine...
Whoa.
Hero of Alexandria created a similar machine, called the *aeolipile*, a few hundred years later.
Also known as the "Hero engine," this self-motivated device must have astonished the locals. Heck, it looks kinda magical even by *today's* standards!
But the principles at work are simple:
The heat of the fire causes the water in the bowl to expand into steam.
The steam speeds up as it's compressed through these pipes.
The exiting steam creates a *push* on the tiny nozzles, making the turbine spin!

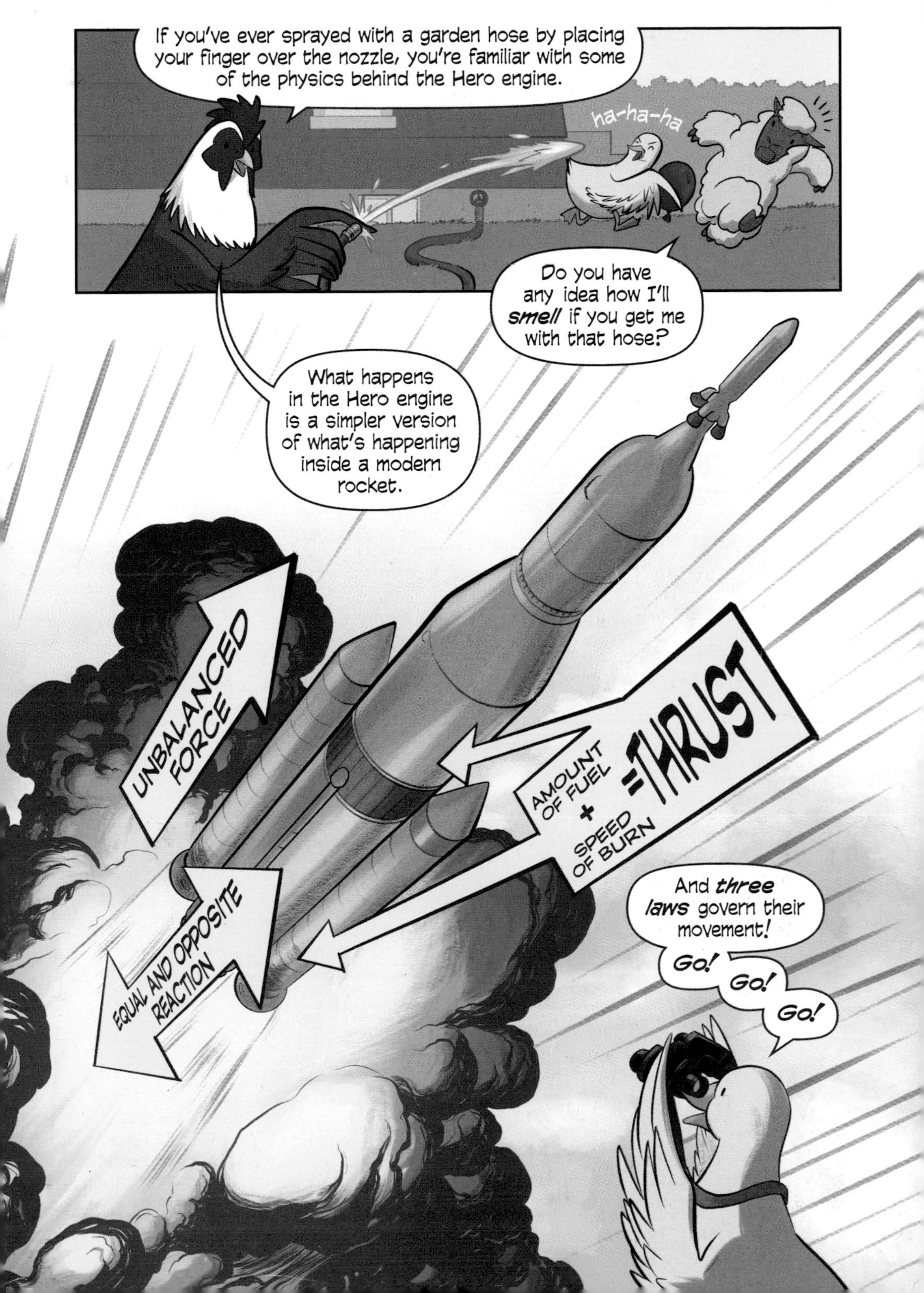

If you've ever sprayed with a garden hose by placing your finger over the nozzle, you're familiar with some of the physics behind the Hero engine.
ha-ha-ha
Do you have any idea how I'll *smell* if you get me with that hose?
What happens in the Hero engine is a simpler version of what's happening inside a modern rocket.
UNBALANCED FORCE
AMOUNT OF FUEL + SPEED OF BURN =THRUST
EQUAL AND OPPOSITE REACTION
And *three laws* govern their movement!
Go!
Go!
Go!

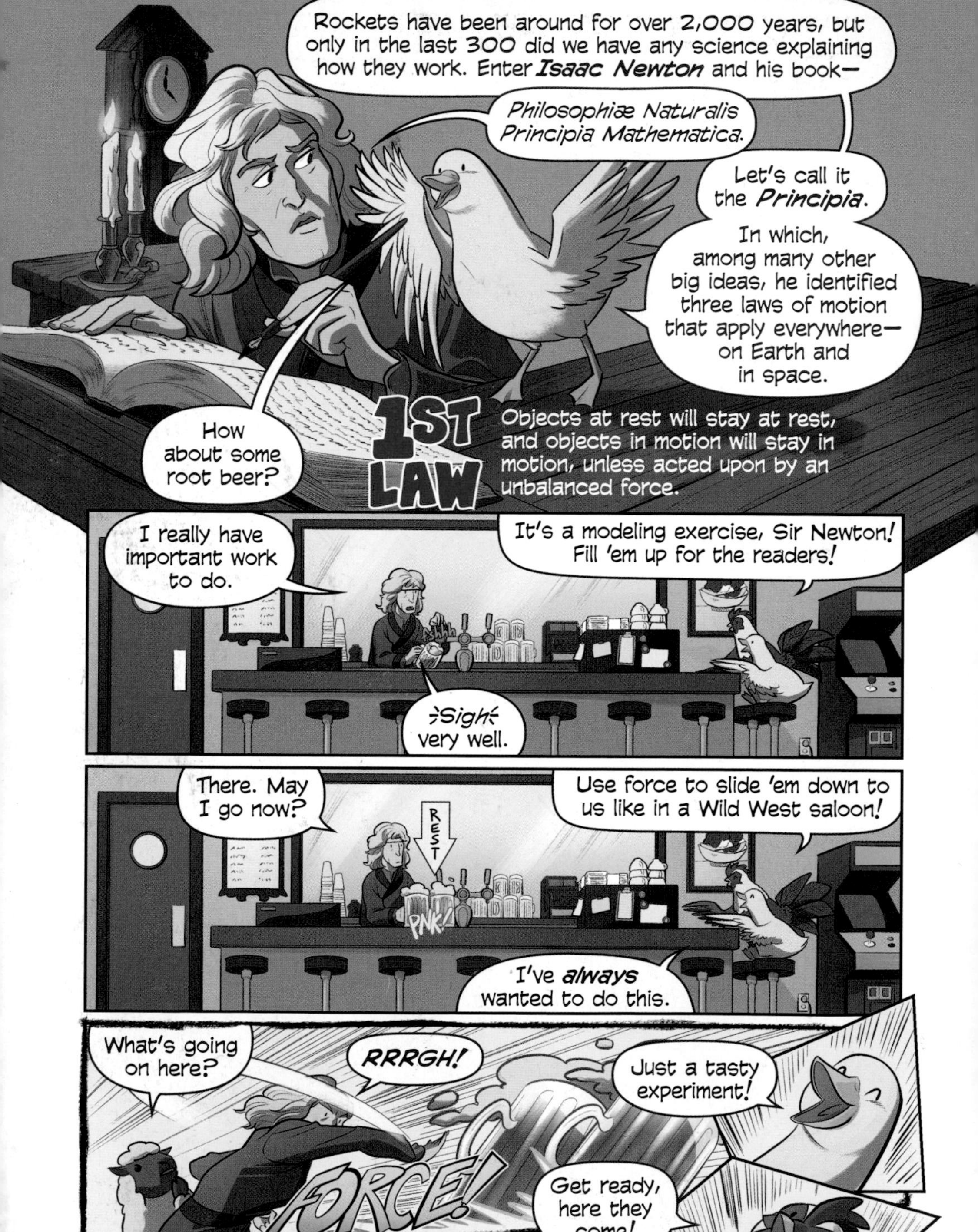

Rockets have been around for over 2,000 years, but only in the last 300 did we have any science explaining how they work. Enter ***Isaac Newton*** and his book—
Philosophiæ Naturalis Principia Mathematica.
Let's call it the ***Principia***.
In which, among many other big ideas, he identified three laws of motion that apply everywhere—on Earth and in space.
How about some root beer?
1ST LAW
Objects at rest will stay at rest, and objects in motion will stay in motion, unless acted upon by an unbalanced force.
I really have important work to do.
It's a modeling exercise, Sir Newton! Fill 'em up for the readers!
fshhh
Sigh very well.
There. May I go now?
Use force to slide 'em down to us like in a Wild West saloon!
REST
PNK!
I've ***always*** wanted to do this.
What's going on here?
RRRGH!
Just a tasty experiment!
FORCE!
Get ready, here they come!

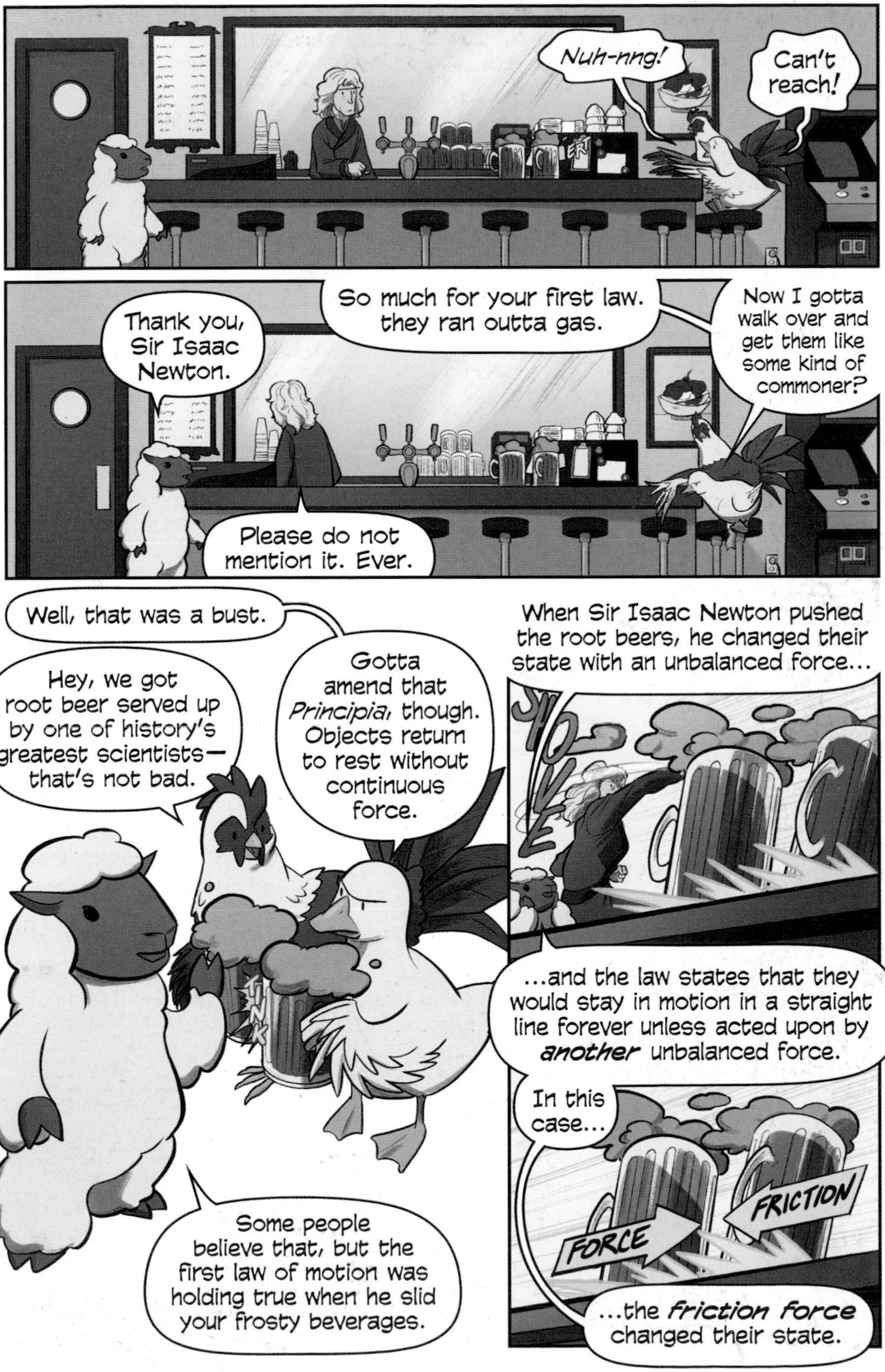

Nuh-nng!
Can't reach!
Thank you, Sir Isaac Newton.
So much for your first law. they ran outta gas.
Now I gotta walk over and get them like some kind of commoner?
Please do not mention it. Ever.
Well, that was a bust.
Hey, we got root beer served up by one of history's greatest scientists—that's not bad.
Gotta amend that *Principia*, though. Objects return to rest without continuous force.
Some people believe that, but the first law of motion was holding true when he slid your frosty beverages.
When Sir Isaac Newton pushed the root beers, he changed their state with an unbalanced force...
SHOVE
...and the law states that they would stay in motion in a straight line forever unless acted upon by ***another*** unbalanced force.
In this case...
FORCE
FRICTION
...the ***friction force*** changed their state.

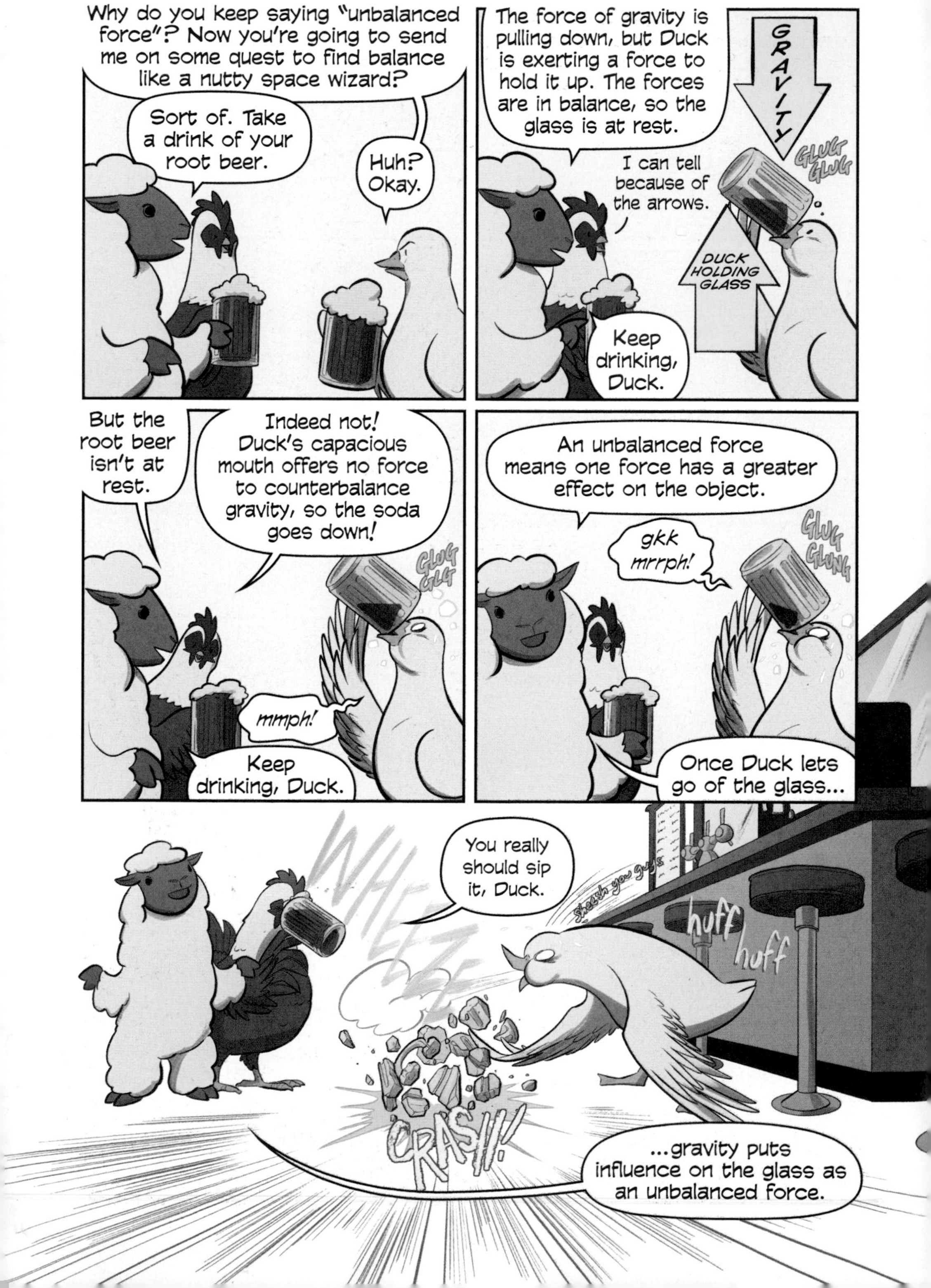

Why do you keep saying "unbalanced force"? Now you're going to send me on some quest to find balance like a nutty space wizard?
Sort of. Take a drink of your root beer.
Huh? Okay.
The force of gravity is pulling down, but Duck is exerting a force to hold it up. The forces are in balance, so the glass is at rest.
GRAVITY
GLUG GLUG
I can tell because of the arrows.
DUCK HOLDING GLASS
Keep drinking, Duck.
But the root beer isn't at rest.
Indeed not! Duck's capacious mouth offers no force to counterbalance gravity, so the soda goes down!
mmph!
Keep drinking, Duck.
An unbalanced force means one force has a greater effect on the object.
gkk mrrph!
Once Duck lets go of the glass...
You really should sip it, Duck.
WHEEZE
huff huff
CRASH!!
...gravity puts influence on the glass as an unbalanced force.

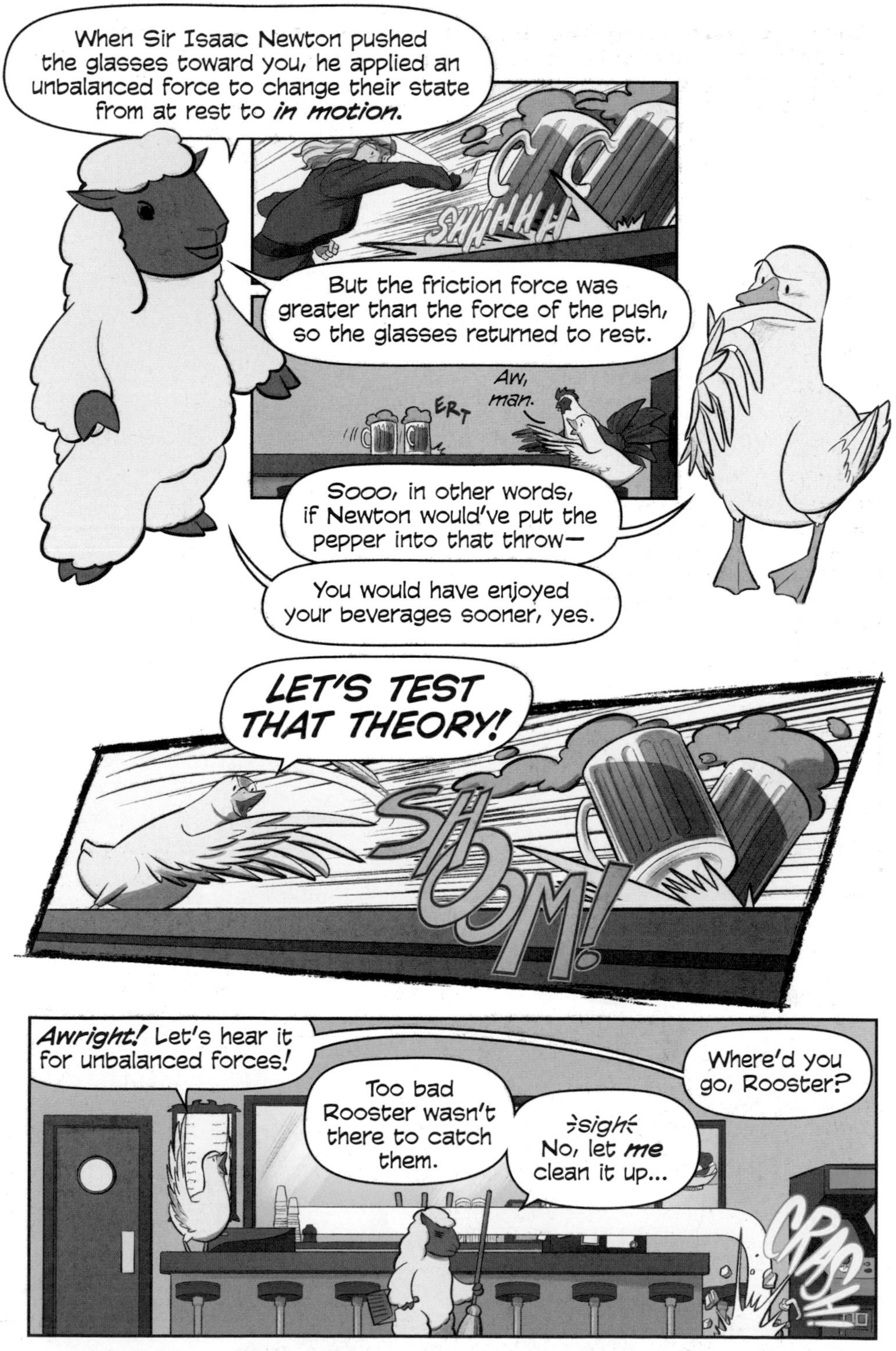

When Sir Isaac Newton pushed the glasses toward you, he applied an unbalanced force to change their state from at rest to *in motion.*
SHHHHH
But the friction force was greater than the force of the push, so the glasses returned to rest.
ERT
Aw, man.
Sooo, in other words, if Newton would've put the pepper into that throw—
You would have enjoyed your beverages sooner, yes.
LET'S TEST THAT THEORY!
SHOOM!
Awright! Let's hear it for unbalanced forces!
Where'd you go, Rooster?
Too bad Rooster wasn't there to catch them.
sigh No, let *me* clean it up...
CRASH!

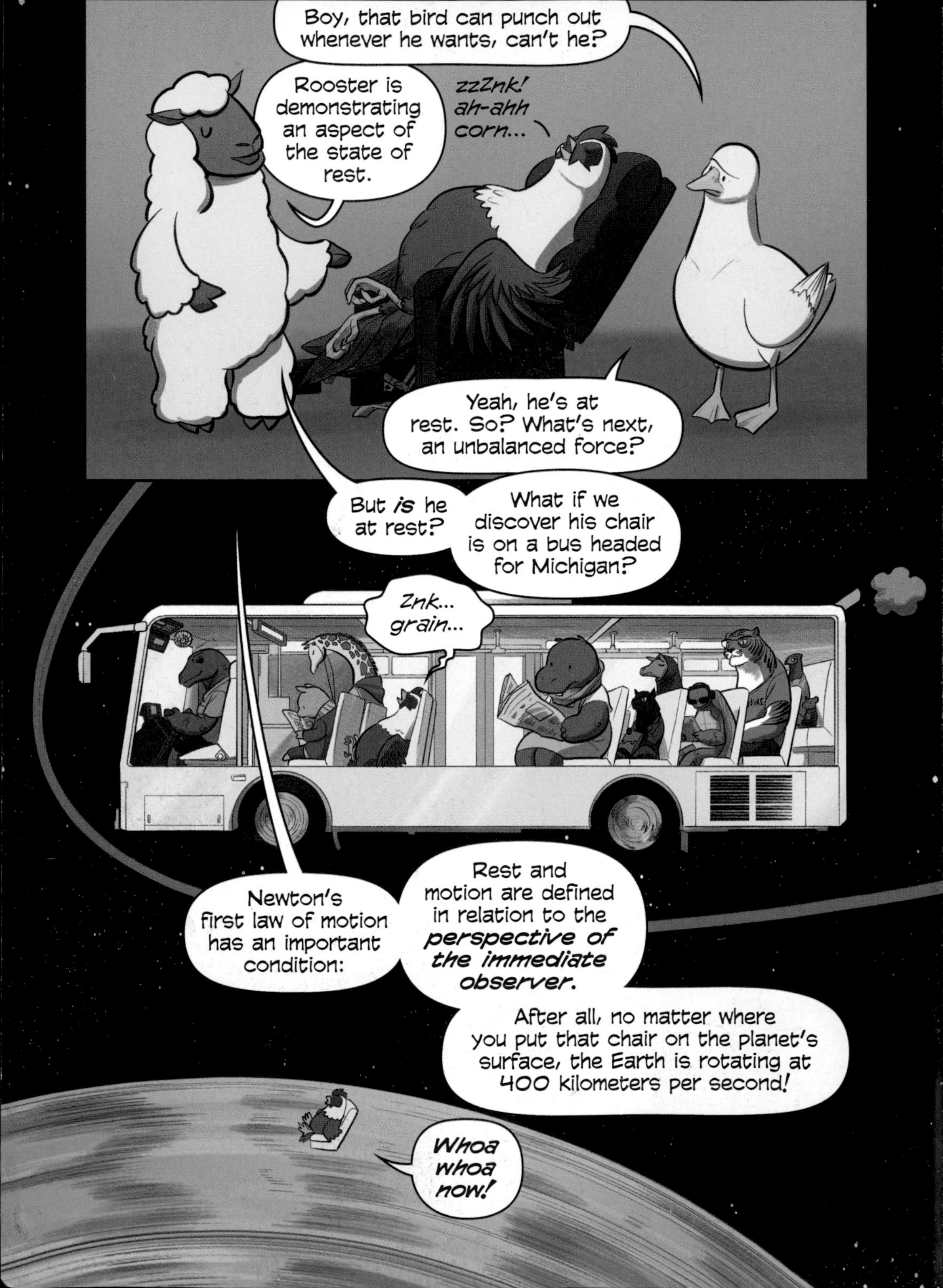
Boy, that bird can punch out whenever he wants, can't he?
Rooster is demonstrating an aspect of the state of rest.
zzZnk! ah-ahh corn...
Yeah, he's at rest. So? What's next, an unbalanced force?
But *is* he at rest?
What if we discover his chair is on a bus headed for Michigan?
Znk... grain...
Newton's first law of motion has an important condition:
Rest and motion are defined in relation to the ***perspective of the immediate observer.***
After all, no matter where you put that chair on the planet's surface, the Earth is rotating at 400 kilometers per second!
Whoa whoa now!

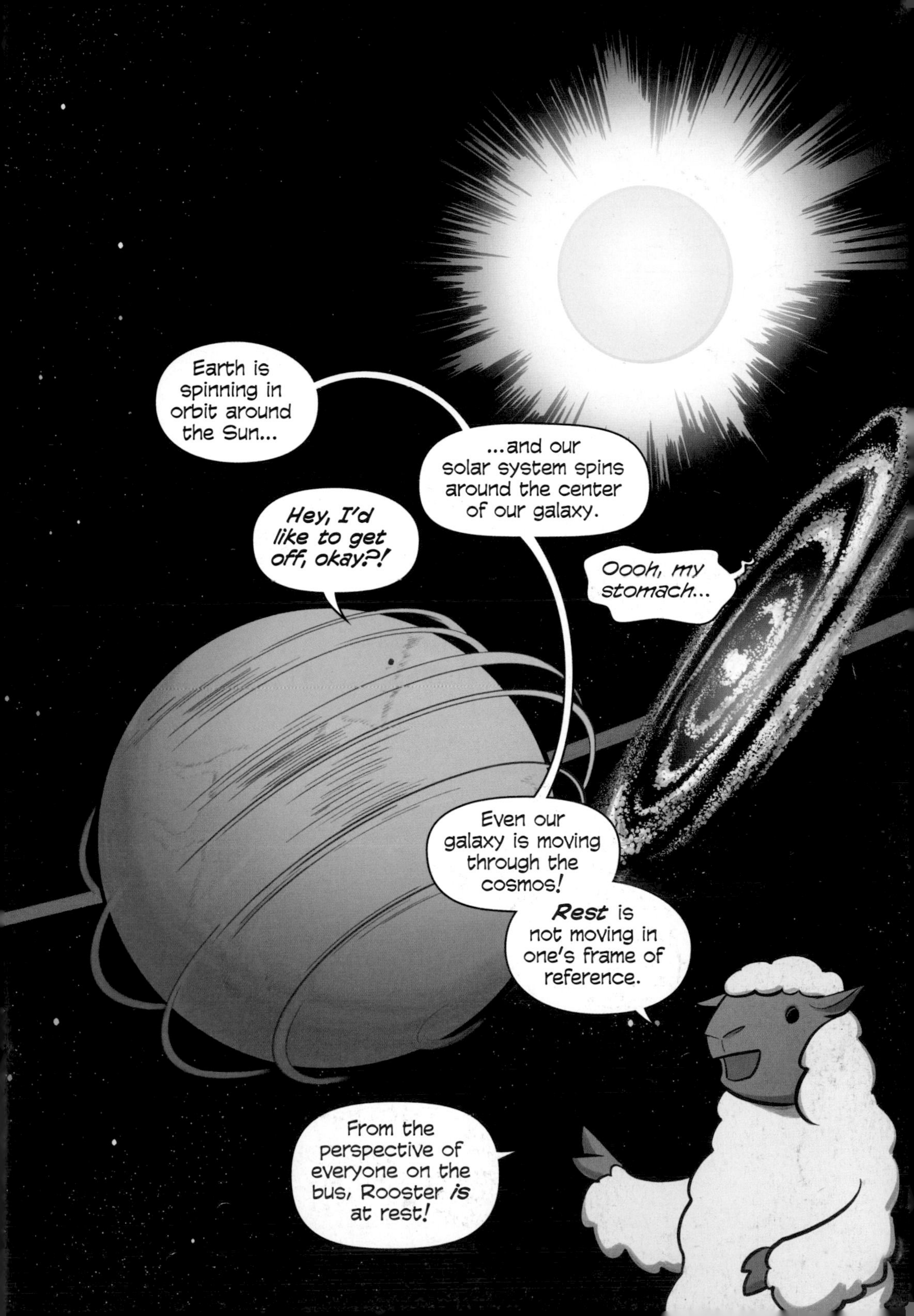
Earth is spinning in orbit around the Sun...
...and our solar system spins around the center of our galaxy.
Hey, I'd like to get off, okay?!
Oooh, my stomach...
Even our galaxy is moving through the cosmos!
Rest is not moving in one's frame of reference.
From the perspective of everyone on the bus, Rooster *is* at rest!

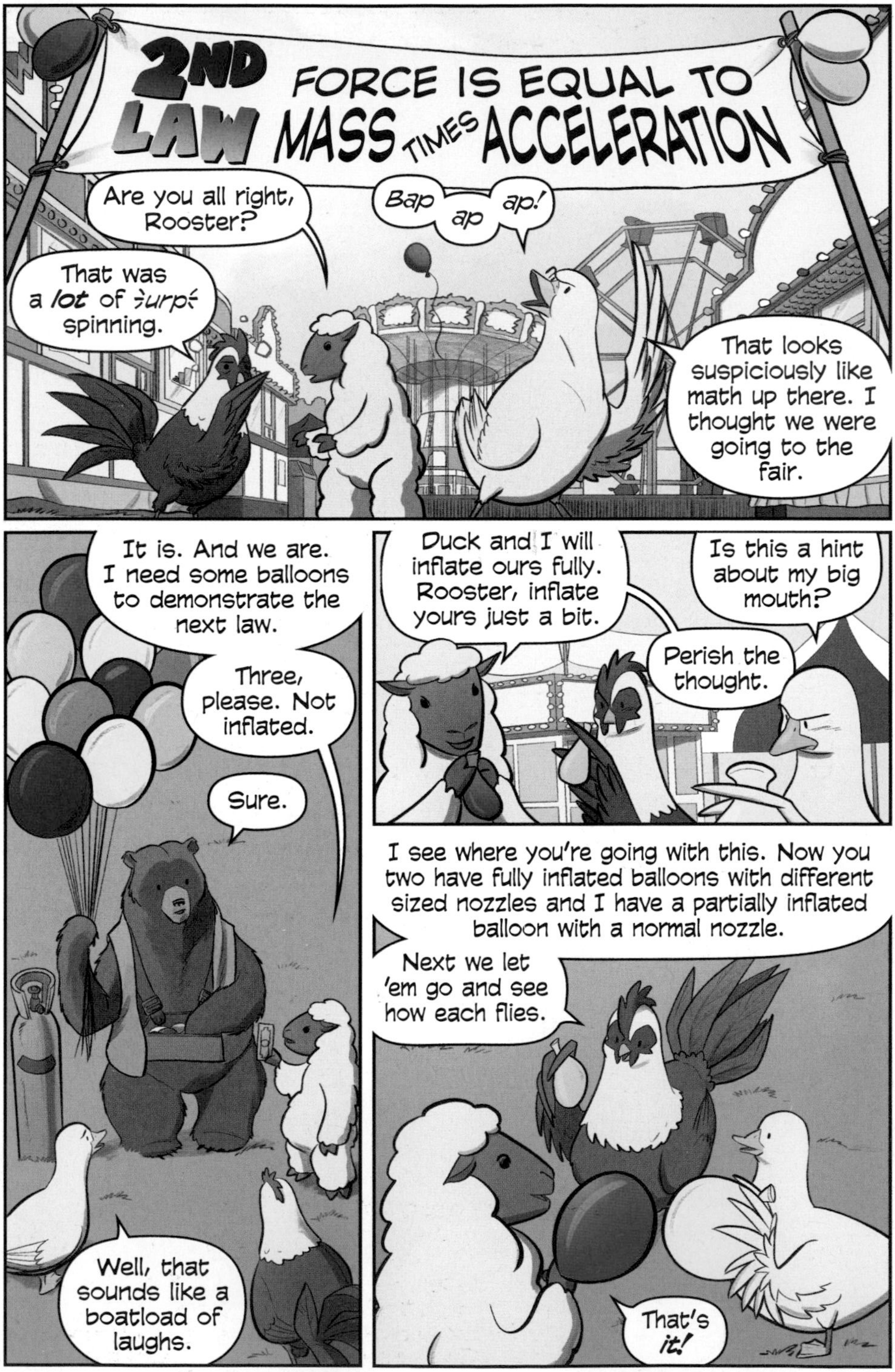
2ND LAW FORCE IS EQUAL TO MASS TIMES ACCELERATION
Are you all right, Rooster?
Bap ap ap!
That was a *lot* of *urp* spinning.
That looks suspiciously like math up there. I thought we were going to the fair.
It is. And we are. I need some balloons to demonstrate the next law.
Three, please. Not inflated.
Sure.
Well, that sounds like a boatload of laughs.
Duck and I will inflate ours fully. Rooster, inflate yours just a bit.
Is this a hint about my big mouth?
Perish the thought.
I see where you're going with this. Now you two have fully inflated balloons with different sized nozzles and I have a partially inflated balloon with a normal nozzle.
Next we let 'em go and see how each flies.
That's *it!*

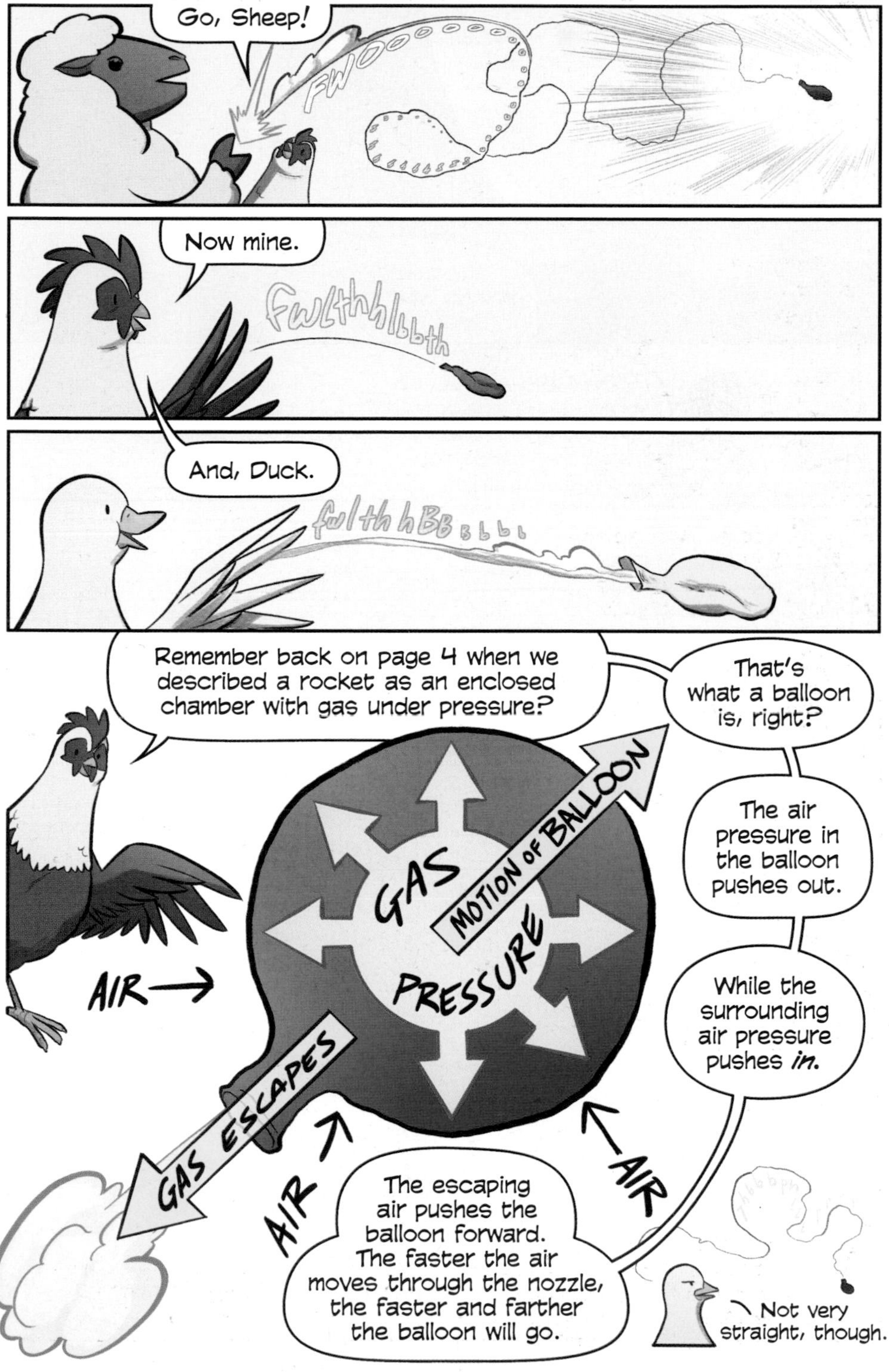
Go, Sheep!
Now mine.
And, Duck.
Remember back on page 4 when we described a rocket as an enclosed chamber with gas under pressure?
That's what a balloon is, right?
The air pressure in the balloon pushes out.
While the surrounding air pressure pushes *in*.
GAS PRESSURE
MOTION OF BALLOON
GAS ESCAPES
AIR
AIR
AIR
The escaping air pushes the balloon forward. The faster the air moves through the nozzle, the faster and farther the balloon will go.
Not very straight, though.

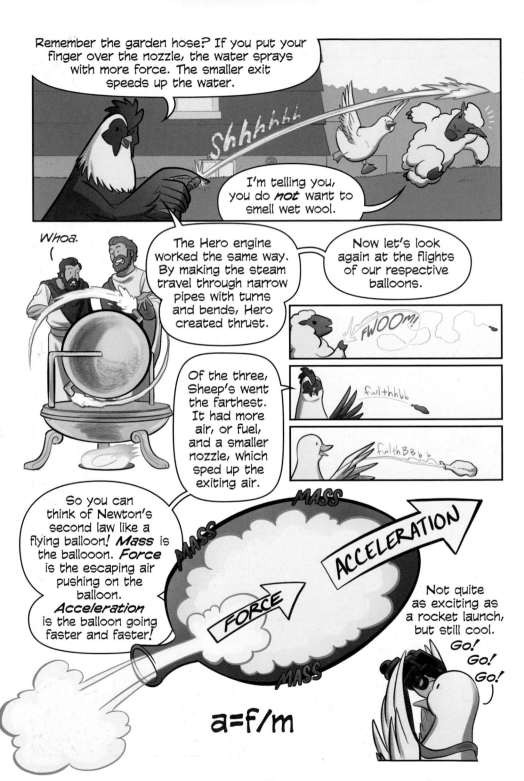

Remember the garden hose? If you put your finger over the nozzle, the water sprays with more force. The smaller exit speeds up the water.

I'm telling you, you do *not* want to smell wet wool.

Whoa.

The Hero engine worked the same way. By making the steam travel through narrow pipes with turns and bends, Hero created thrust.

Now let's look again at the flights of our respective balloons.

FWOOM!

Of the three, Sheep's went the farthest. It had more air, or fuel, and a smaller nozzle, which sped up the exiting air.

fwlthhbb

fwlthBBbb

So you can think of Newton's second law like a flying balloon! *Mass* is the balloon. *Force* is the escaping air pushing on the balloon. *Acceleration* is the balloon going faster and faster!

MASS

MASS

ACCELERATION

FORCE

MASS

Not quite as exciting as a rocket launch, but still cool.

Go! Go! Go!

$$a = f/m$$

14

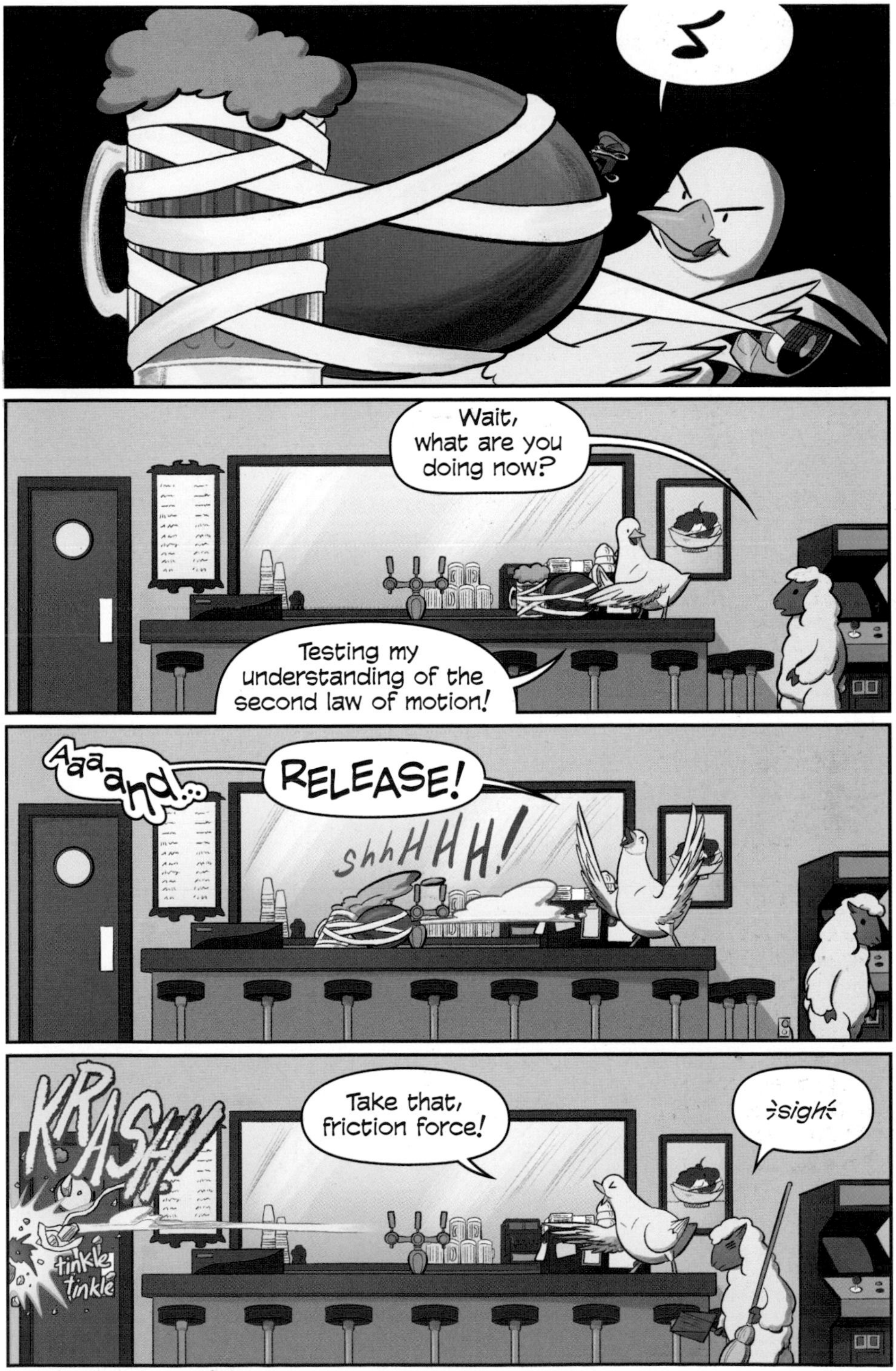
Wait, what are you doing now?
Testing my understanding of the second law of motion!
Aaaand...
RELEASE!
shhHHHH!
KRASH!
tinkle tinkle
Take that, friction force!
sigh

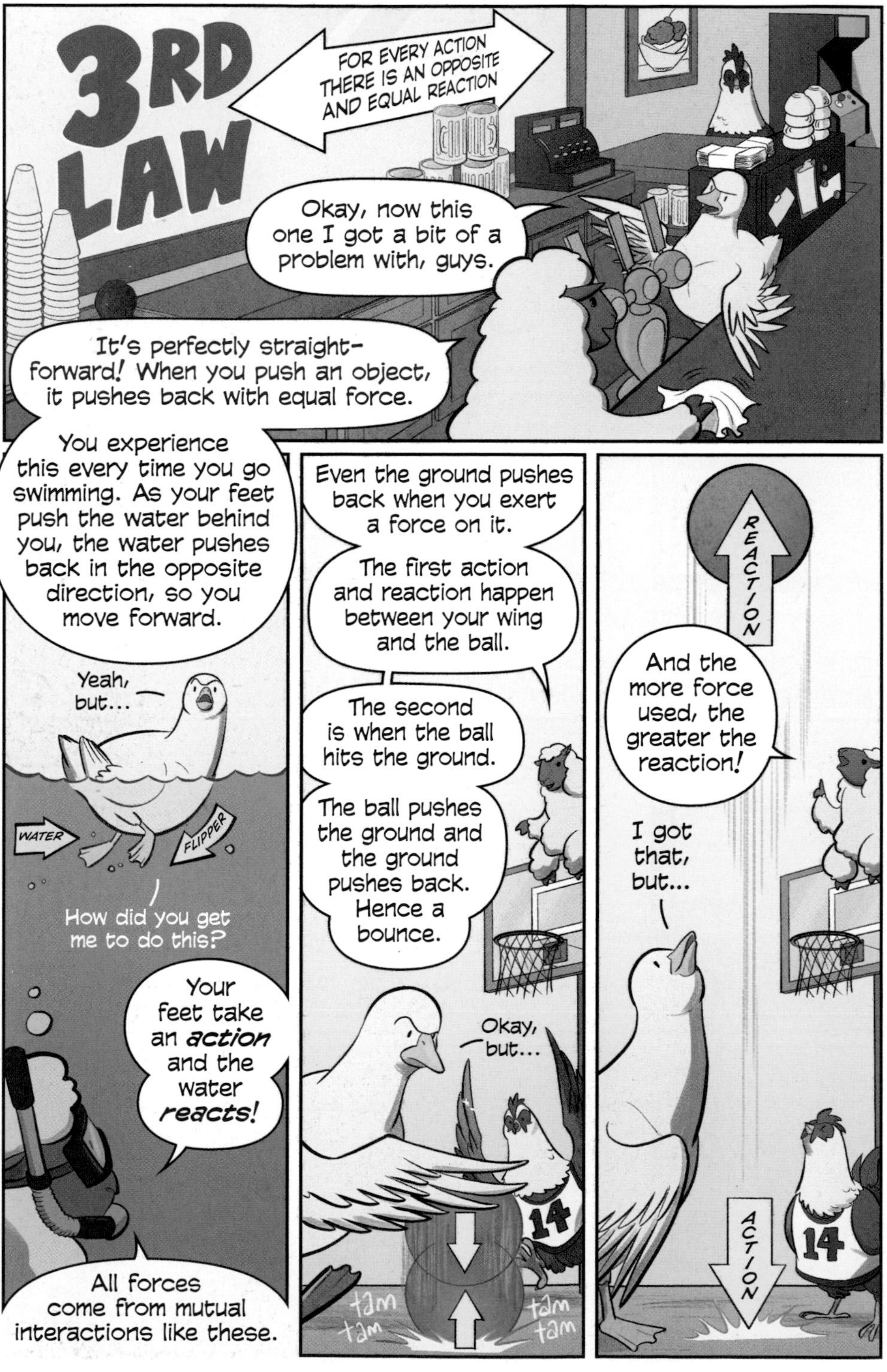
3RD LAW
FOR EVERY ACTION THERE IS AN OPPOSITE AND EQUAL REACTION
Okay, now this one I got a bit of a problem with, guys.
It's perfectly straight-forward! When you push an object, it pushes back with equal force.
You experience this every time you go swimming. As your feet push the water behind you, the water pushes back in the opposite direction, so you move forward.
Yeah, but...
WATER
FLIPPER
How did you get me to do this?
Your feet take an action and the water reacts!
All forces come from mutual interactions like these.
Even the ground pushes back when you exert a force on it.
The first action and reaction happen between your wing and the ball.
The second is when the ball hits the ground.
The ball pushes the ground and the ground pushes back. Hence a bounce.
Okay, but...
14
tam tam
tam tam
REACTION
And the more force used, the greater the reaction!
I got that, but...
14
ACTION

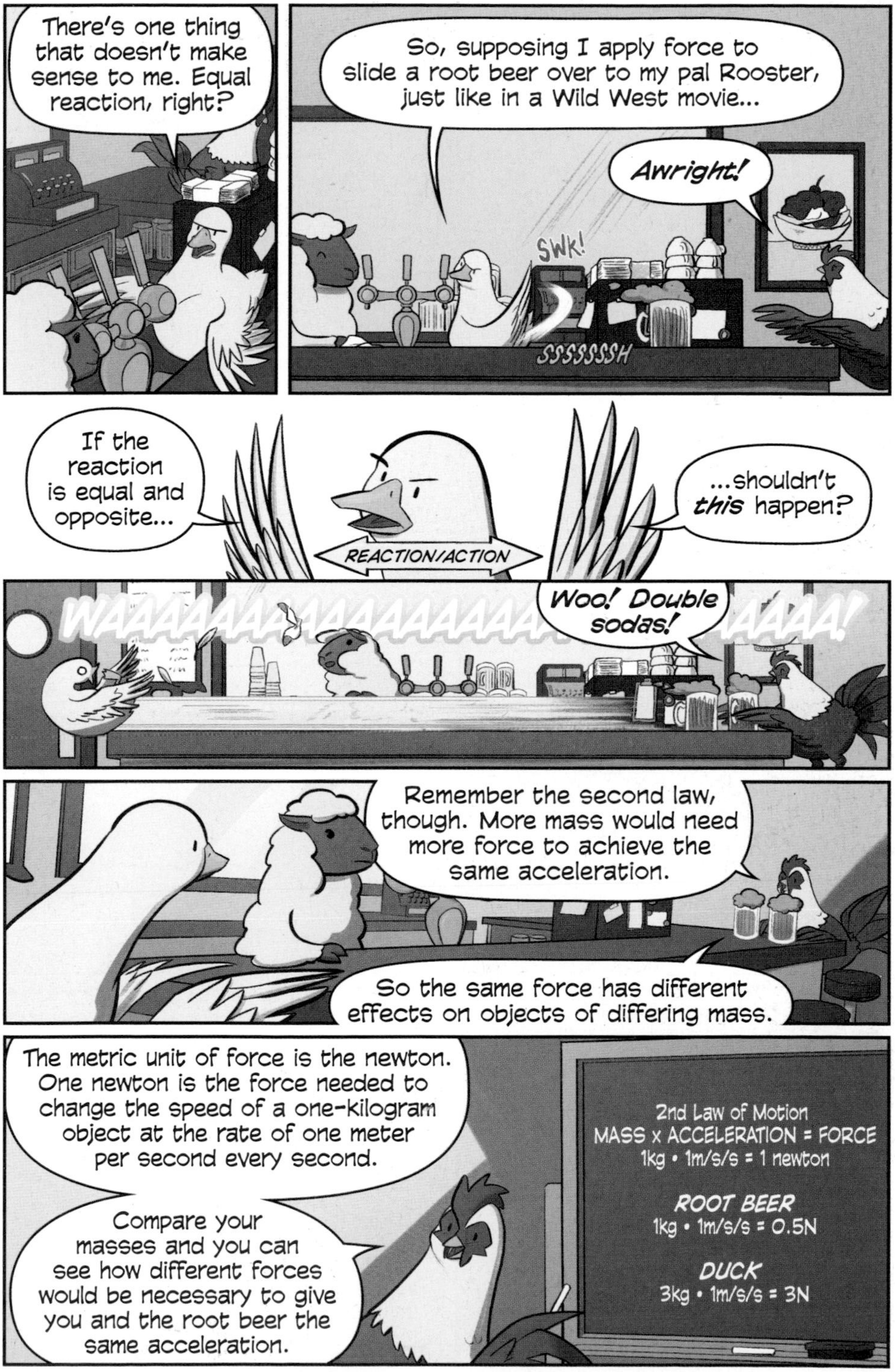

There's one thing that doesn't make sense to me. Equal reaction, right?
So, supposing I apply force to slide a root beer over to my pal Rooster, just like in a Wild West movie...
Awright!
SWK!
SSSSSSSH
If the reaction is equal and opposite...
REACTION/ACTION
...shouldn't *this* happen?
WAAAAAAAAAAAAAAAA
Woo! Double sodas!
AAAAA!
Remember the second law, though. More mass would need more force to achieve the same acceleration.
So the same force has different effects on objects of differing mass.
The metric unit of force is the newton. One newton is the force needed to change the speed of a one-kilogram object at the rate of one meter per second every second.
Compare your masses and you can see how different forces would be necessary to give you and the root beer the same acceleration.
2nd Law of Motion
MASS x ACCELERATION = FORCE
1kg • 1m/s/s = 1 newton
ROOT BEER
1kg • 1m/s/s = 0.5N
DUCK
3kg • 1m/s/s = 3N

So now let's look at the same equation with force as a consistent value.

Remember, it was the *same force* acting on two different masses.

2nd Law of Motion
MASS x ACCELERATION = FORCE
1kg • 1m/s/s = 1 newton

ROOT BEER
0.5N = 0.5kg • 1m/s/s

DUCK
0.5N = 3kg • 0.1666m/s/s

Less acceleration!

The same force results in less acceleration on more mass. So, while the third law held— it was an opposite and equal reaction— it wasn't as dramatic a reaction on you because you're a more massive object.

If the reaction were the same regardless of mass, every time even a tiny meteor hit the Earth, the whole planet would be shoved out of orbit!

Oh no! Not again!

PLOOP

ZOOM!

Hmm... That's a whole lot of math up there...

You actually encounter this pretty regularly in real life.

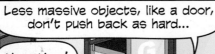

Less massive objects, like a door, don't push back as hard...

Yoga time! *All right!*

KICK!

GYM

...while more massive objects offer greater resistance to changing their state of motion or rest!

WHAM!

Sorry! ≥huff huff≤

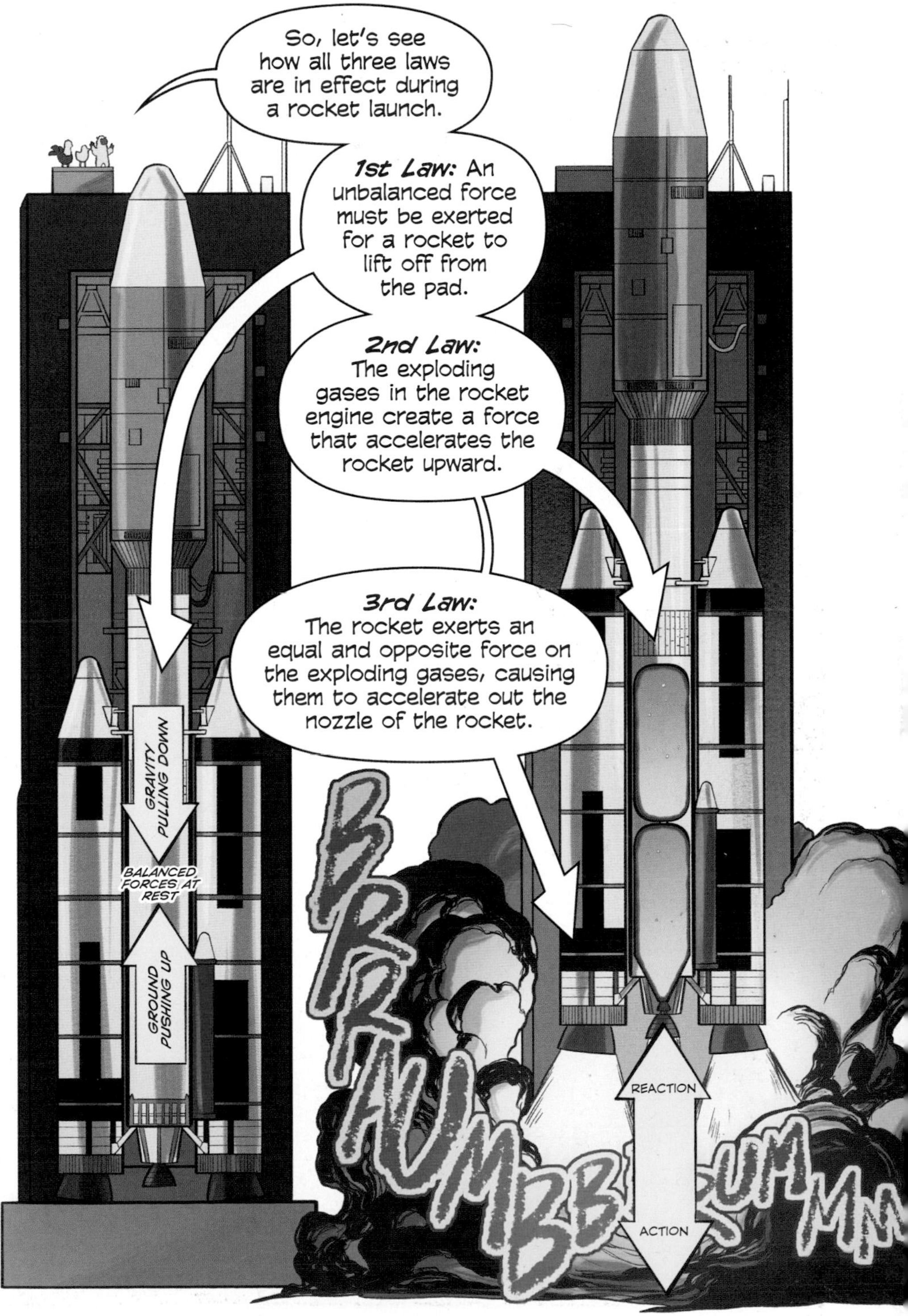
So, let's see how all three laws are in effect during a rocket launch.
1st Law: An unbalanced force must be exerted for a rocket to lift off from the pad.
2nd Law: The exploding gases in the rocket engine create a force that accelerates the rocket upward.
3rd Law: The rocket exerts an equal and opposite force on the exploding gases, causing them to accelerate out the nozzle of the rocket.
GRAVITY PULLING DOWN
BALANCED FORCES AT REST
GROUND PUSHING UP
REACTION
ACTION
BRRUMBBRUMMM

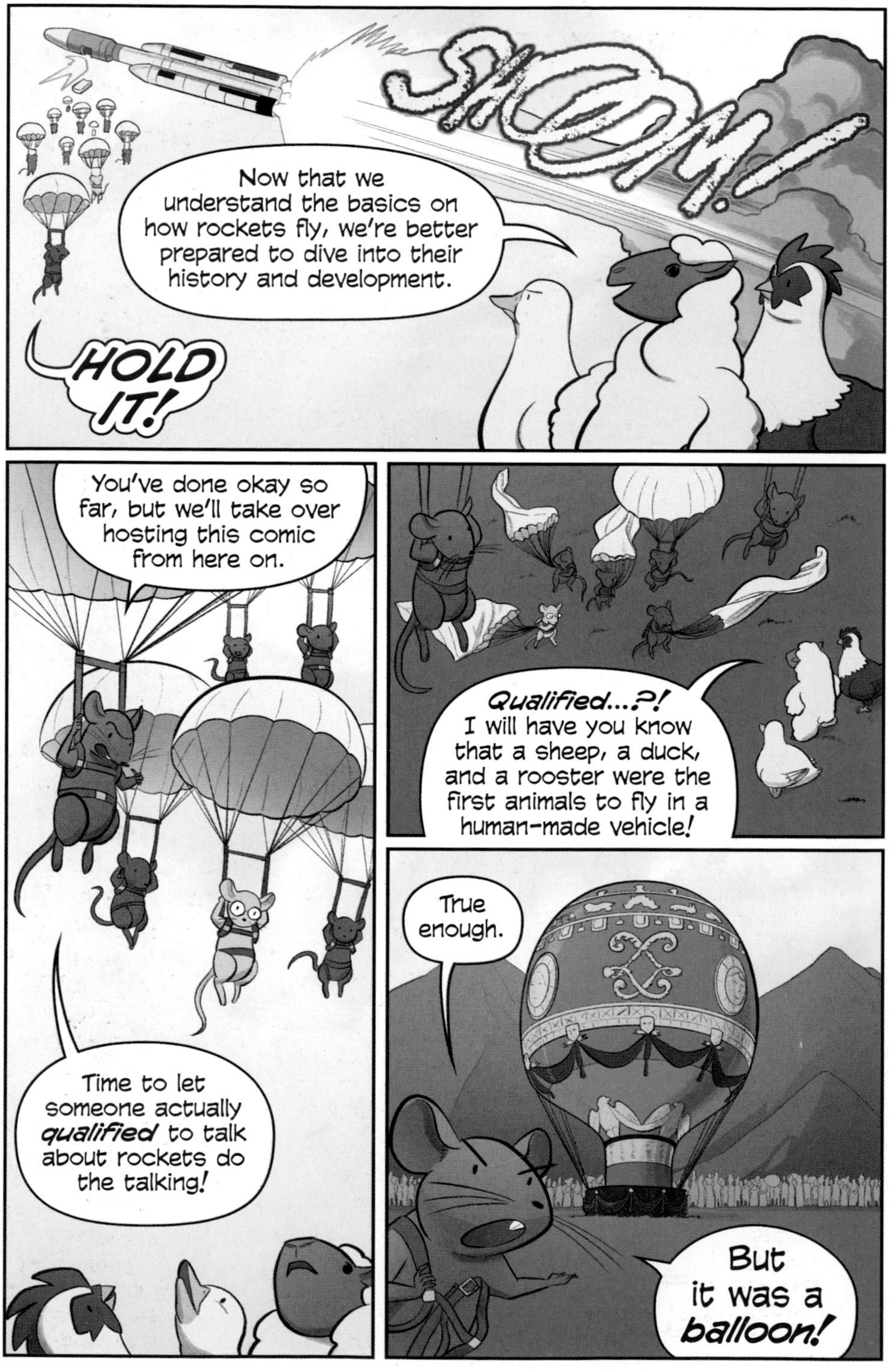
SHOOM!
Now that we understand the basics on how rockets fly, we're better prepared to dive into their history and development.
HOLD IT!
You've done okay so far, but we'll take over hosting this comic from here on.
Time to let someone actually *qualified* to talk about rockets do the talking!
Qualified...?! I will have you know that a sheep, a duck, and a rooster were the first animals to fly in a human-made vehicle!
True enough.
But it was a *balloon!*

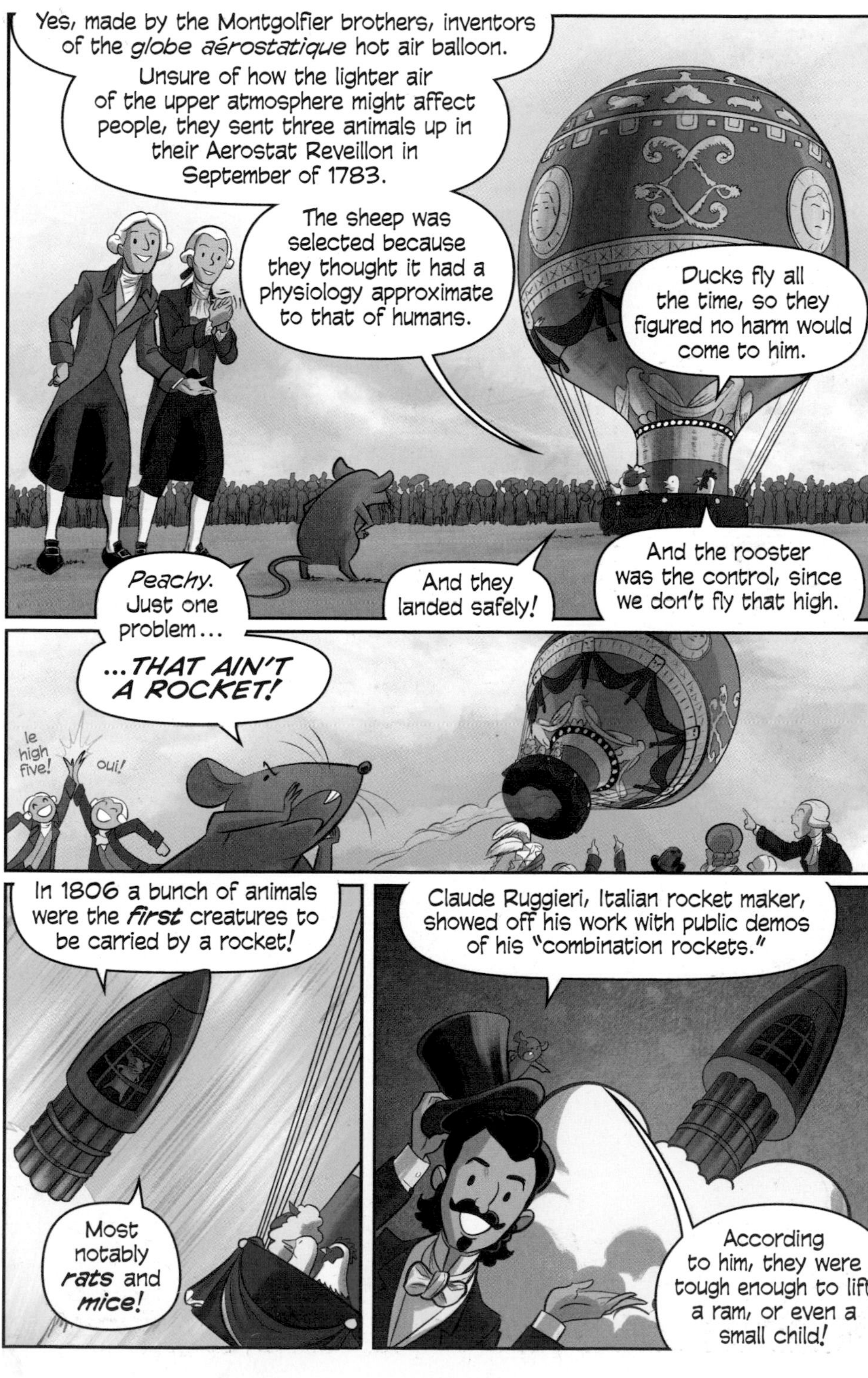
Yes, made by the Montgolfier brothers, inventors of the *globe aérostatique* hot air balloon.
Unsure of how the lighter air of the upper atmosphere might affect people, they sent three animals up in their Aerostat Reveillon in September of 1783.
The sheep was selected because they thought it had a physiology approximate to that of humans.
Ducks fly all the time, so they figured no harm would come to him.
And the rooster was the control, since we don't fly that high.
And they landed safely!
Peachy. Just one problem...
...THAT AIN'T A ROCKET!
le high five!
oui!
In 1806 a bunch of animals were the ***first*** creatures to be carried by a rocket!
Most notably ***rats*** and ***mice!***
Claude Ruggieri, Italian rocket maker, showed off his work with public demos of his "combination rockets."
According to him, they were tough enough to lift a ram, or even a small child!

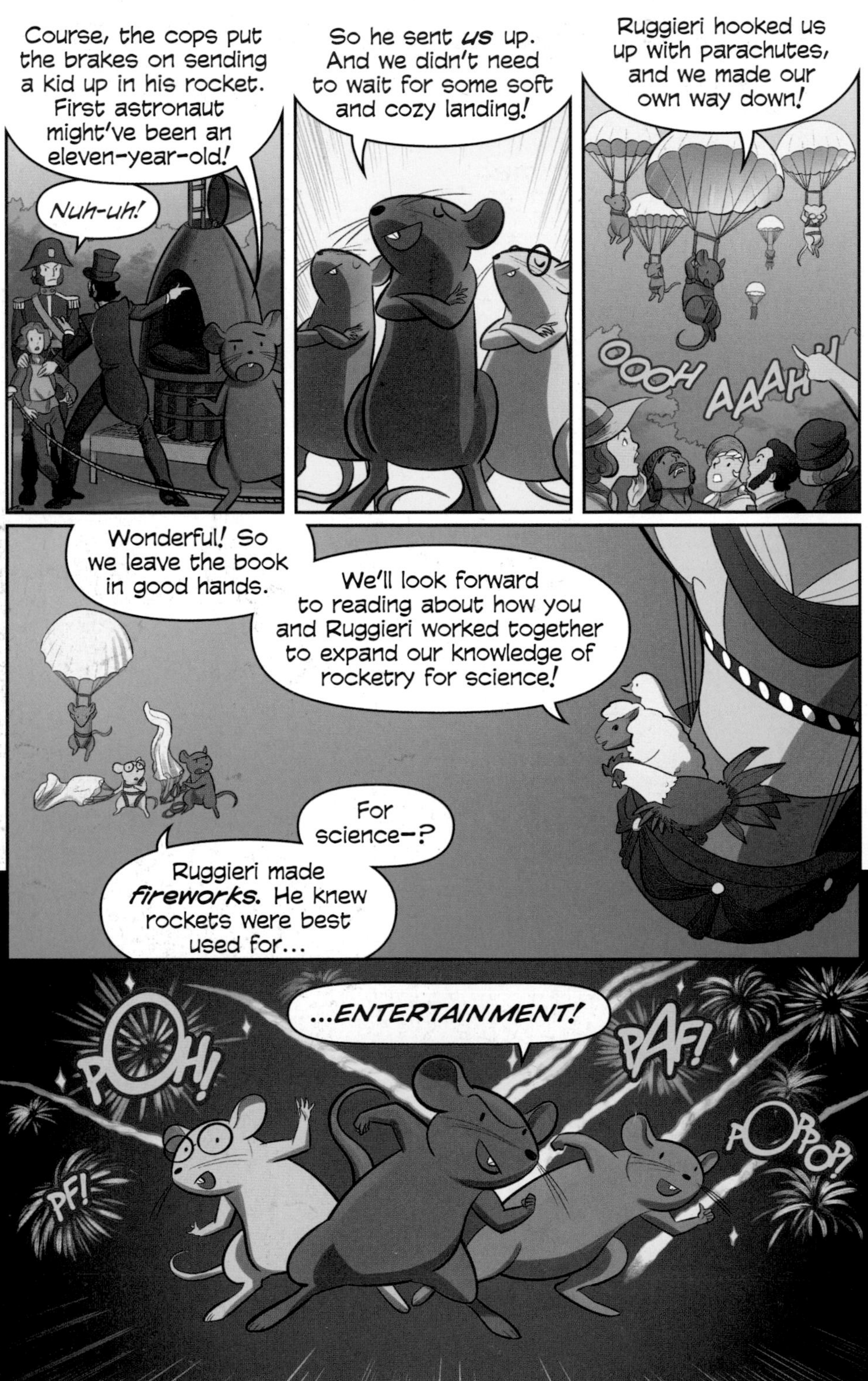

Course, the cops put the brakes on sending a kid up in his rocket. First astronaut might've been an eleven-year-old!
Nuh-uh!
So he sent *us* up. And we didn't need to wait for some soft and cozy landing!
Ruggieri hooked us up with parachutes, and we made our own way down!
OOOH
AAAH
Wonderful! So we leave the book in good hands.
We'll look forward to reading about how you and Ruggieri worked together to expand our knowledge of rocketry for science!
For science—?
Ruggieri made *fireworks*. He knew rockets were best used for...
...ENTERTAINMENT!
POH!
PAF!
POPPOP!
PF!

CHAPTER 2: ROCKETS AS ENTERTAINMENT

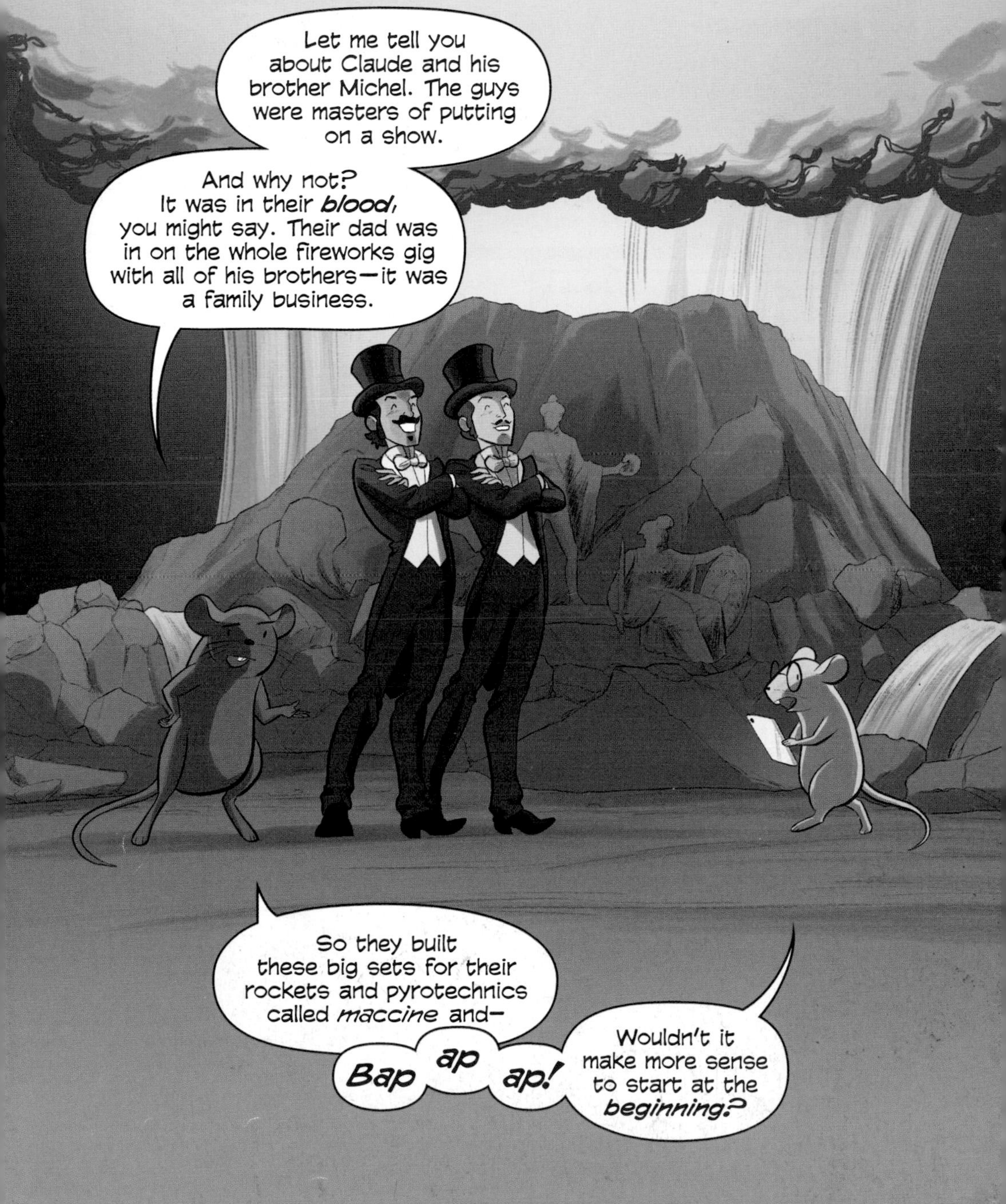
Let me tell you about Claude and his brother Michel. The guys were masters of putting on a show.
And why not? It was in their *blood*, you might say. Their dad was in on the whole fireworks gig with all of his brothers—it was a family business.
So they built these big sets for their rockets and pyrotechnics called *maccine* and—
Bap ap ap!
Wouldn't it make more sense to start at the *beginning?*

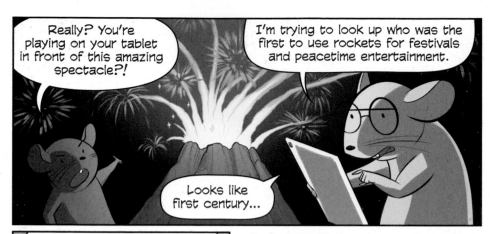

Really? You're playing on your tablet in front of this amazing spectacle?!

I'm trying to look up who was the first to use rockets for festivals and peacetime entertainment.

Looks like first century...

First-century China, to be precise. Can you guess how they might have used these bamboo tubes and simple gunpowder?

You're kidding me. This stinky stuff?

They would fill the tubes with powder and throw them into fires to create explosions during religious festivals.

Well, *DUH!* How else are you gonna honor the facilitators of cosmic power than with a big, awesome

KA BOOM?!

Um, actually, the noise was probably meant to scare away troublesome spirits...

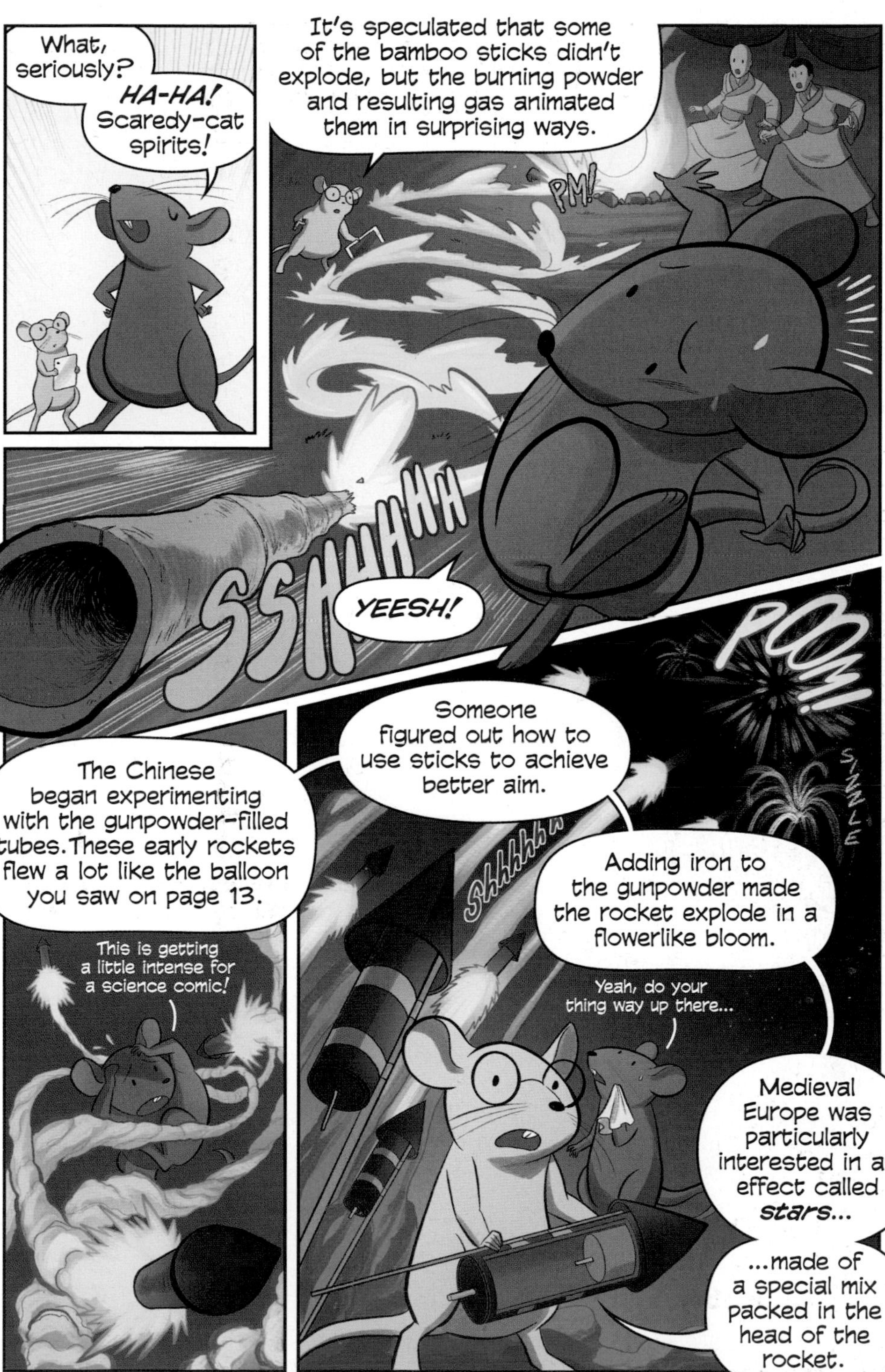

What, seriously? HA-HA! Scaredy-cat spirits!
It's speculated that some of the bamboo sticks didn't explode, but the burning powder and resulting gas animated them in surprising ways.
PM!
SSHHHHH
YEESH!
POOM!!
Someone figured out how to use sticks to achieve better aim.
The Chinese began experimenting with the gunpowder-filled tubes. These early rockets flew a lot like the balloon you saw on page 13.
SIZZLE
This is getting a little intense for a science comic!
Shhhhhh
Adding iron to the gunpowder made the rocket explode in a flowerlike bloom.
Yeah, do your thing way up there...
Medieval Europe was particularly interested in an effect called *stars*...
...made of a special mix packed in the head of the rocket.

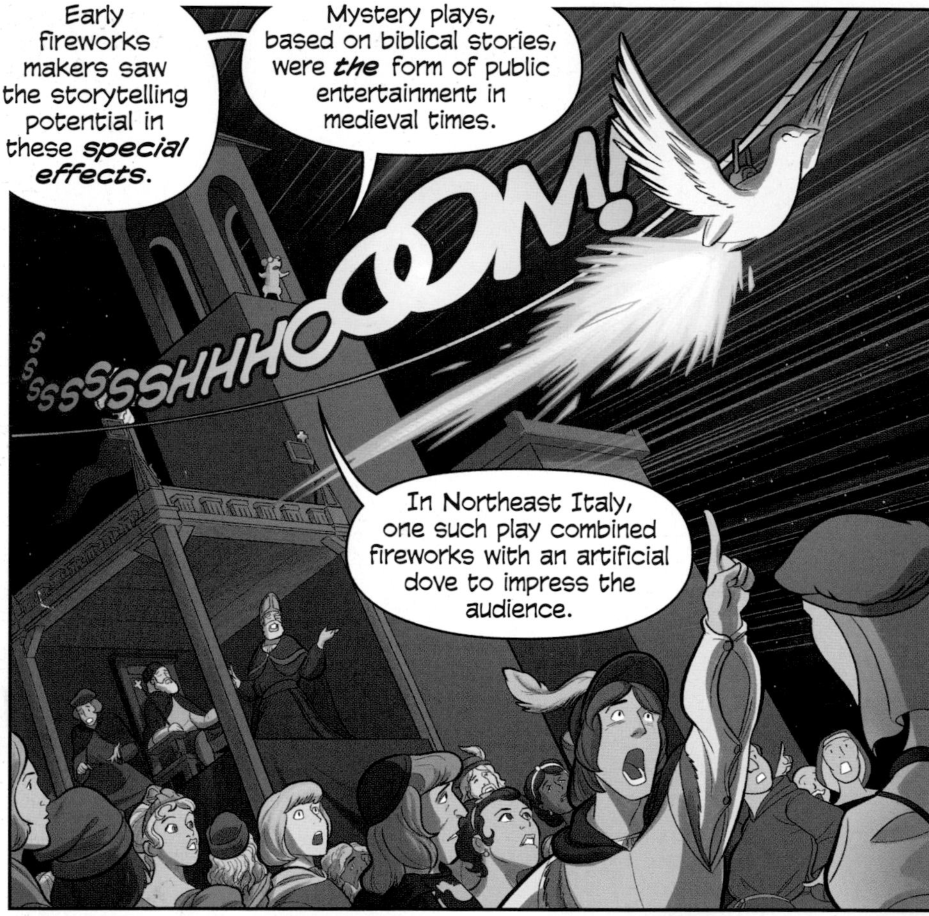
Early fireworks makers saw the storytelling potential in these *special effects*.
Mystery plays, based on biblical stories, were *the* form of public entertainment in medieval times.
SSSSSSHHHOOOOM!
In Northeast Italy, one such play combined fireworks with an artificial dove to impress the audience.

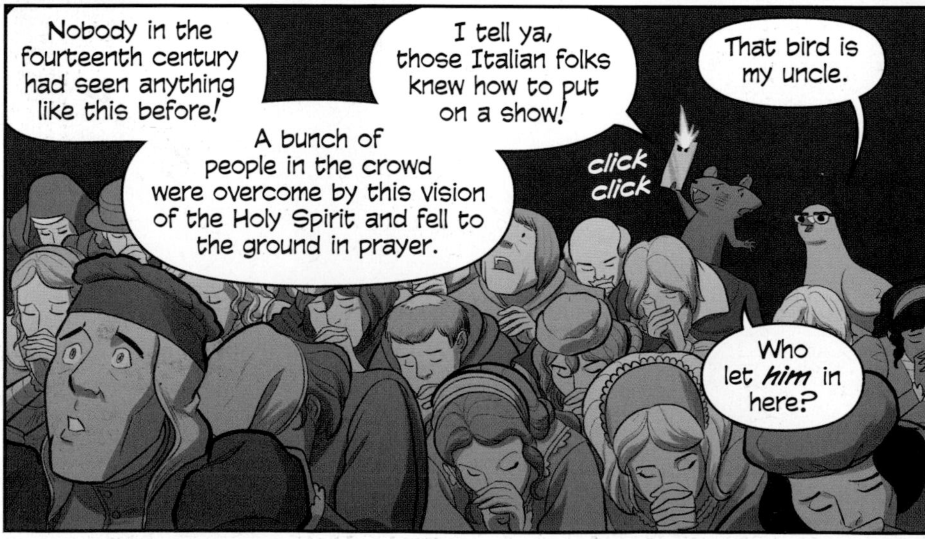
Nobody in the fourteenth century had seen anything like this before!
A bunch of people in the crowd were overcome by this vision of the Holy Spirit and fell to the ground in prayer.
I tell ya, those Italian folks knew how to put on a show!
click click
That bird is my uncle.
Who let *him* in here?

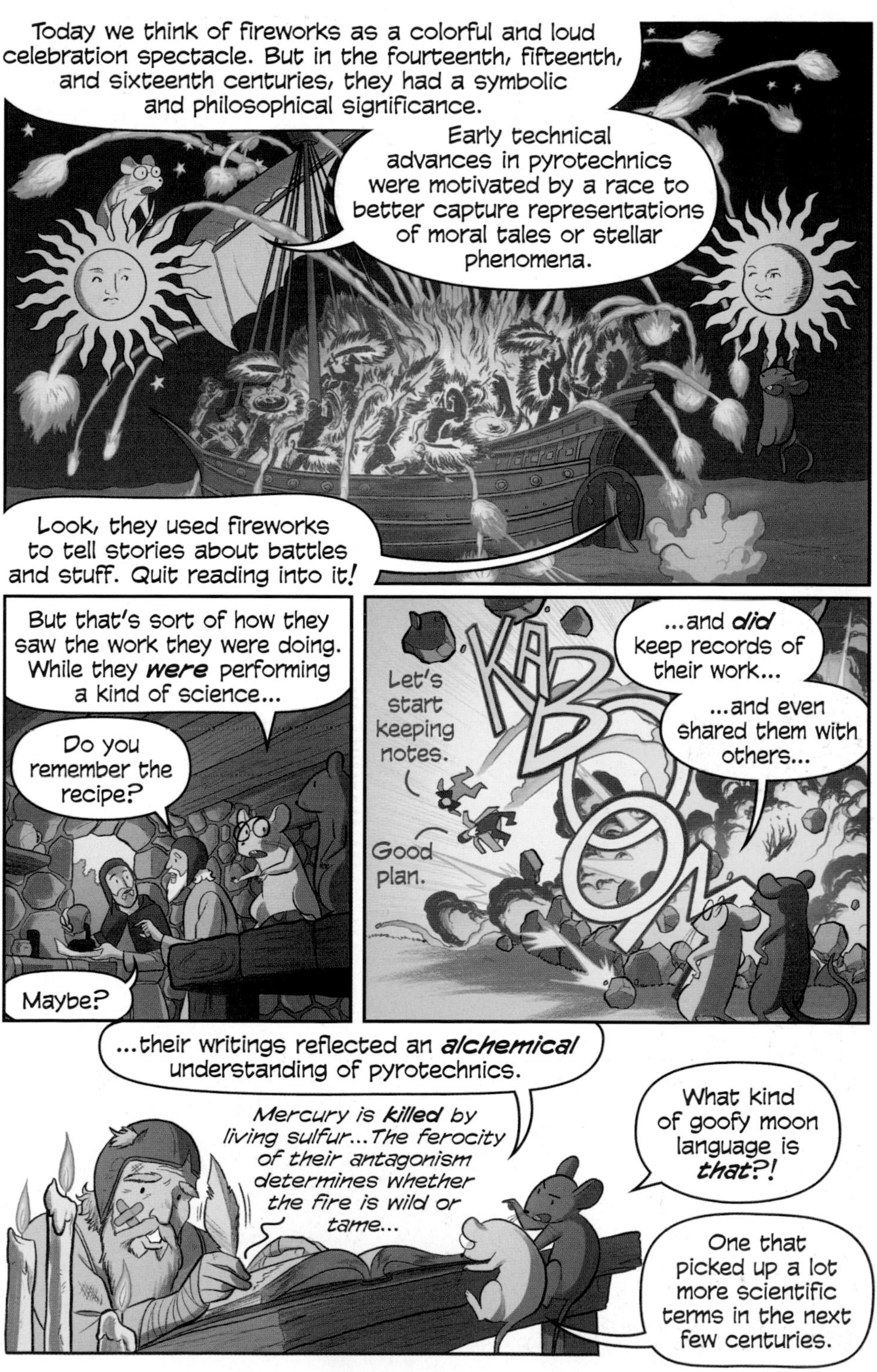

Today we think of fireworks as a colorful and loud celebration spectacle. But in the fourteenth, fifteenth, and sixteenth centuries, they had a symbolic and philosophical significance.
Early technical advances in pyrotechnics were motivated by a race to better capture representations of moral tales or stellar phenomena.
Look, they used fireworks to tell stories about battles and stuff. Quit reading into it!
But that's sort of how they saw the work they were doing. While they *were* performing a kind of science...
Do you remember the recipe?
Maybe?
KABOOM
Let's start keeping notes.
Good plan.
...and *did* keep records of their work...
...and even shared them with others...
...their writings reflected an *alchemical* understanding of pyrotechnics.
*Mercury is **killed** by living sulfur... The ferocity of their antagonism determines whether the fire is wild or tame...*
What kind of goofy moon language is ***that***?!
One that picked up a lot more scientific terms in the next few centuries.

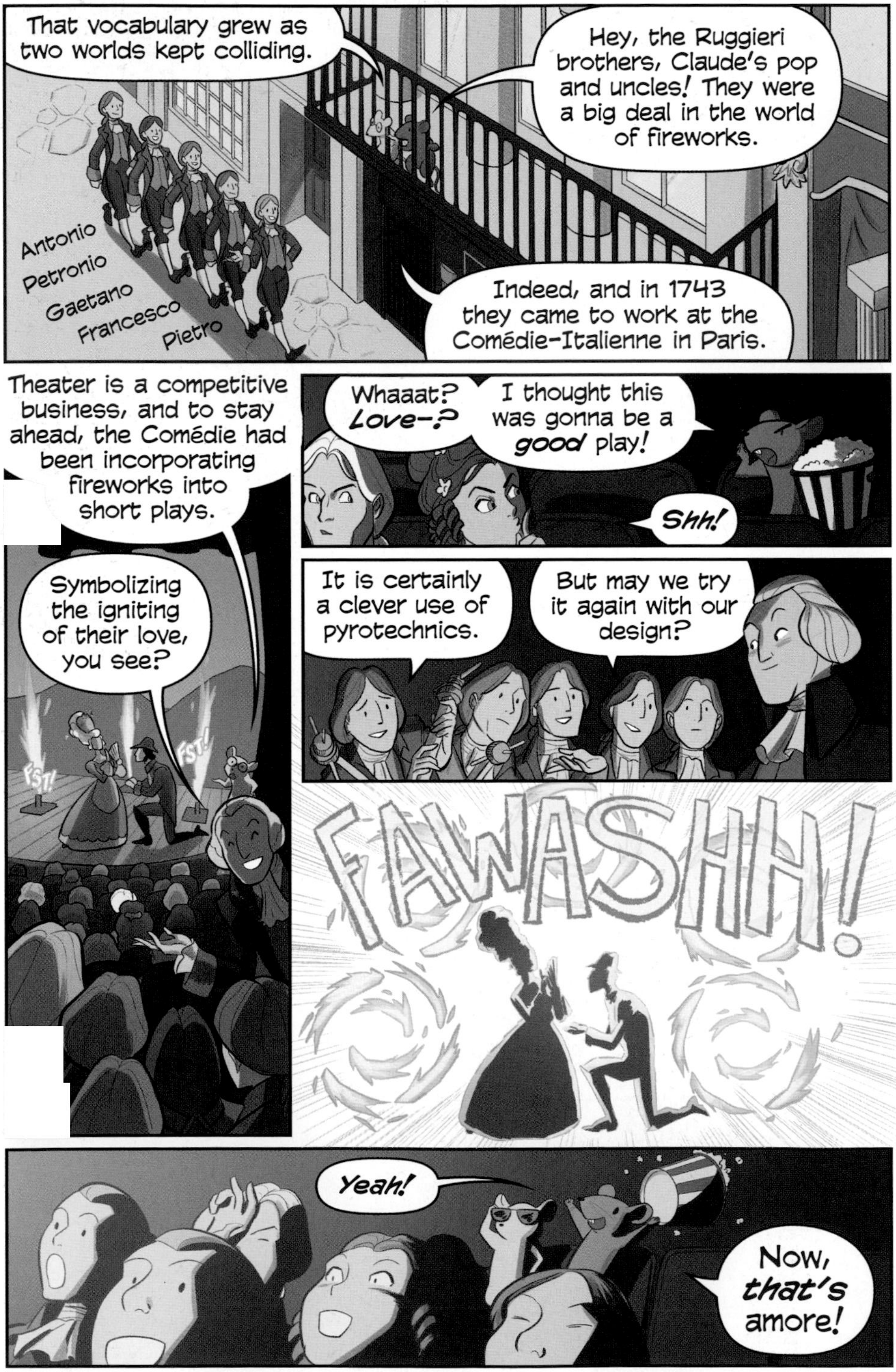
That vocabulary grew as two worlds kept colliding.
Hey, the Ruggieri brothers, Claude's pop and uncles! They were a big deal in the world of fireworks.
Antonio
Petronio
Gaetano
Francesco
Pietro
Indeed, and in 1743 they came to work at the Comédie-Italienne in Paris.
Theater is a competitive business, and to stay ahead, the Comédie had been incorporating fireworks into short plays.
Whaaat? *Love-?*
I thought this was gonna be a *good* play!
Shh!
Symbolizing the igniting of their love, you see?
FST!
FST!
It is certainly a clever use of pyrotechnics.
But may we try it again with our design?
FAWASHH!
Yeah!
Now, *that's* amore!

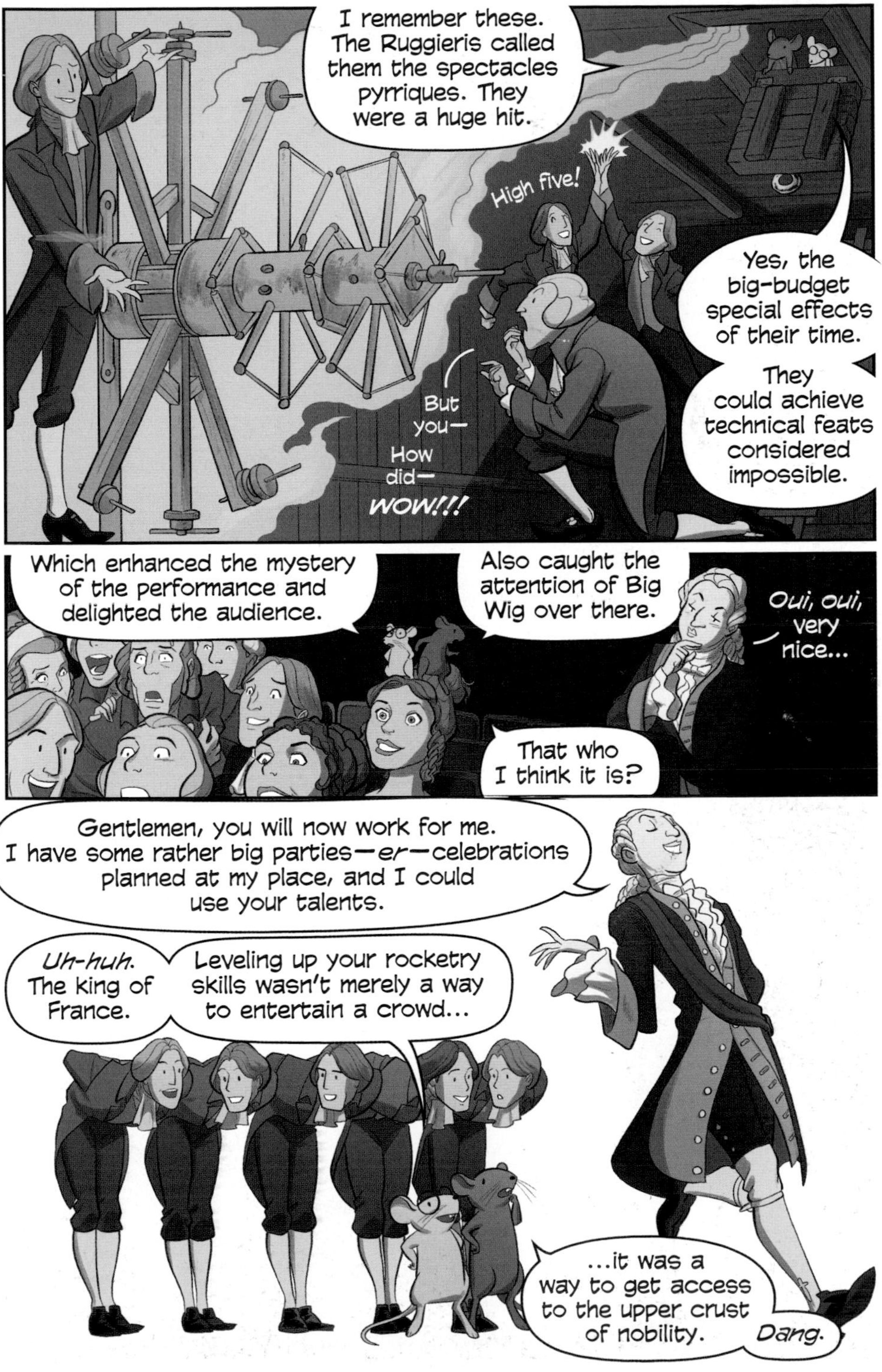
I remember these. The Ruggieris called them the spectacles pyrriques. They were a huge hit.
High five!
Yes, the big-budget special effects of their time.
They could achieve technical feats considered impossible.
But you—
How did—
WOW!!!
Which enhanced the mystery of the performance and delighted the audience.
Also caught the attention of Big Wig over there.
Oui, oui, very nice...
That who I think it is?
Gentlemen, you will now work for me. I have some rather big parties—er—celebrations planned at my place, and I could use your talents.
Uh-huh. The king of France.
Leveling up your rocketry skills wasn't merely a way to entertain a crowd...
...it was a way to get access to the upper crust of nobility.
Dang.

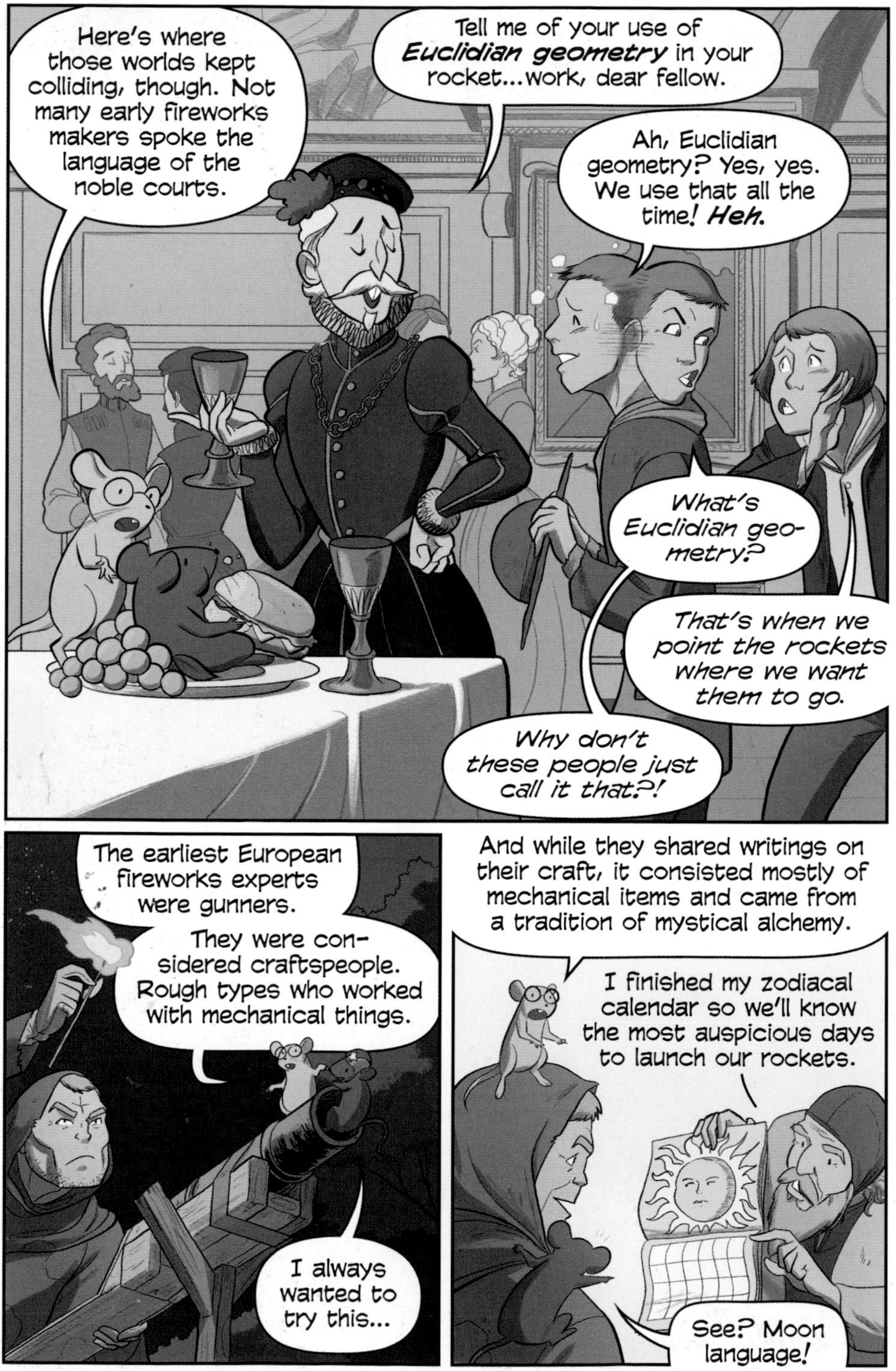
Here's where those worlds kept colliding, though. Not many early fireworks makers spoke the language of the noble courts.
Tell me of your use of ***Euclidian geometry*** in your rocket...work, dear fellow.
Ah, Euclidian geometry? Yes, yes. We use that all the time! ***Heh.***
What's Euclidian geo-metry?
That's when we point the rockets where we want them to go.
Why don't these people just call it that?!
The earliest European fireworks experts were gunners.
They were con-sidered craftspeople. Rough types who worked with mechanical things.
I always wanted to try this...
And while they shared writings on their craft, it consisted mostly of mechanical items and came from a tradition of mystical alchemy.
I finished my zodiacal calendar so we'll know the most auspicious days to launch our rockets.
See? Moon language!

The nobility of the time made a distinction between what they considered mechanical endeavors and the liberal arts taught at universities.

$1 + 2 = 3$
Mathematics

Music

He gave it to me
Grammar

B
x
A 60 60 C
Geometry

Rhetoric

Astronomy

Logic

To gain more favor with the nobles and promote their own status, they started incorporating language we recognize as scientific today...

Ah—welcome to my *laboratory*, my lord.

I was just writing about the various inventions being developed in the realm of pyrotechnics.

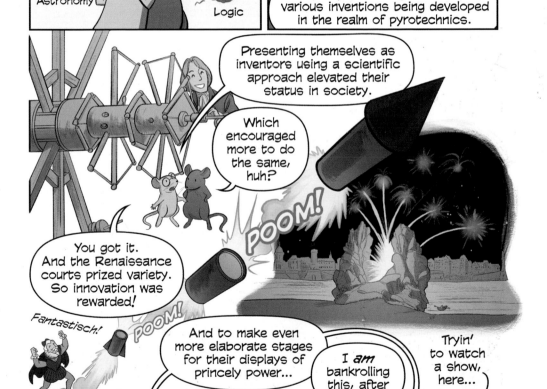

Presenting themselves as inventors using a scientific approach elevated their status in society.

Which encouraged more to do the same, huh?

You got it. And the Renaissance courts prized variety. So innovation was rewarded!

POOM!

POOM!

Fantastisch!

And to make even more elaborate stages for their displays of princely power...

I *am* bankrolling this, after all.

Tryin' to watch a show, here...

This incentivized creation of new rocket technologies like Johann Schmidlap's step rockets.

...they had to learn architecture, physics, and more chemistry!

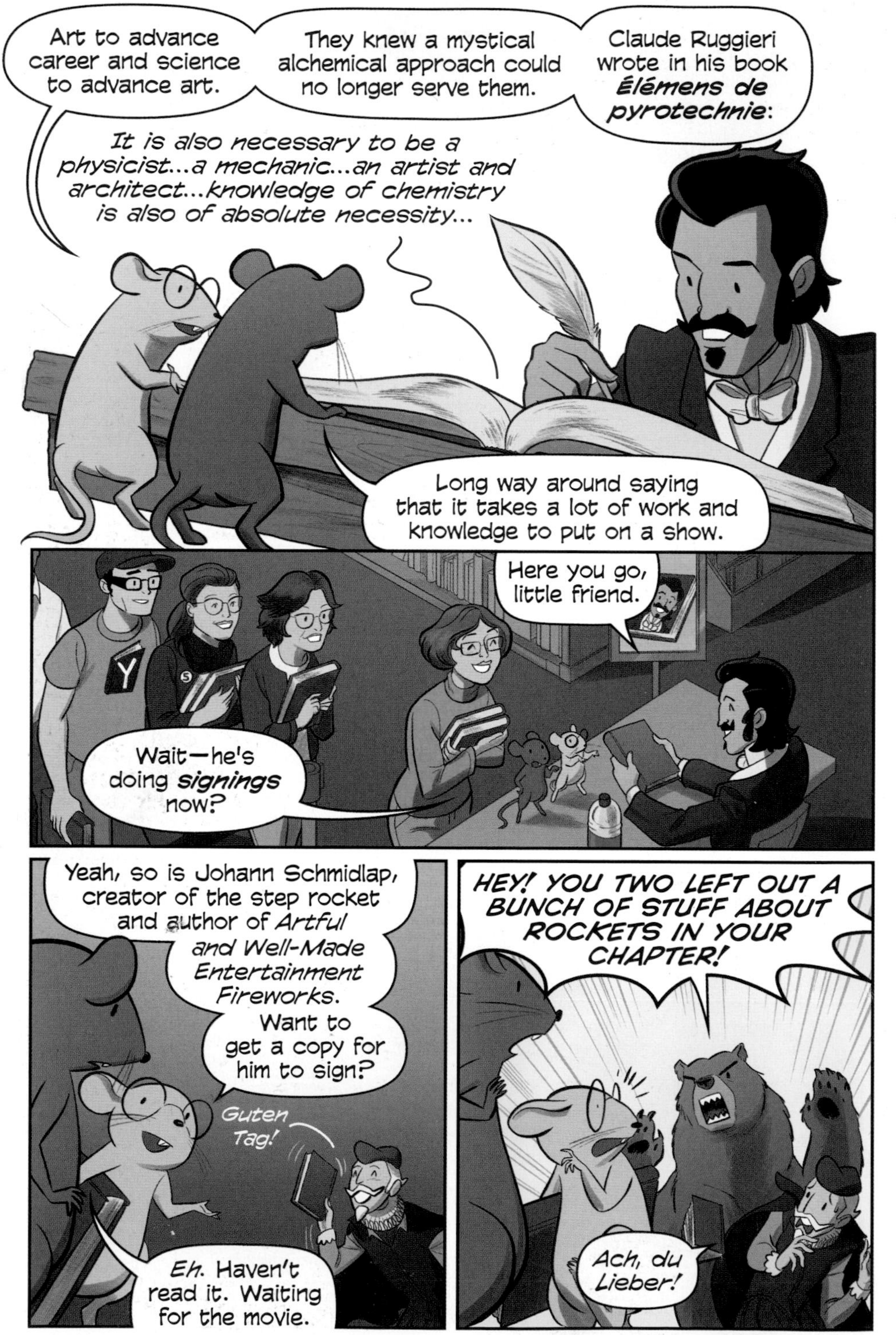
Art to advance career and science to advance art.
They knew a mystical alchemical approach could no longer serve them.
Claude Ruggieri wrote in his book ***Élémens de pyrotechnie***:
It is also necessary to be a physicist...a mechanic...an artist and architect...knowledge of chemistry is also of absolute necessity...
Long way around saying that it takes a lot of work and knowledge to put on a show.
Here you go, little friend.
Wait—he's doing ***signings*** now?
Yeah, so is Johann Schmidlap, creator of the step rocket and author of *Artful and Well-Made Entertainment Fireworks*.
Want to get a copy for him to sign?
Guten Tag!
Eh. Haven't read it. Waiting for the movie.
HEY! YOU TWO LEFT OUT A BUNCH OF STUFF ABOUT ROCKETS IN YOUR CHAPTER!
Ach, du Lieber!

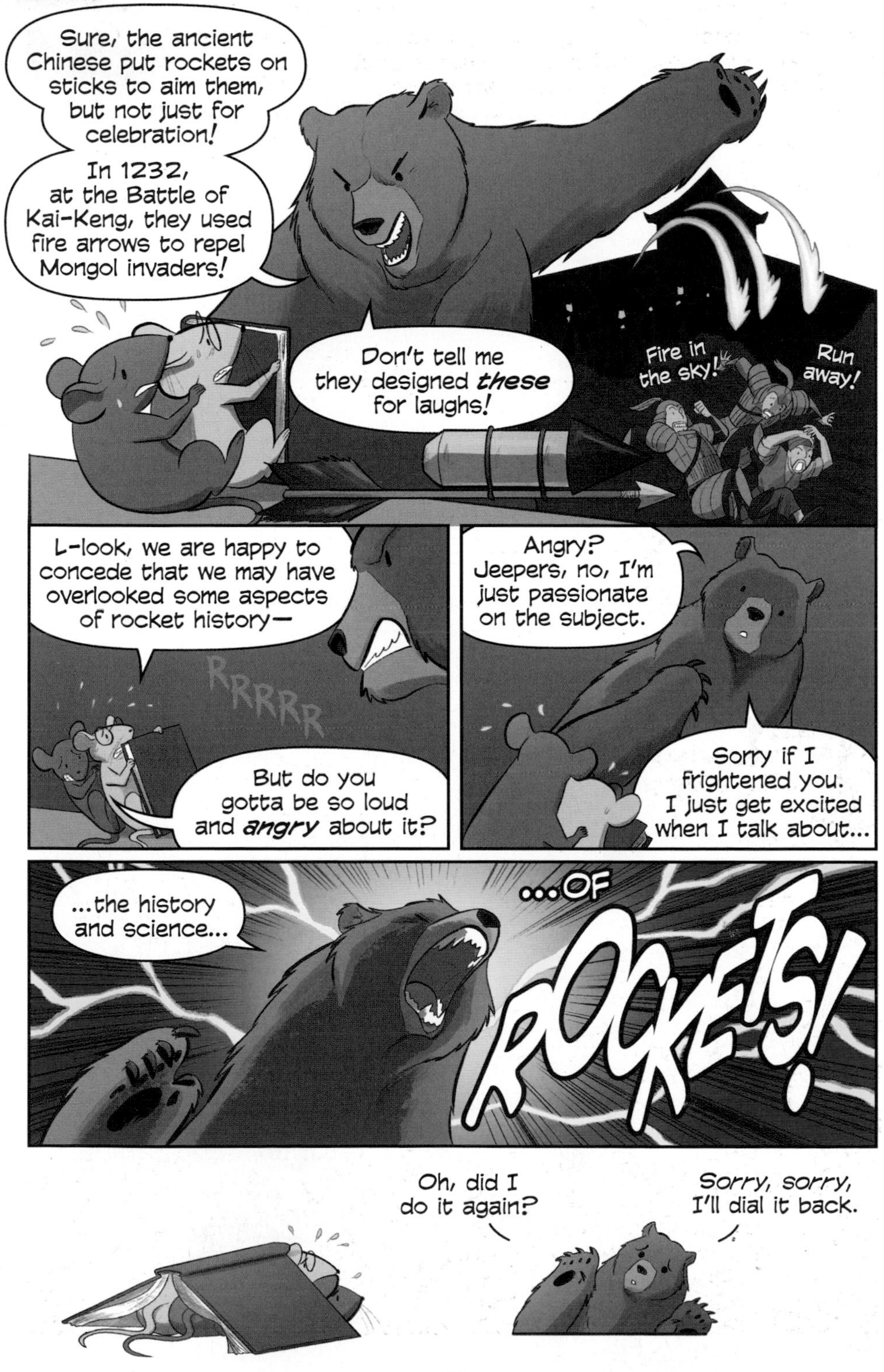
Sure, the ancient Chinese put rockets on sticks to aim them, but not just for celebration!
In 1232, at the Battle of Kai-Keng, they used fire arrows to repel Mongol invaders!
Don't tell me they designed *these* for laughs!
Fire in the sky!
Run away!
L-look, we are happy to concede that we may have overlooked some aspects of rocket history—
RRRRR
But do you gotta be so loud and *angry* about it?
Angry? Jeepers, no, I'm just passionate on the subject.
Sorry if I frightened you. I just get excited when I talk about...
...the history and science...
...OF ROCKETS!
Oh, did I do it again?
Sorry, sorry, I'll dial it back.

CHAPTER 3: ROCKETS IN WARFARE

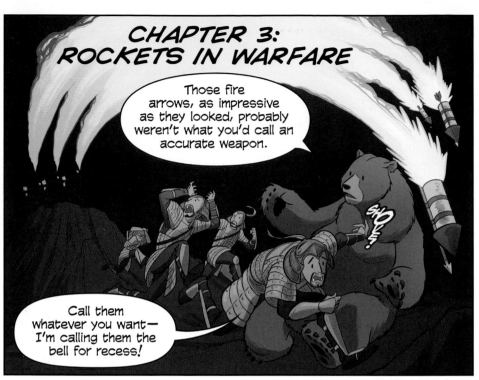

Those fire arrows, as impressive as they looked, probably weren't what you'd call an accurate weapon.

SHOVE!

Call them whatever you want— I'm calling them the bell for recess!

This isn't a shortcoming when firing rockets to create displays in the sky, but it becomes an engineering challenge once you introduce a target.

Suppose I wanted to fire a rocket at that oatmeal there.

Why? Oatmeal is delicious.

You're still here?

Look, any breakfast cereal without marshmallows is an insult to breakfast!

You just like the cartoon characters on the boxes.

So what if I do?

BACK TO MY DEMO! Early rocketeers found greater accuracy by attaching a stick to the rocket...

We're with ya.

SShff!

POOM

Arced it a little too far, pal.

Some attached fins to the rockets, which could add spin, like passing a football...

The long bomb!

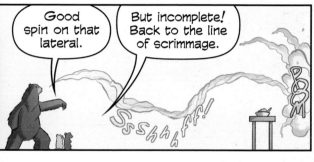

Good spin on that lateral.

But incomplete! Back to the line of scrimmage.

Ssshhff!

POOM

...while others tried firing rockets from hollow tubes to guide them!

I'm outta here!

SHF!

POOM

Ah! Foiled by recoil!

Once you give a rocket a target, stabilizing flight becomes an interesting problem.

And while nobody enjoys war, a lot of advances came out of developing rockets for that purpose.

Let's start by learning to think in 3-D.

Our mouths are gonna go to war on this oatmeal.

Please tell me he's out of rockets.

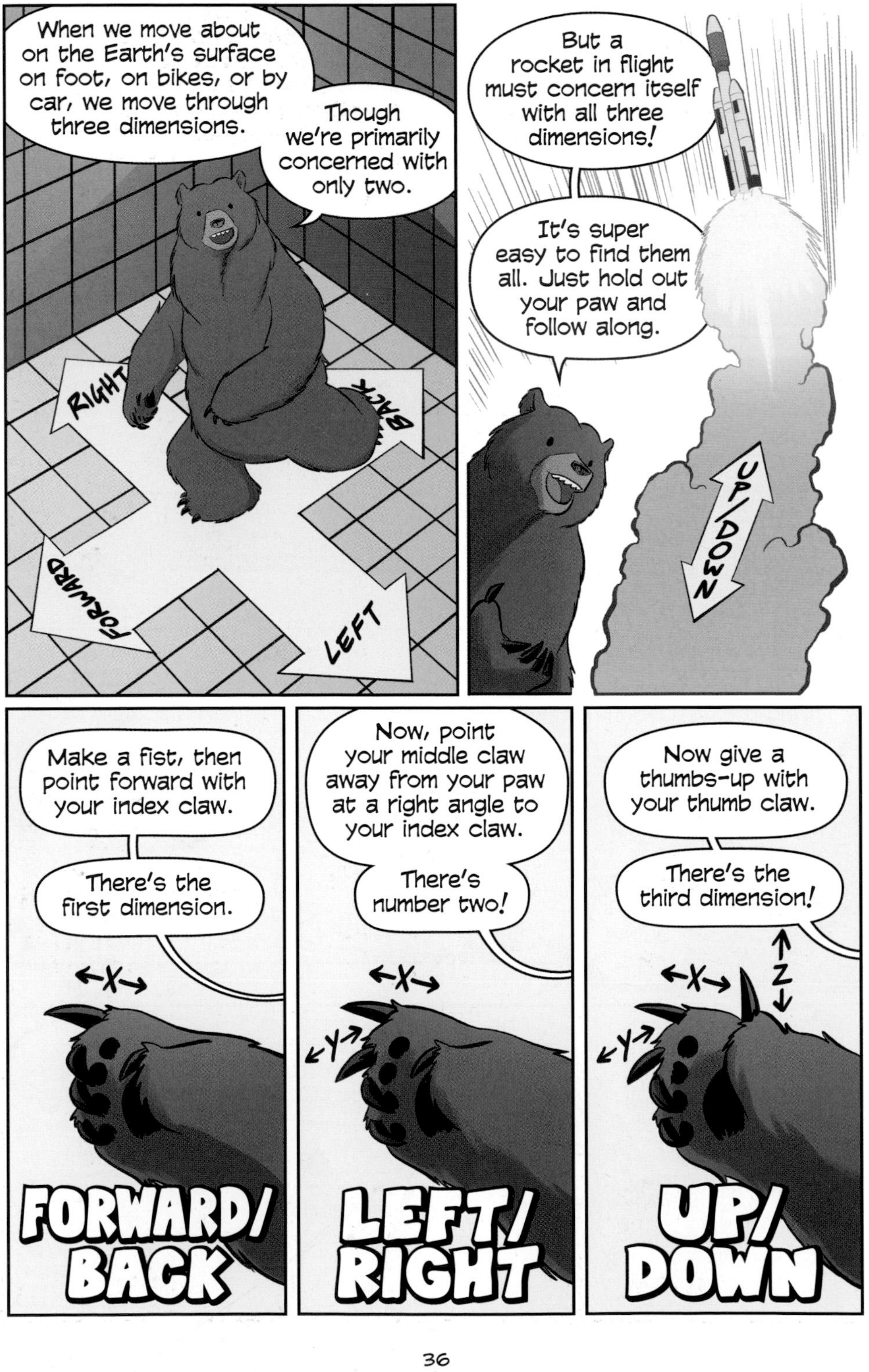
When we move about on the Earth's surface on foot, on bikes, or by car, we move through three dimensions.
Though we're primarily concerned with only two.
RIGHT
BACK
FORWARD
LEFT
But a rocket in flight must concern itself with all three dimensions!
It's super easy to find them all. Just hold out your paw and follow along.
UP/DOWN
Make a fist, then point forward with your index claw.
There's the first dimension.
X
FORWARD/ BACK
Now, point your middle claw away from your paw at a right angle to your index claw.
There's number two!
X
Y
LEFT/ RIGHT
Now give a thumbs-up with your thumb claw.
There's the third dimension!
X
Y
Z
UP/ DOWN

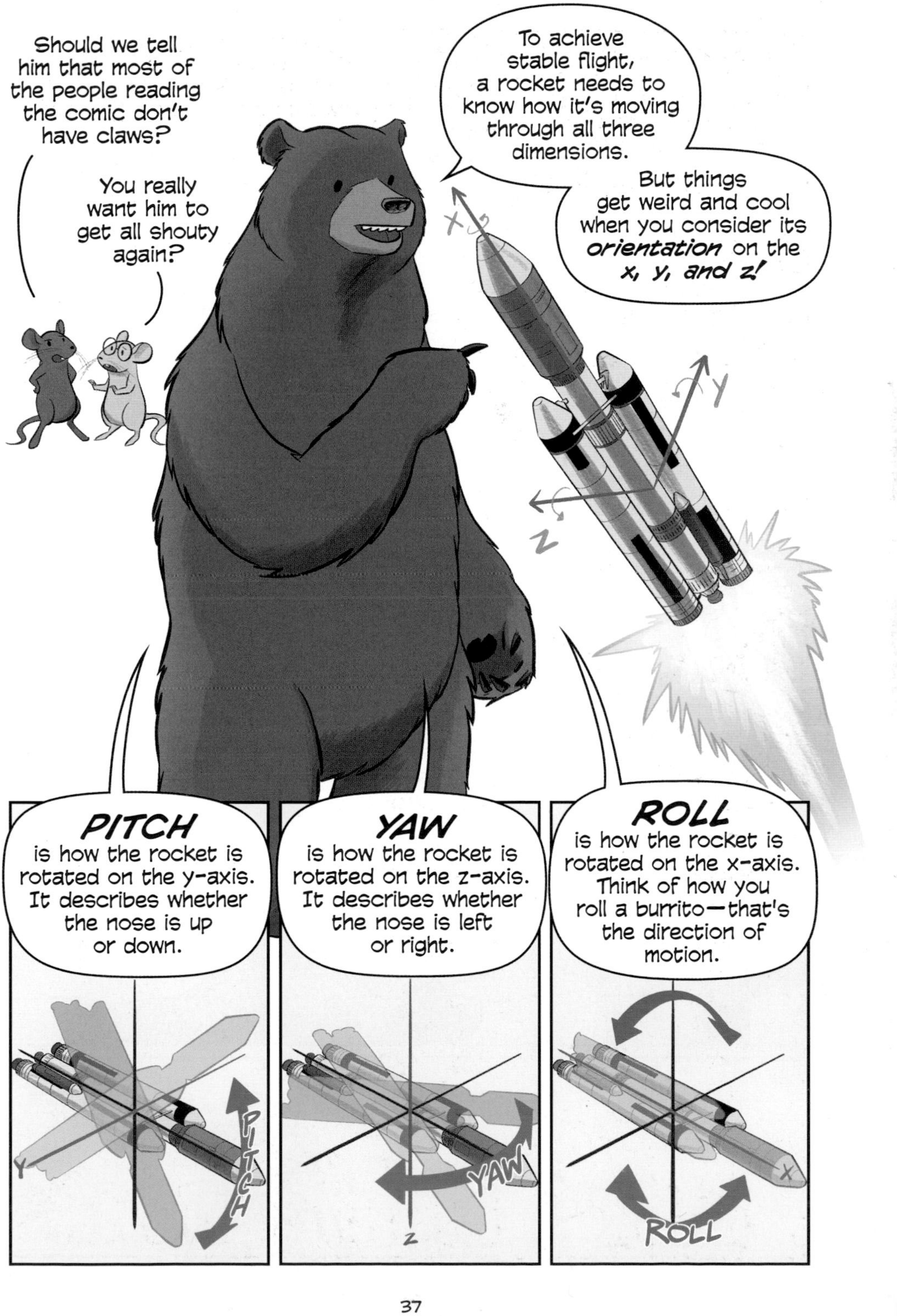

Should we tell him that most of the people reading the comic don't have claws?
You really want him to get all shouty again?
To achieve stable flight, a rocket needs to know how it's moving through all three dimensions.
But things get weird and cool when you consider its *orientation* on the *x, y, and z!*
X
Y
Z
PITCH is how the rocket is rotated on the y-axis. It describes whether the nose is up or down.
Y
PITCH
YAW is how the rocket is rotated on the z-axis. It describes whether the nose is left or right.
YAW
Z
ROLL is how the rocket is rotated on the x-axis. Think of how you roll a burrito—that's the direction of motion.
X
ROLL

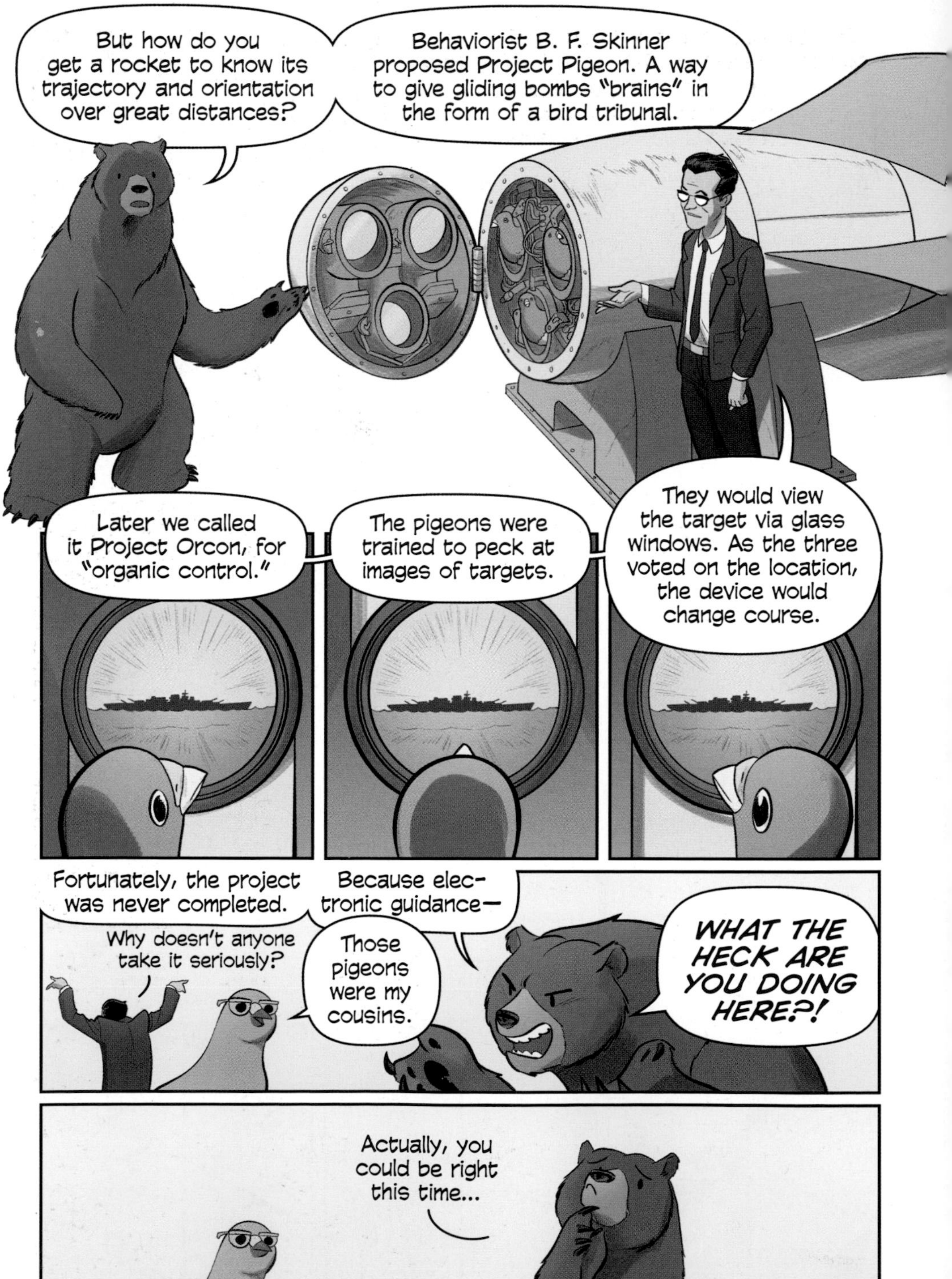

But how do you get a rocket to know its trajectory and orientation over great distances?
Behaviorist B. F. Skinner proposed Project Pigeon. A way to give gliding bombs "brains" in the form of a bird tribunal.
Later we called it Project Orcon, for "organic control."
The pigeons were trained to peck at images of targets.
They would view the target via glass windows. As the three voted on the location, the device would change course.
Fortunately, the project was never completed.
Because elec-tronic guidance—
Why doesn't anyone take it seriously?
Those pigeons were my cousins.
WHAT THE HECK ARE YOU DOING HERE?!
Actually, you could be right this time...

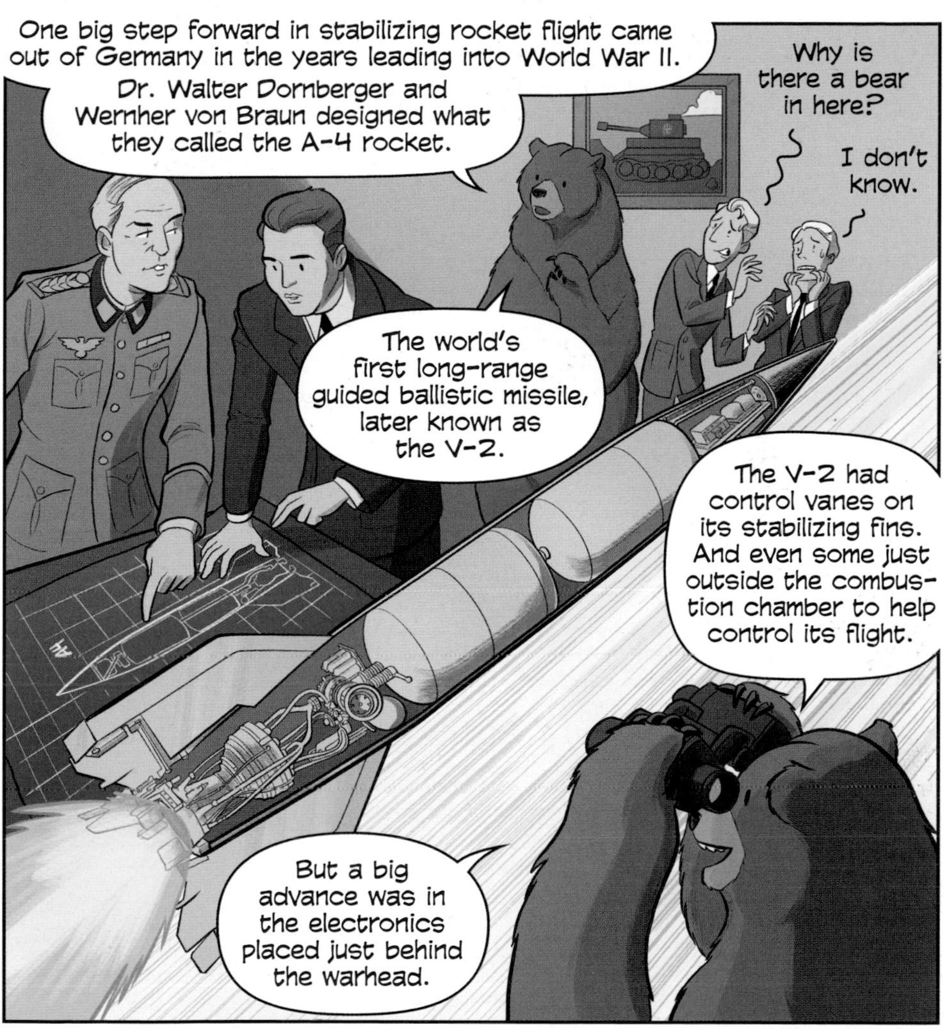
One big step forward in stabilizing rocket flight came out of Germany in the years leading into World War II.
Dr. Walter Dornberger and Wernher von Braun designed what they called the A-4 rocket.
Why is there a bear in here?
I don't know.
The world's first long-range guided ballistic missile, later known as the V-2.
The V-2 had control vanes on its stabilizing fins. And even some just outside the combustion chamber to help control its flight.
But a big advance was in the electronics placed just behind the warhead.

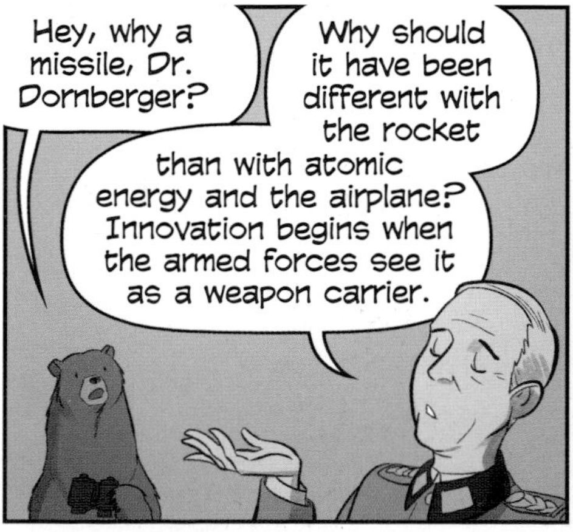
Hey, why a missile, Dr. Dornberger?
Why should it have been different with the rocket
than with atomic energy and the airplane? Innovation begins when the armed forces see it as a weapon carrier.

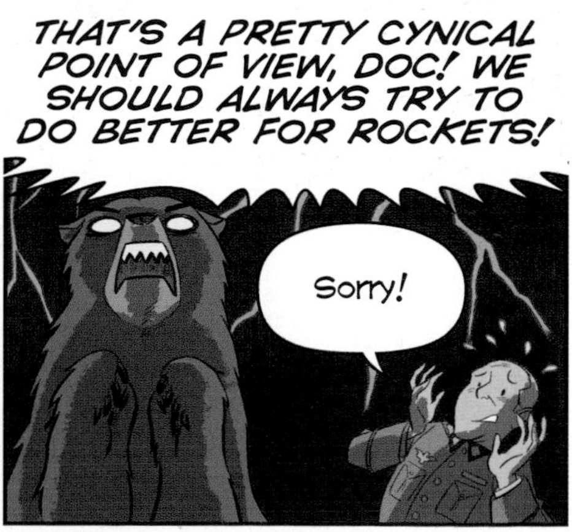
THAT'S A PRETTY CYNICAL POINT OF VIEW, DOC! WE SHOULD ALWAYS TRY TO DO BETTER FOR ROCKETS!
Sorry!

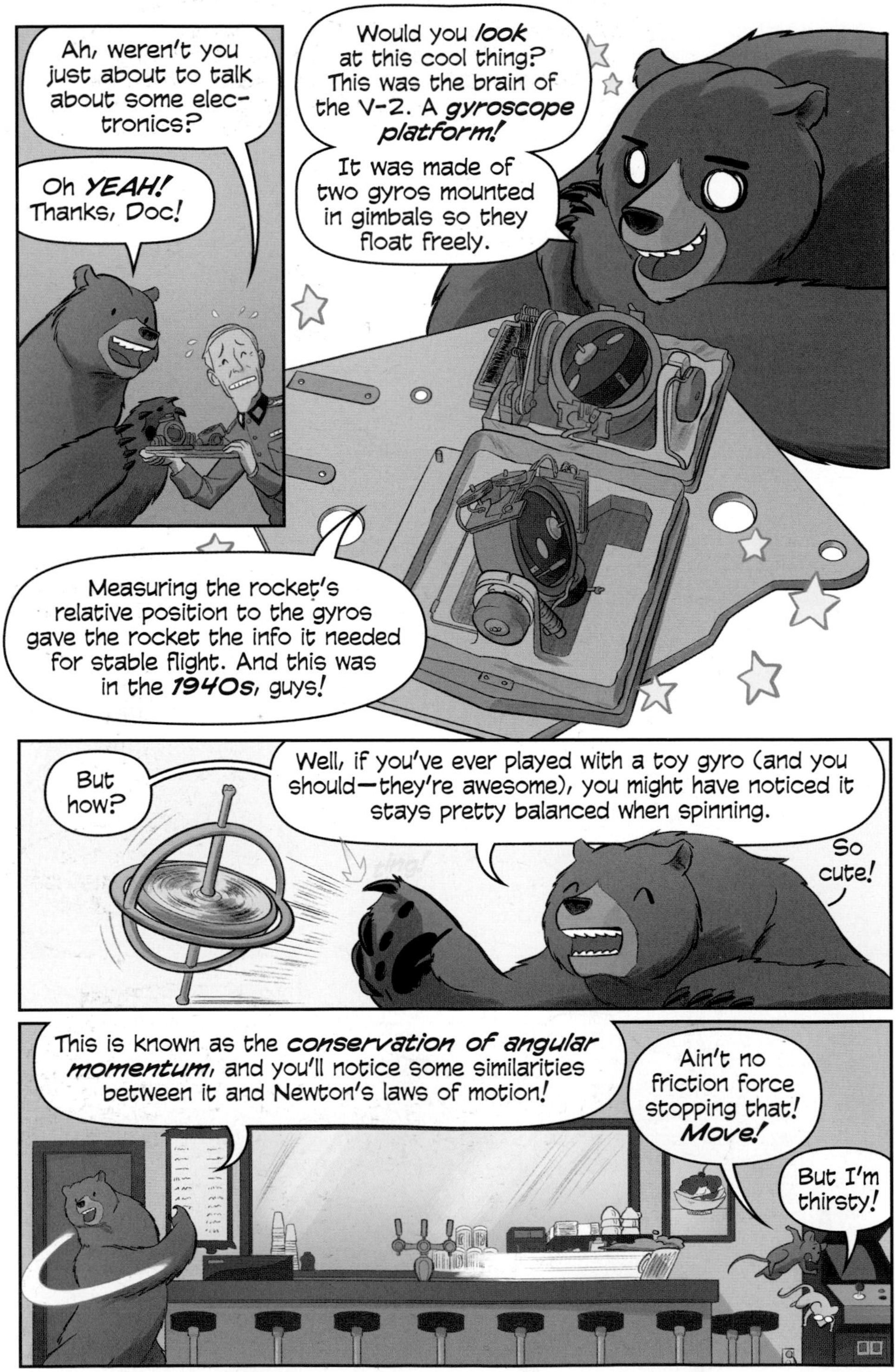

Ah, weren't you just about to talk about some electronics?
Oh *YEAH!* Thanks, Doc!
Would you *look* at this cool thing? This was the brain of the V-2. A ***gyroscope platform!***
It was made of two gyros mounted in gimbals so they float freely.
Measuring the rocket's relative position to the gyros gave the rocket the info it needed for stable flight. And this was in the ***1940s***, guys!
But how?
Well, if you've ever played with a toy gyro (and you should—they're awesome), you might have noticed it stays pretty balanced when spinning.
So cute!
This is known as the ***conservation of angular momentum***, and you'll notice some similarities between it and Newton's laws of motion!
Ain't no friction force stopping that! ***Move!***
But I'm thirsty!

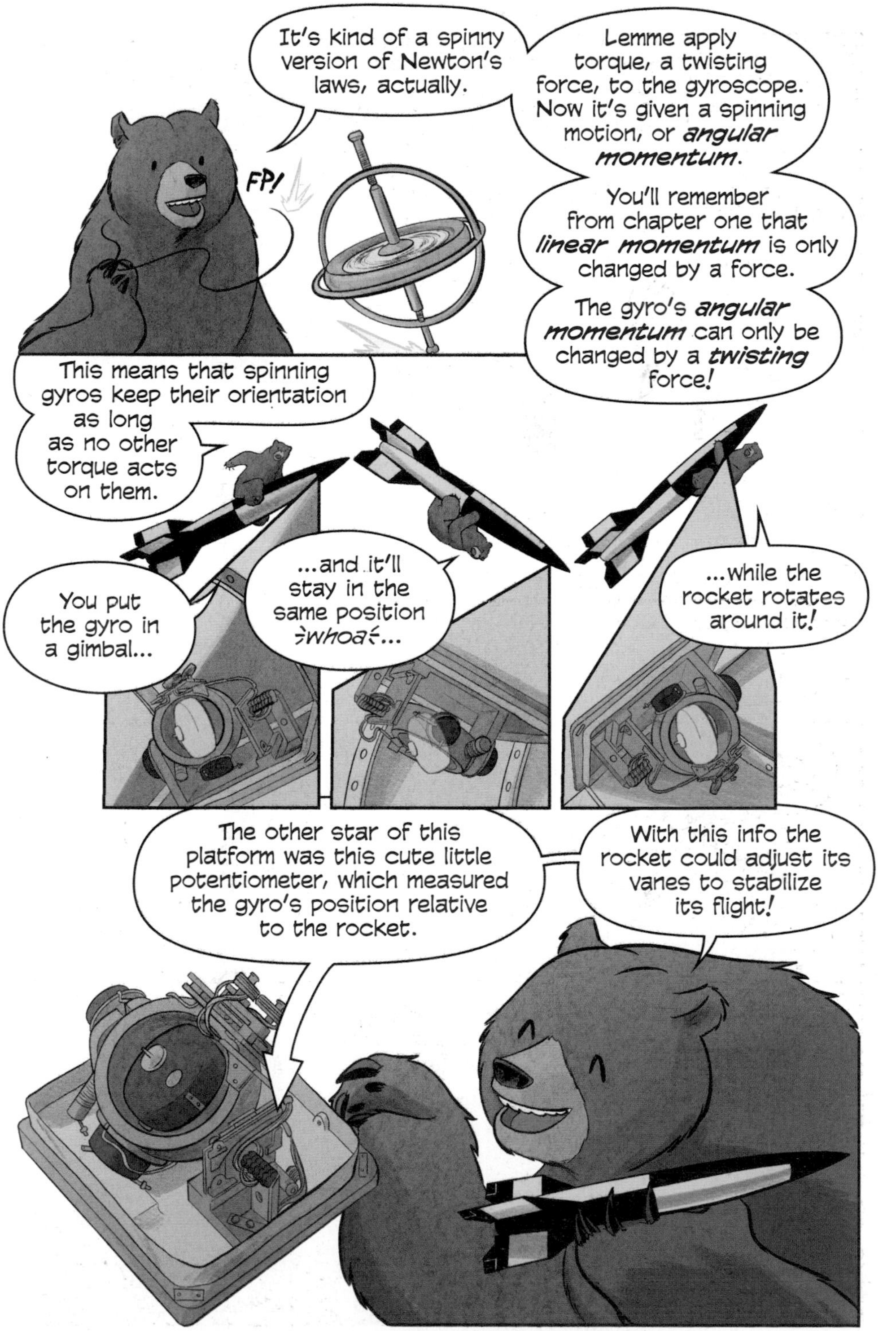
It's kind of a spinny version of Newton's laws, actually.
FP!
Lemme apply torque, a twisting force, to the gyroscope. Now it's given a spinning motion, or *angular momentum*.
You'll remember from chapter one that *linear momentum* is only changed by a force.
The gyro's *angular momentum* can only be changed by a *twisting* force!
This means that spinning gyros keep their orientation as long as no other torque acts on them.
You put the gyro in a gimbal...
...and it'll stay in the same position *whoa*...
...while the rocket rotates around it!
The other star of this platform was this cute little potentiometer, which measured the gyro's position relative to the rocket.
With this info the rocket could adjust its vanes to stabilize its flight!

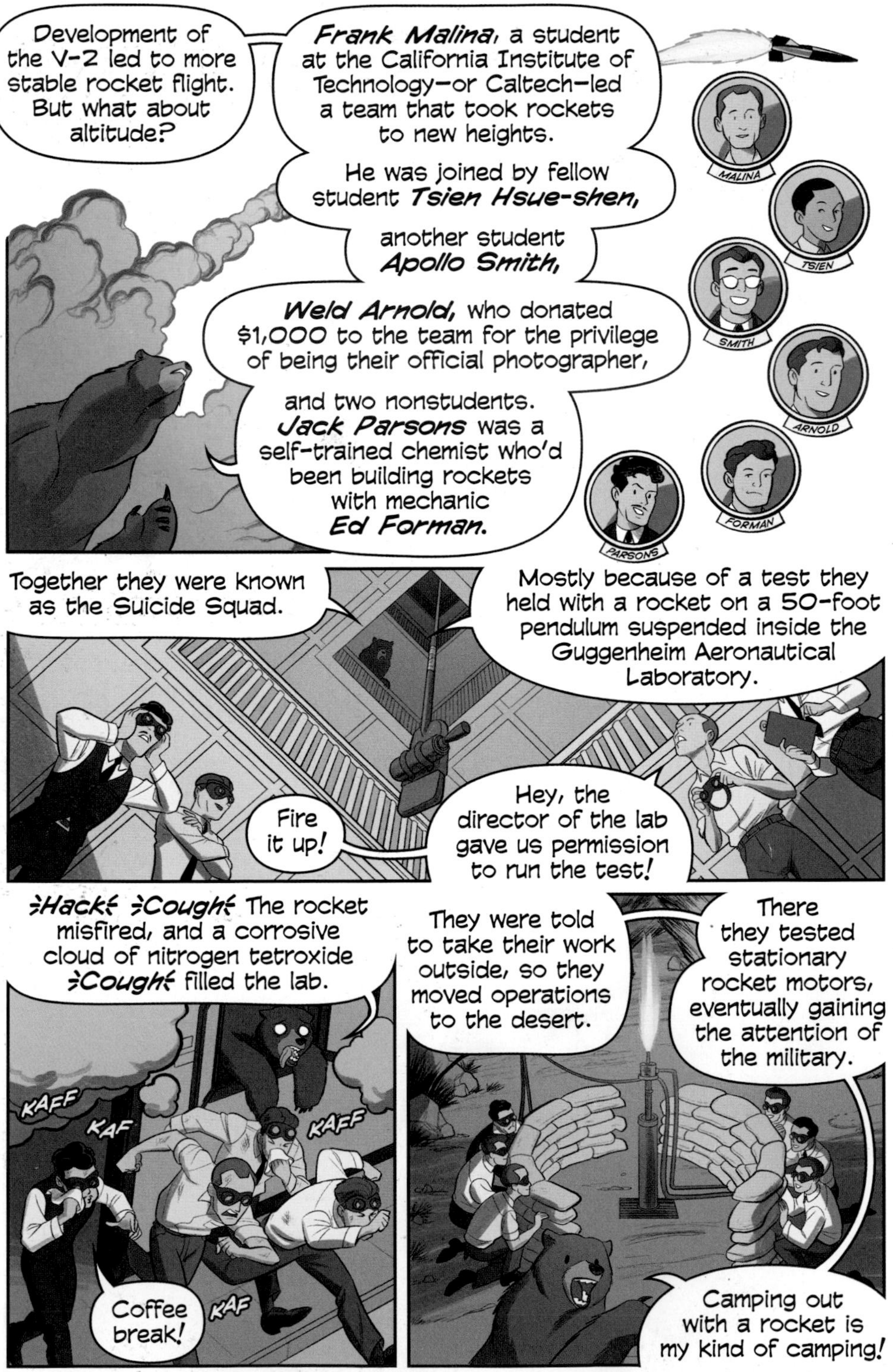

Development of the V-2 led to more stable rocket flight. But what about altitude?
Frank Malina, a student at the California Institute of Technology—or Caltech—led a team that took rockets to new heights.
He was joined by fellow student Tsien Hsue-shen,
another student Apollo Smith,
Weld Arnold, who donated $1,000 to the team for the privilege of being their official photographer,
and two nonstudents. Jack Parsons was a self-trained chemist who'd been building rockets with mechanic Ed Forman.
MALINA
TSIEN
SMITH
ARNOLD
FORMAN
PARSONS
Together they were known as the Suicide Squad.
Mostly because of a test they held with a rocket on a 50-foot pendulum suspended inside the Guggenheim Aeronautical Laboratory.
Fire it up!
Hey, the director of the lab gave us permission to run the test!
Hack Cough The rocket misfired, and a corrosive cloud of nitrogen tetroxide Cough filled the lab.
KAFF
KAF
KAFF
Coffee break!
KAF
They were told to take their work outside, so they moved operations to the desert.
There they tested stationary rocket motors, eventually gaining the attention of the military.
Camping out with a rocket is my kind of camping!

They grew the team and founded the Jet Propulsion Laboratory.

Together they developed the *jet-assisted take-off rocket.*

JATO

PRIVATE A, F

CORPORAL E, F

WAC CORPORAL

These fellas could deliver instruments into the upper atmosphere.

The WAC Corporal was named for the Women's Army Corps. We thought of it as a sister to the Corporal E.

Cool!

Malina and his team came up with a neat use for the WAC Corporal and a recently acquired German V-2.

Launched in 1950, it was the first rocket to launch from Cape Canaveral!

VROOM

The Corporal would gain more acceleration by launching from the in-flight V-2.

This Bumper WAC was the first human-made object to reach outer space!

JPL made rockets for the military, but these achievements pointed to higher goals...

One might say the era of rocket propulsion development...

...was now giving way to the era of space vehicles and man in extra-terrestrial space.

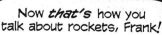

Now *that's* how you talk about rockets, Frank!

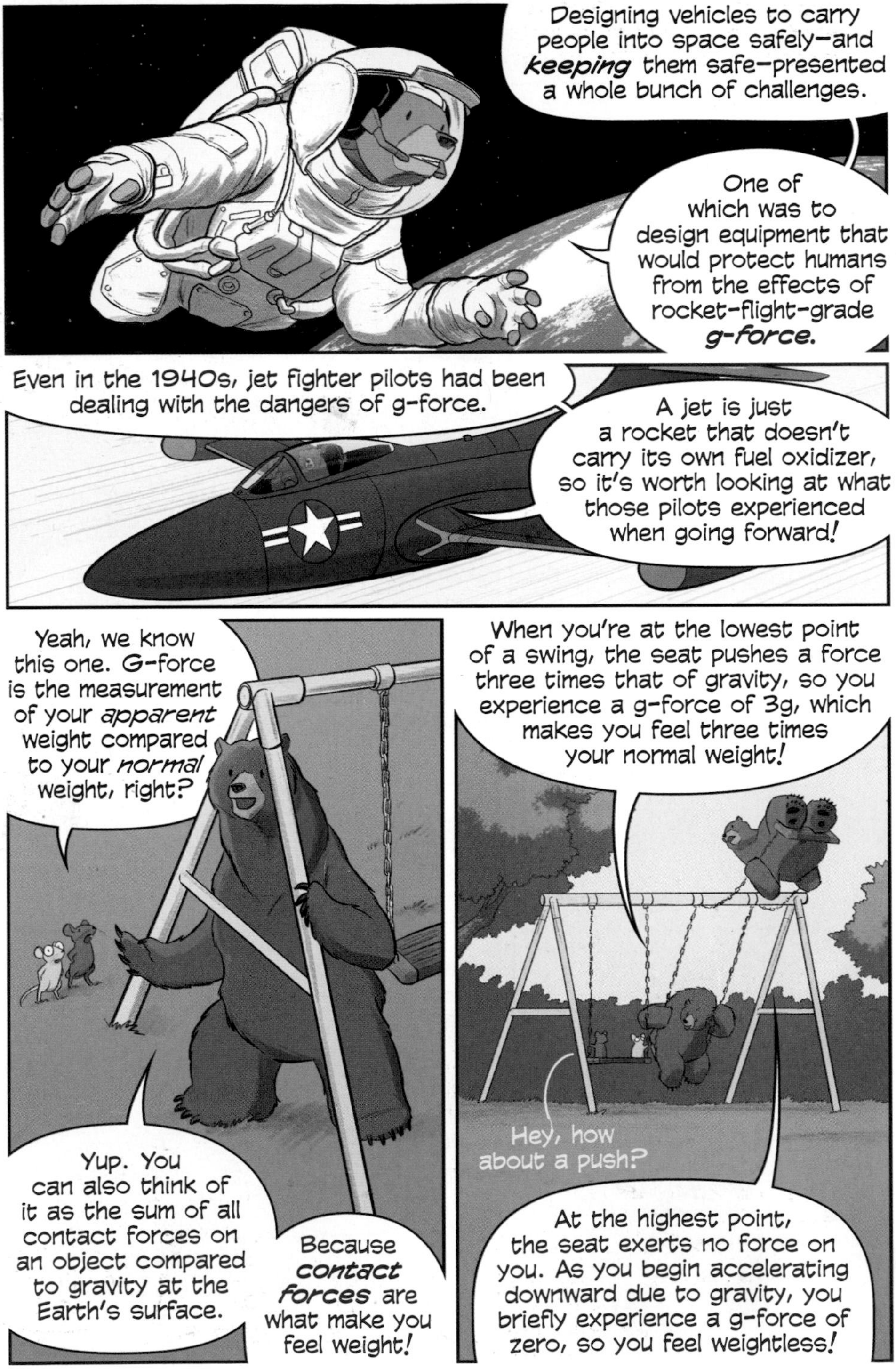

Designing vehicles to carry people into space safely—and *keeping* them safe—presented a whole bunch of challenges.
One of which was to design equipment that would protect humans from the effects of rocket-flight-grade *g-force.*
Even in the 1940s, jet fighter pilots had been dealing with the dangers of g-force.
A jet is just a rocket that doesn't carry its own fuel oxidizer, so it's worth looking at what those pilots experienced when going forward!
Yeah, we know this one. G-force is the measurement of your *apparent* weight compared to your *normal* weight, right?
Yup. You can also think of it as the sum of all contact forces on an object compared to gravity at the Earth's surface.
Because *contact forces* are what make you feel weight!
When you're at the lowest point of a swing, the seat pushes a force three times that of gravity, so you experience a g-force of 3g, which makes you feel three times your normal weight!
Hey, how about a push?
At the highest point, the seat exerts no force on you. As you begin accelerating downward due to gravity, you briefly experience a g-force of zero, so you feel weightless!

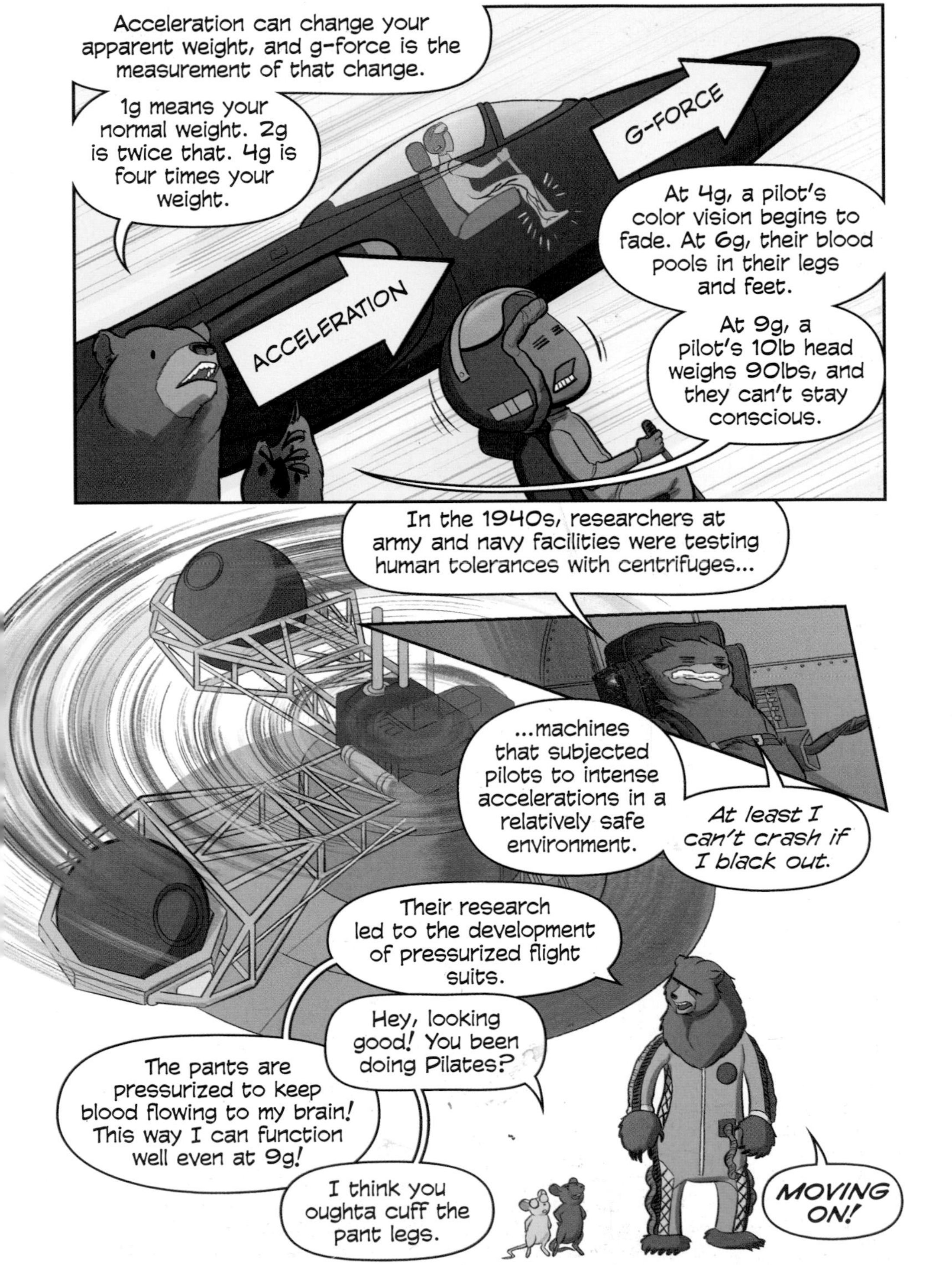
Acceleration can change your apparent weight, and g-force is the measurement of that change.
1g means your normal weight. 2g is twice that. 4g is four times your weight.
G-FORCE
ACCELERATION
At 4g, a pilot's color vision begins to fade. At 6g, their blood pools in their legs and feet.
At 9g, a pilot's 10lb head weighs 90lbs, and they can't stay conscious.
In the 1940s, researchers at army and navy facilities were testing human tolerances with centrifuges...
...machines that subjected pilots to intense accelerations in a relatively safe environment.
At least I can't crash if I black out.
Their research led to the development of pressurized flight suits.
Hey, looking good! You been doing Pilates?
The pants are pressurized to keep blood flowing to my brain! This way I can function well even at 9g!
I think you oughta cuff the pant legs.
MOVING ON!

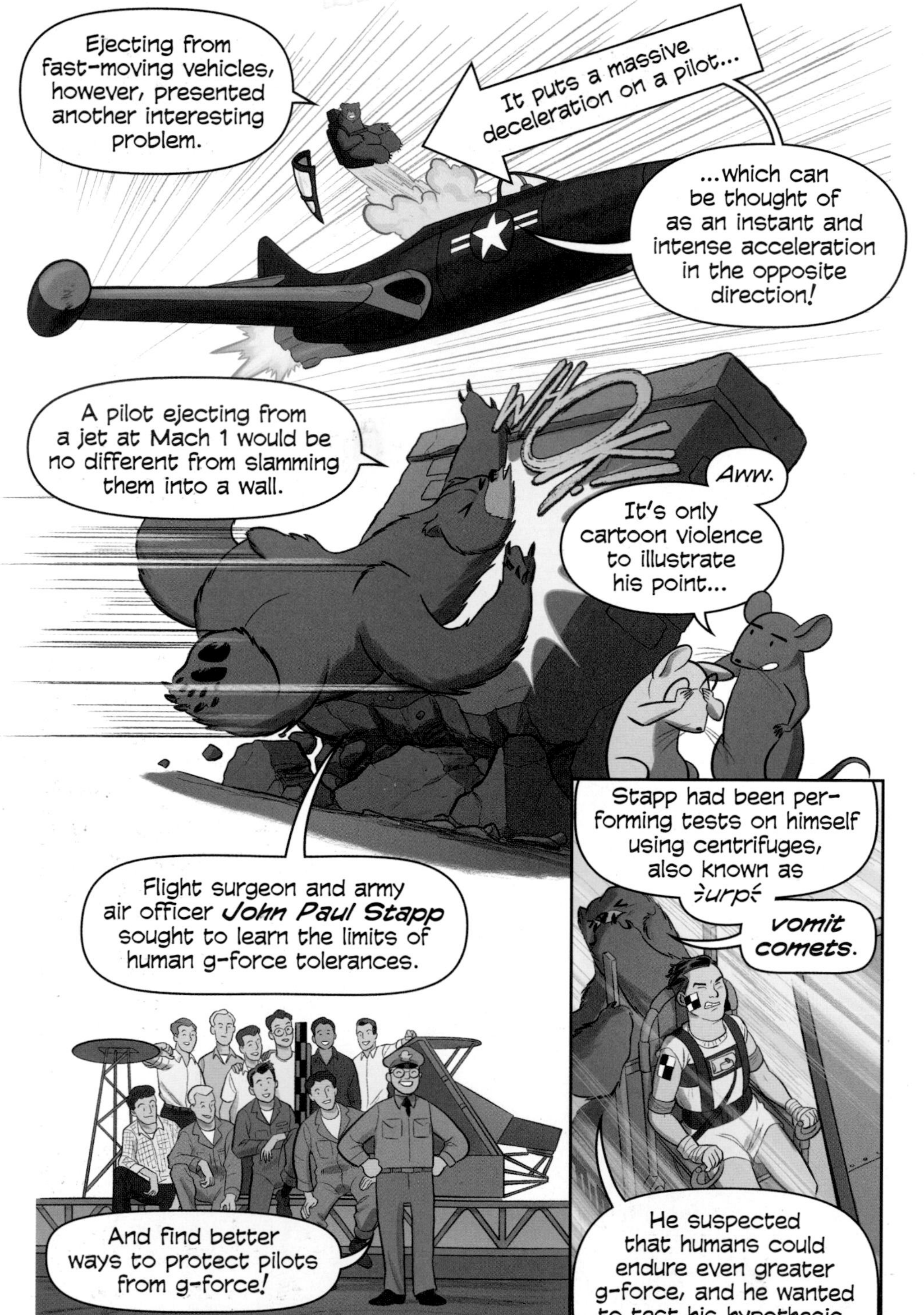
Ejecting from fast-moving vehicles, however, presented another interesting problem.
It puts a massive deceleration on a pilot...
...which can be thought of as an instant and intense acceleration in the opposite direction!
WHOK
A pilot ejecting from a jet at Mach 1 would be no different from slamming them into a wall.
Aww.
It's only cartoon violence to illustrate his point...
Flight surgeon and army air officer *John Paul Stapp* sought to learn the limits of human g-force tolerances.
And find better ways to protect pilots from g-force!
Stapp had been performing tests on himself using centrifuges, also known as
urp
vomit comets.
He suspected that humans could endure even greater g-force, and he wanted to test his hypothesis.

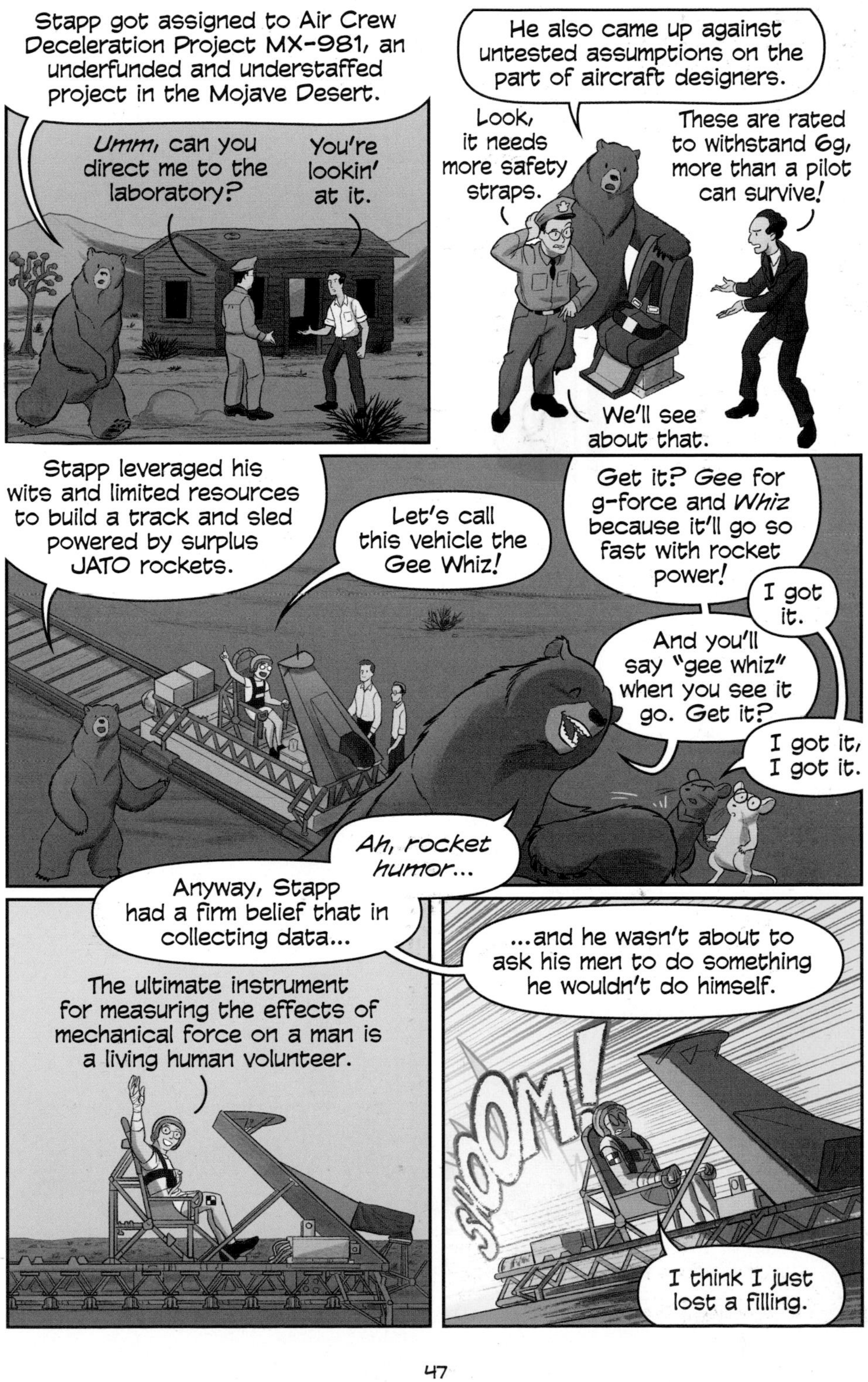

Stapp got assigned to Air Crew Deceleration Project MX-981, an underfunded and understaffed project in the Mojave Desert.
Umm, can you direct me to the laboratory?
You're lookin' at it.
He also came up against untested assumptions on the part of aircraft designers.
Look, it needs more safety straps.
These are rated to withstand 6g, more than a pilot can survive!
We'll see about that.
Stapp leveraged his wits and limited resources to build a track and sled powered by surplus JATO rockets.
Let's call this vehicle the Gee Whiz!
Get it? *Gee* for g-force and *Whiz* because it'll go so fast with rocket power!
I got it.
And you'll say "gee whiz" when you see it go. Get it?
I got it, I got it.
Ah, rocket humor...
Anyway, Stapp had a firm belief that in collecting data...
The ultimate instrument for measuring the effects of mechanical force on a man is a living human volunteer.
...and he wasn't about to ask his men to do something he wouldn't do himself.
SHOOOM!
I think I just lost a filling.

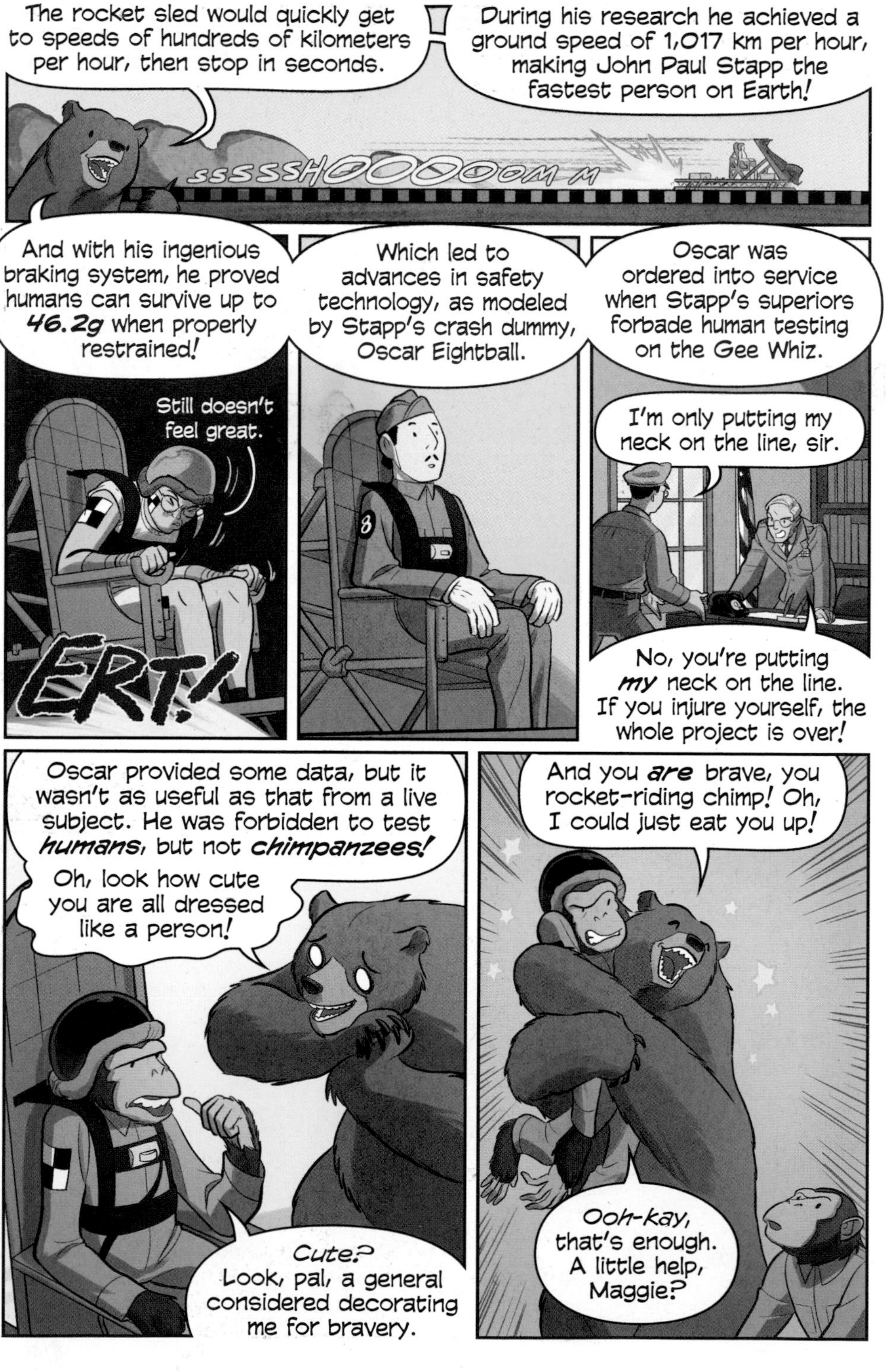

The rocket sled would quickly get to speeds of hundreds of kilometers per hour, then stop in seconds.
During his research he achieved a ground speed of 1,017 km per hour, making John Paul Stapp the fastest person on Earth!
sssSSSHOOOOOOOOM M
And with his ingenious braking system, he proved humans can survive up to *46.2g* when properly restrained!
Still doesn't feel great.
ERT!
Which led to advances in safety technology, as modeled by Stapp's crash dummy, Oscar Eightball.
Oscar was ordered into service when Stapp's superiors forbade human testing on the Gee Whiz.
I'm only putting my neck on the line, sir.
No, you're putting *my* neck on the line. If you injure yourself, the whole project is over!
Oscar provided some data, but it wasn't as useful as that from a live subject. He was forbidden to test *humans*, but not *chimpanzees!*
Oh, look how cute you are all dressed like a person!
Cute? Look, pal, a general considered decorating me for bravery.
And you *are* brave, you rocket-riding chimp! Oh, I could just eat you up!
Ooh-kay, that's enough. A little help, Maggie?

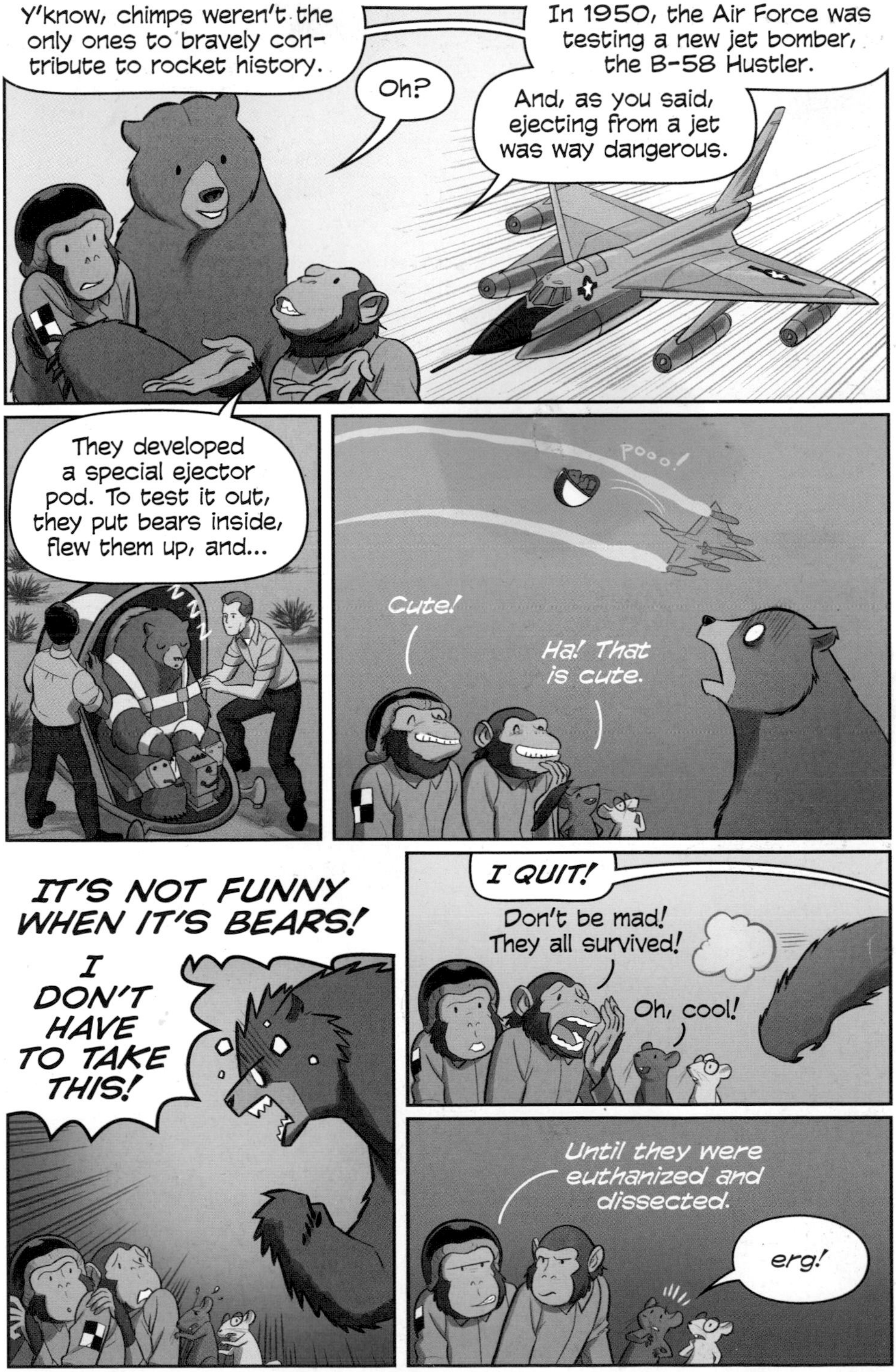
Y'know, chimps weren't the only ones to bravely contribute to rocket history.
Oh?
In 1950, the Air Force was testing a new jet bomber, the B-58 Hustler.
And, as you said, ejecting from a jet was way dangerous.
They developed a special ejector pod. To test it out, they put bears inside, flew them up, and...
POOO!
Cute!
Ha! That is cute.
IT'S NOT FUNNY WHEN IT'S BEARS!
I DON'T HAVE TO TAKE THIS!
I QUIT!
Don't be mad! They all survived!
Oh, cool!
Until they were euthanized and dissected.
erg!

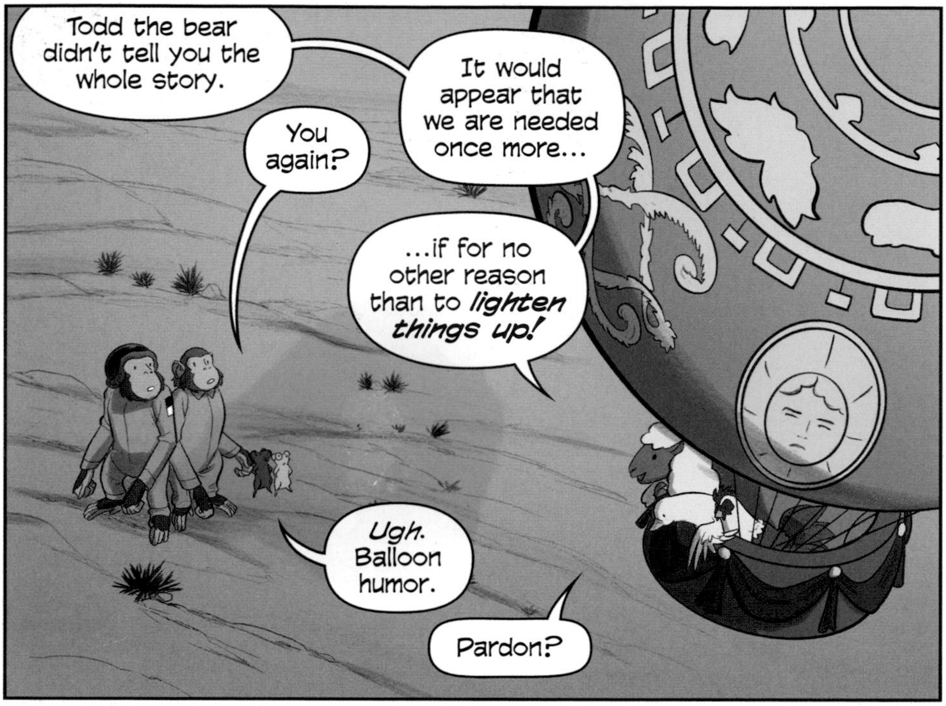
Todd the bear didn't tell you the whole story.
You again?
It would appear that we are needed once more...
...if for no other reason than to *lighten things up!*
Ugh. Balloon humor.
Pardon?

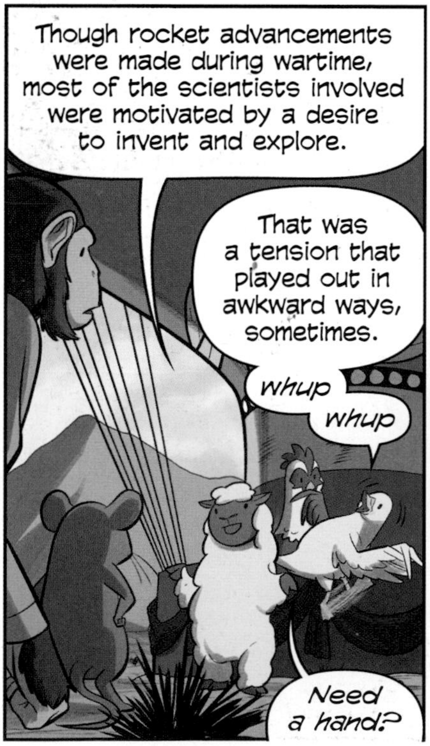
Though rocket advancements were made during wartime, most of the scientists involved were motivated by a desire to invent and explore.
That was a tension that played out in awkward ways, sometimes.
whup
whup
Need a hand?

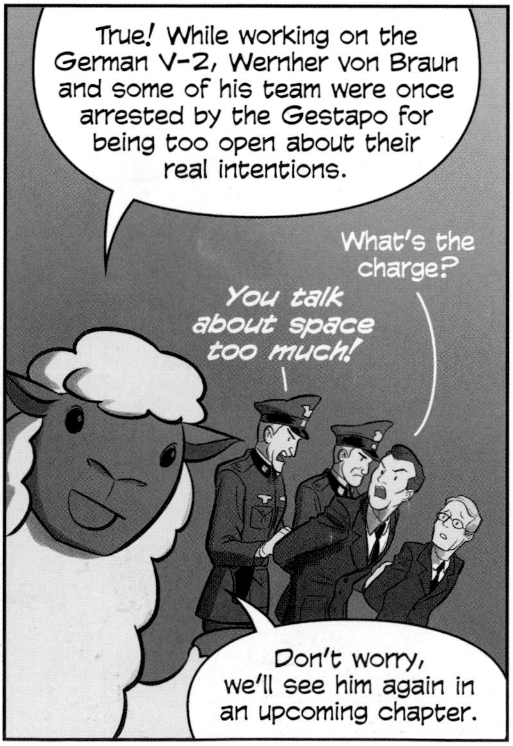
True! While working on the German V-2, Wernher von Braun and some of his team were once arrested by the Gestapo for being too open about their real intentions.
What's the charge?
You talk about space too much!
Don't worry, we'll see him again in an upcoming chapter.

CHAPTER 4: ROCKET INVENTORS

Ooh, cool diagrams.

I love these cutaway drawings...

$$\Delta V = U_{eq} \; ln(R) = 785 \times ln(1.5) \approx 318 \, m/s$$

There were many who contributed to rocket advancements without military funding.

Three in particular made similar breakthroughs around the same time.

American scientist Robert Goddard was driven by a desire to see humans explore the Moon and beyond...

Robert, you forgot your coat again!

...? Thank you, dear.

...sometimes at the expense of other things.

After earning his PhD in physics, and joining the faculty at Clark University in Massachusetts, he set on his mission.

Gonna launch me some rockets!

For the next several years, Goddard experimented with solid and liquid fuel rockets in Worcester.

Wicked burn!

FWAM!

Robert, your coat!

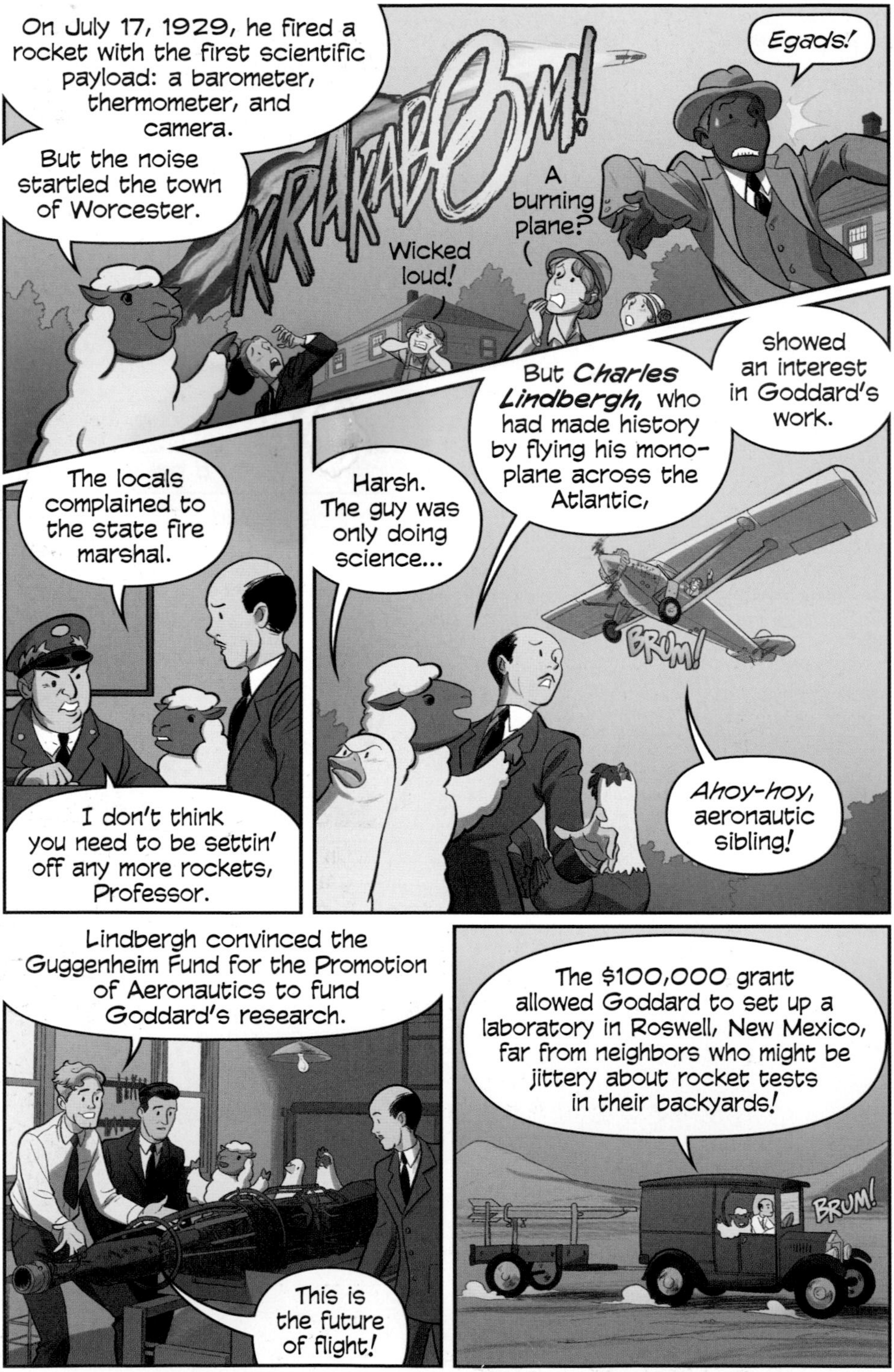
On July 17, 1929, he fired a rocket with the first scientific payload: a barometer, thermometer, and camera.
But the noise startled the town of Worcester.
KRAKABOOM!
Wicked loud!
A burning plane?
Egads!
The locals complained to the state fire marshal.
I don't think you need to be settin' off any more rockets, Professor.
Harsh. The guy was only doing science...
But *Charles Lindbergh,* who had made history by flying his monoplane across the Atlantic,
showed an interest in Goddard's work.
BROM!
Ahoy-hoy, aeronautic sibling!
Lindbergh convinced the Guggenheim Fund for the Promotion of Aeronautics to fund Goddard's research.
This is the future of flight!
The $100,000 grant allowed Goddard to set up a laboratory in Roswell, New Mexico, far from neighbors who might be jittery about rocket tests in their backyards!
BRUM!

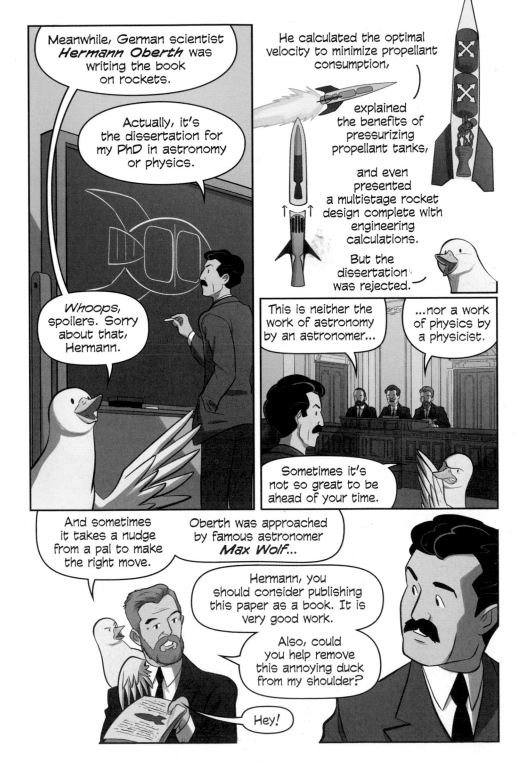

Meanwhile, German scientist *Hermann Oberth* was writing the book on rockets.

Actually, it's the dissertation for my PhD in astronomy or physics.

Whoops, spoilers. Sorry about that, Hermann.

He calculated the optimal velocity to minimize propellant consumption,

explained the benefits of pressurizing propellant tanks,

and even presented a multistage rocket design complete with engineering calculations.

But the dissertation was rejected.

This is neither the work of astronomy by an astronomer...

...nor a work of physics by a physicist.

Sometimes it's not so great to be ahead of your time.

And sometimes it takes a nudge from a pal to make the right move.

Oberth was approached by famous astronomer *Max Wolf*...

Hermann, you should consider publishing this paper as a book. It is very good work.

Also, could you help remove this annoying duck from my shoulder?

Hey!

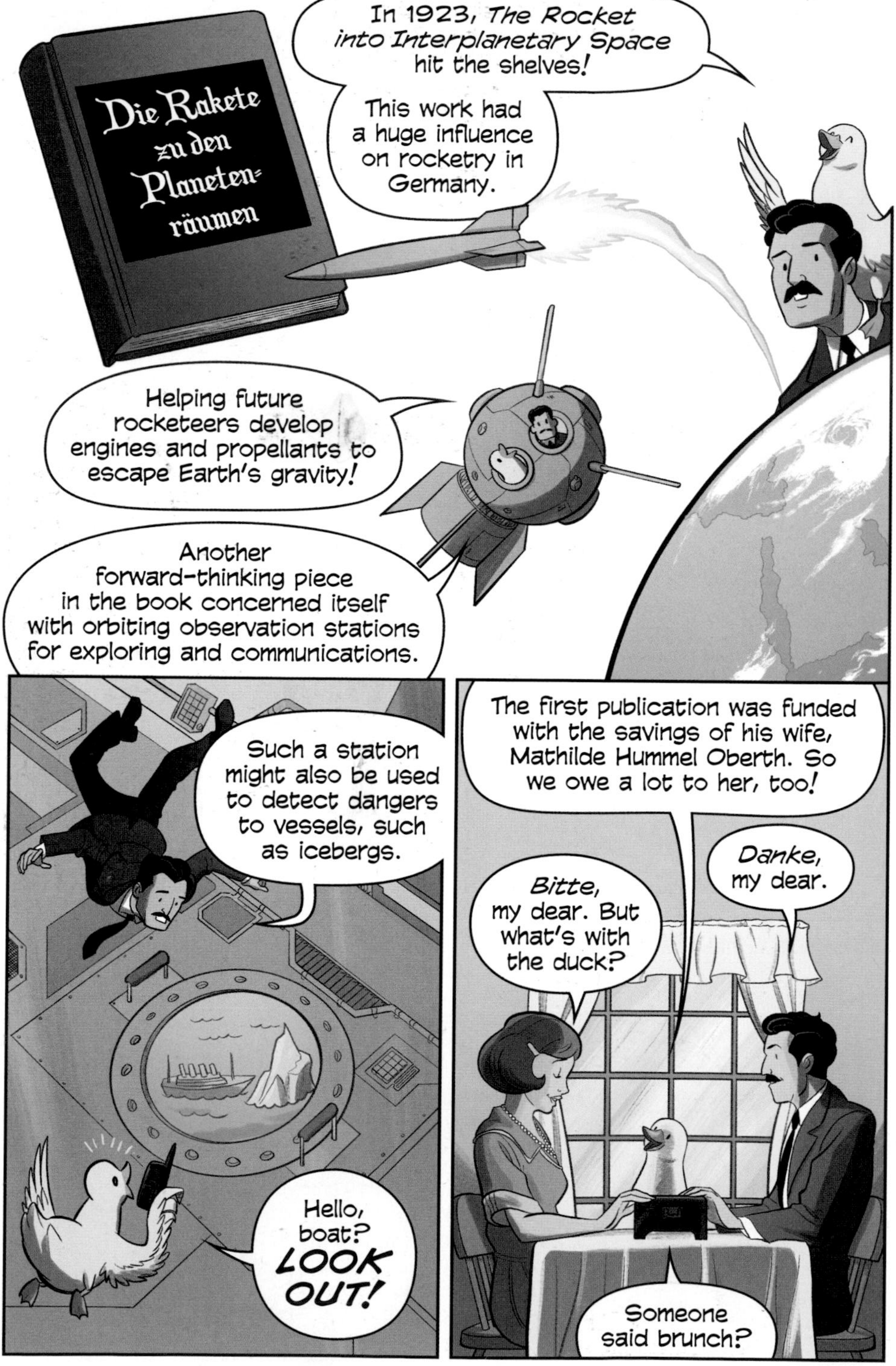

Die Rakete zu den Planeten= räumen
In 1923, *The Rocket into Interplanetary Space* hit the shelves!
This work had a huge influence on rocketry in Germany.
Helping future rocketeers develop engines and propellants to escape Earth's gravity!
Another forward-thinking piece in the book concerned itself with orbiting observation stations for exploring and communications.
Such a station might also be used to detect dangers to vessels, such as icebergs.
Hello, boat? ***LOOK OUT!***
The first publication was funded with the savings of his wife, Mathilde Hummel Oberth. So we owe a lot to her, too!
Bitte, my dear. But what's with the duck?
Danke, my dear.
Someone said brunch?

Before either of those guys, there was the Russian theorist *Konstantin Tsiolkovsky.*

In his 1883 manuscript *Free Space*, he drew a proposal for a spacecraft powered by rockets, featuring accommodations for weightless crew and even an air lock.

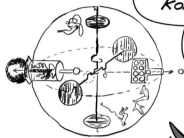

Regarded in Russia as the founder of cosmonautics, he had a big impact on rocketry, and he was mostly self-taught!

At age eleven, he became nearly deaf after contracting scarlet fever, making it impossible for him to attend higher learning institutions of the time.

At sixteen, he moved to Moscow, where he primarily hung out at what is now the Russian State Library. His near deafness isolated him, and he became withdrawn.

It's okay. My books are my teachers.

Later he became a high school teacher and began his writings on rockets.

"Research into Interplanetary Space by Means of Rocket Power" was one of his first important articles.

He discovered the rocket equation, describing how a rocket moves with variable mass of expended propellant given exhaust velocity.

And he wrote this in 1903, the same year as the Wright brothers' first flight!

BRUM!

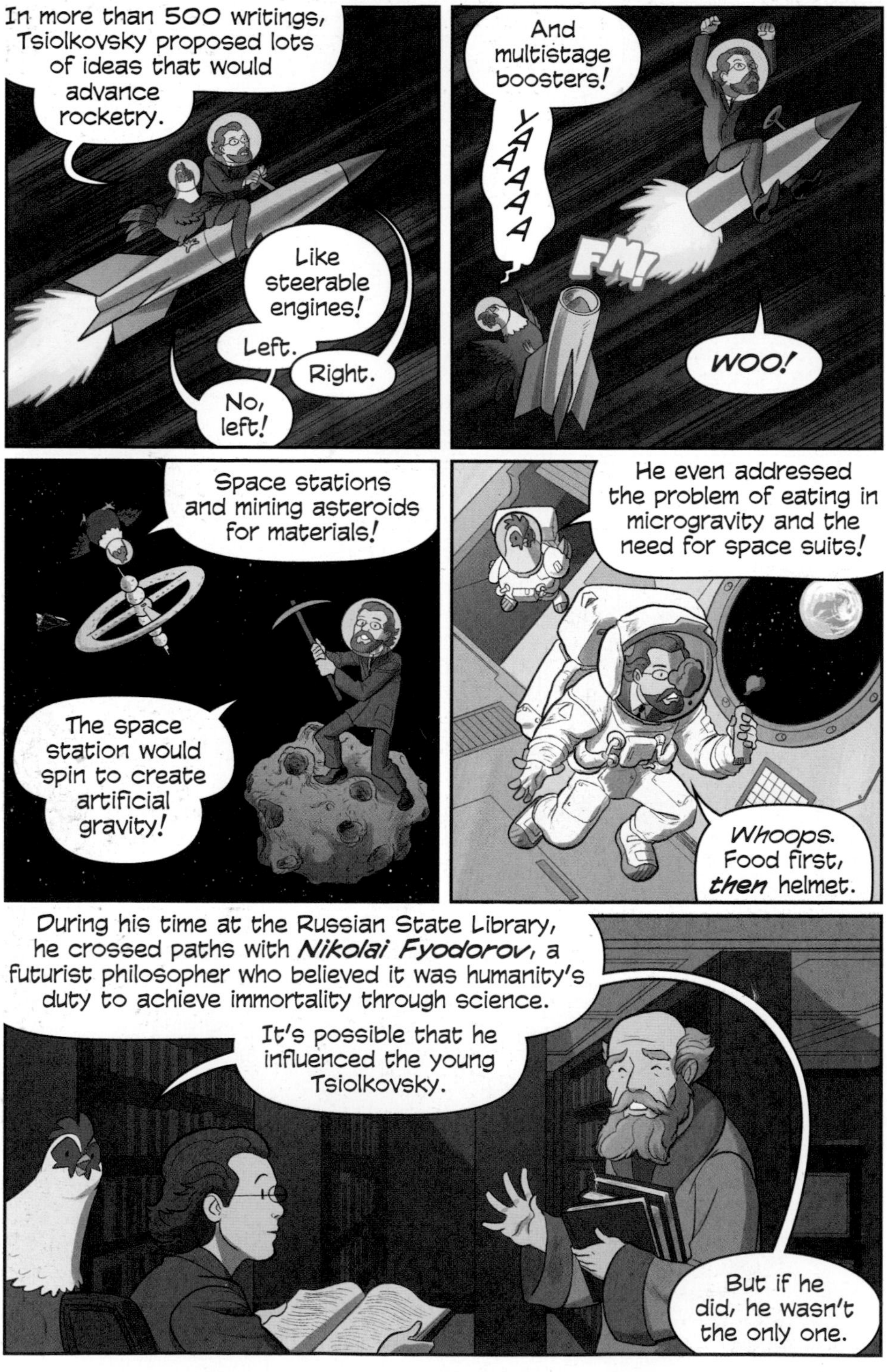
In more than 500 writings, Tsiolkovsky proposed lots of ideas that would advance rocketry.
Like steerable engines!
Left.
Right.
No, left!
And multistage boosters!
YAAAAA
FM!
WOO!
Space stations and mining asteroids for materials!
The space station would spin to create artificial gravity!
He even addressed the problem of eating in microgravity and the need for space suits!
Whoops. Food first, *then* helmet.
During his time at the Russian State Library, he crossed paths with *Nikolai Fyodorov*, a futurist philosopher who believed it was humanity's duty to achieve immortality through science.
It's possible that he influenced the young Tsiolkovsky.
But if he did, he wasn't the only one.

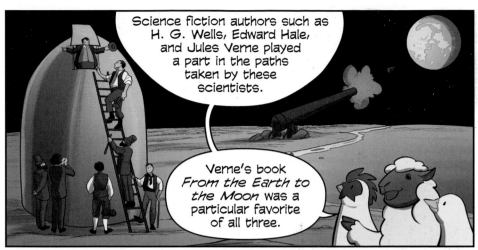

Science fiction authors such as H. G. Wells, Edward Hale, and Jules Verne played a part in the paths taken by these scientists.

Verne's book *From the Earth to the Moon* was a particular favorite of all three.

A young Goddard would be inspired by the fact that Verne attempted to work out the math on getting the ship there.

A young Oberth couldn't get enough of the book.

I read it at least five or six times.

While Tsiolkovsky took it as a challenge to be met.

The cannon would have to be impossibly long...

Whoa, whoa! Are you "Well, actually"–ing Jules Verne?

On the contrary!

The book inspired me to develop my theories of space flight!

It's a wonderful story. Would you like to borrow my copy?

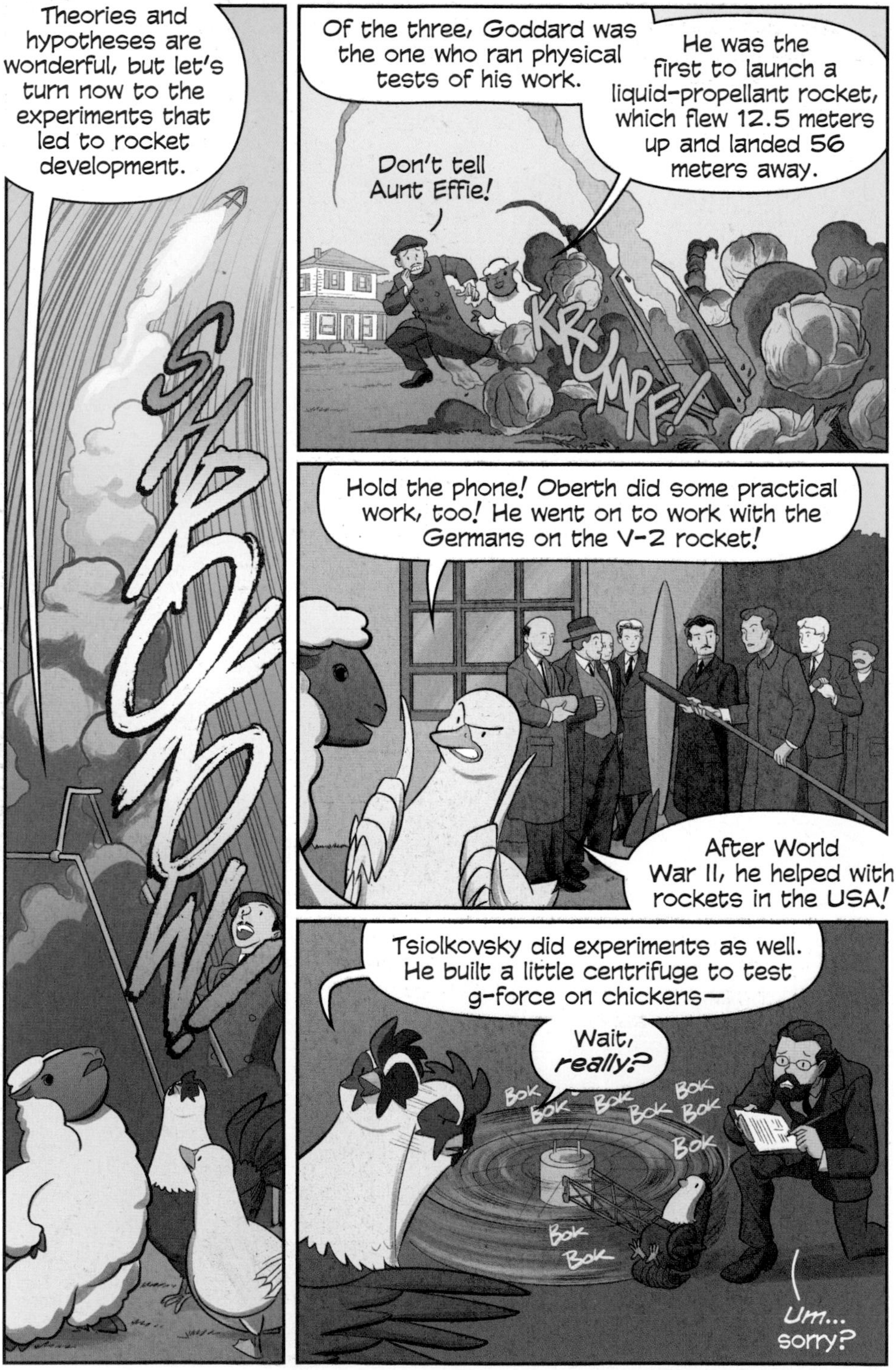
Theories and hypotheses are wonderful, but let's turn now to the experiments that led to rocket development.
SHHOOOOW!
Of the three, Goddard was the one who ran physical tests of his work.
He was the first to launch a liquid-propellant rocket, which flew 12.5 meters up and landed 56 meters away.
Don't tell Aunt Effie!
KRUMPF!
Hold the phone! Oberth did some practical work, too! He went on to work with the Germans on the V-2 rocket!
After World War II, he helped with rockets in the USA!
Tsiolkovsky did experiments as well. He built a little centrifuge to test g-force on chickens—
Wait, *really?*
BOK BOK BOK BOK BOK BOK BOK
BOK BOK
Um... sorry?

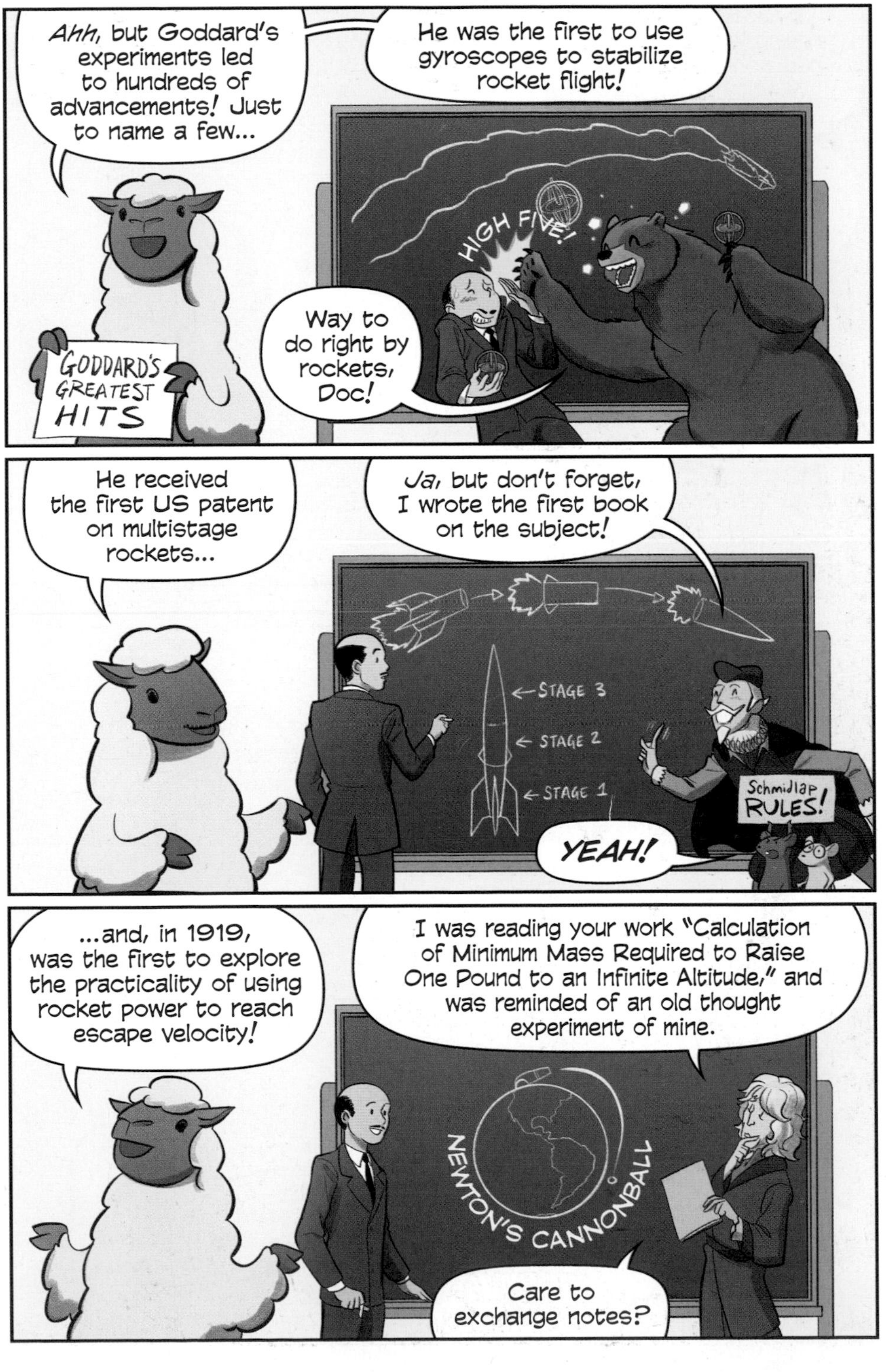
Ahh, but Goddard's experiments led to hundreds of advancements! Just to name a few...
He was the first to use gyroscopes to stabilize rocket flight!
GODDARD'S GREATEST HITS
HIGH FIVE!
Way to do right by rockets, Doc!
He received the first US patent on multistage rockets...
Ja, but don't forget, I wrote the first book on the subject!
STAGE 3
STAGE 2
STAGE 1
Schmidlap RULES!
YEAH!
...and, in 1919, was the first to explore the practicality of using rocket power to reach escape velocity!
I was reading your work "Calculation of Minimum Mass Required to Raise One Pound to an Infinite Altitude," and was reminded of an old thought experiment of mine.
NEWTON'S CANNONBALL
Care to exchange notes?

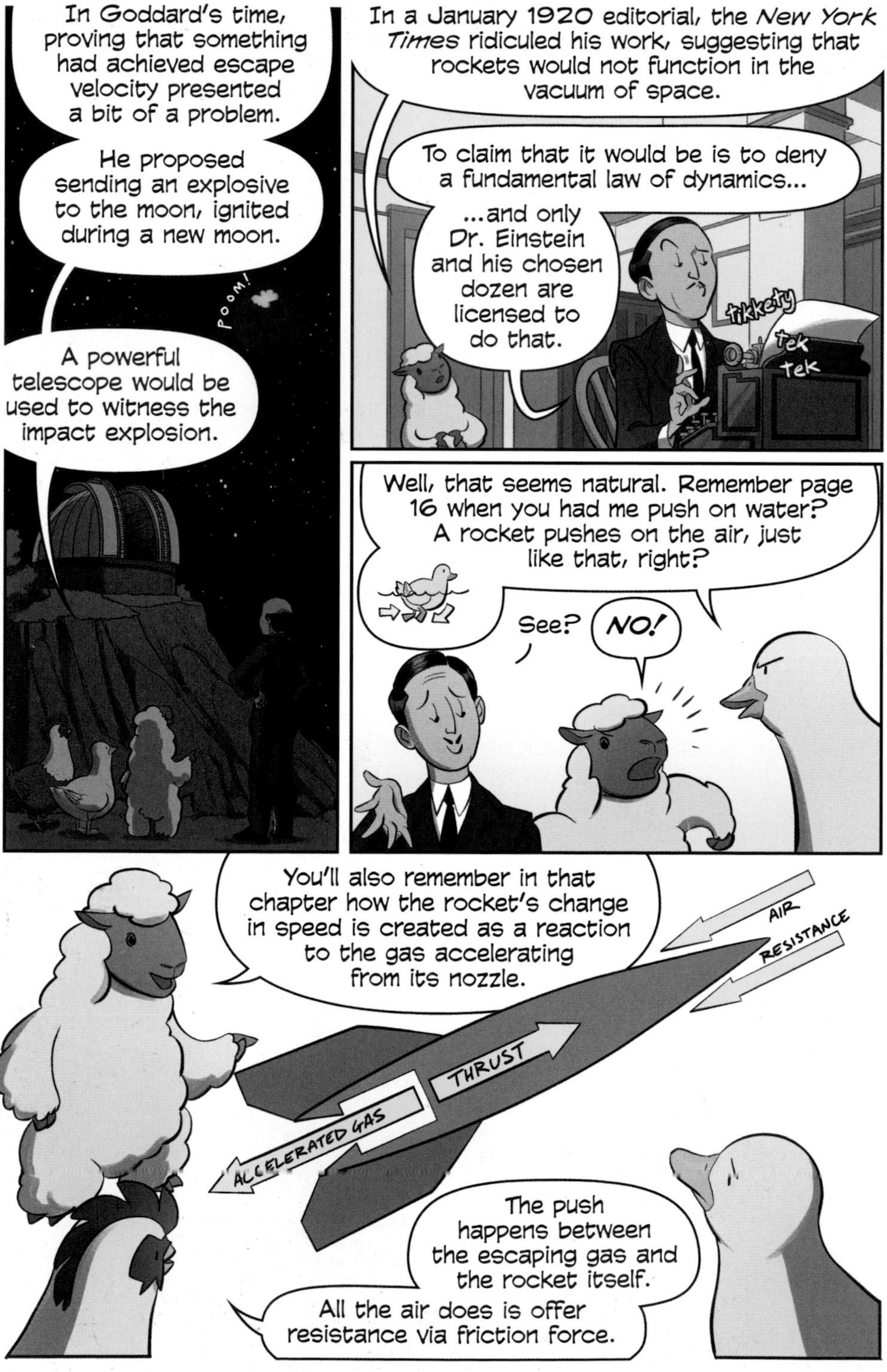
In Goddard's time, proving that something had achieved escape velocity presented a bit of a problem.
He proposed sending an explosive to the moon, ignited during a new moon.
POOM!
A powerful telescope would be used to witness the impact explosion.
In a January 1920 editorial, the *New York Times* ridiculed his work, suggesting that rockets would not function in the vacuum of space.
To claim that it would be is to deny a fundamental law of dynamics...
...and only Dr. Einstein and his chosen dozen are licensed to do that.
tikkety
tek
tek
Well, that seems natural. Remember page 16 when you had me push on water? A rocket pushes on the air, just like that, right?
See?
NO!
You'll also remember in that chapter how the rocket's change in speed is created as a reaction to the gas accelerating from its nozzle.
AIR RESISTANCE
THRUST
ACCELERATED GAS
The push happens between the escaping gas and the rocket itself.
All the air does is offer resistance via friction force.

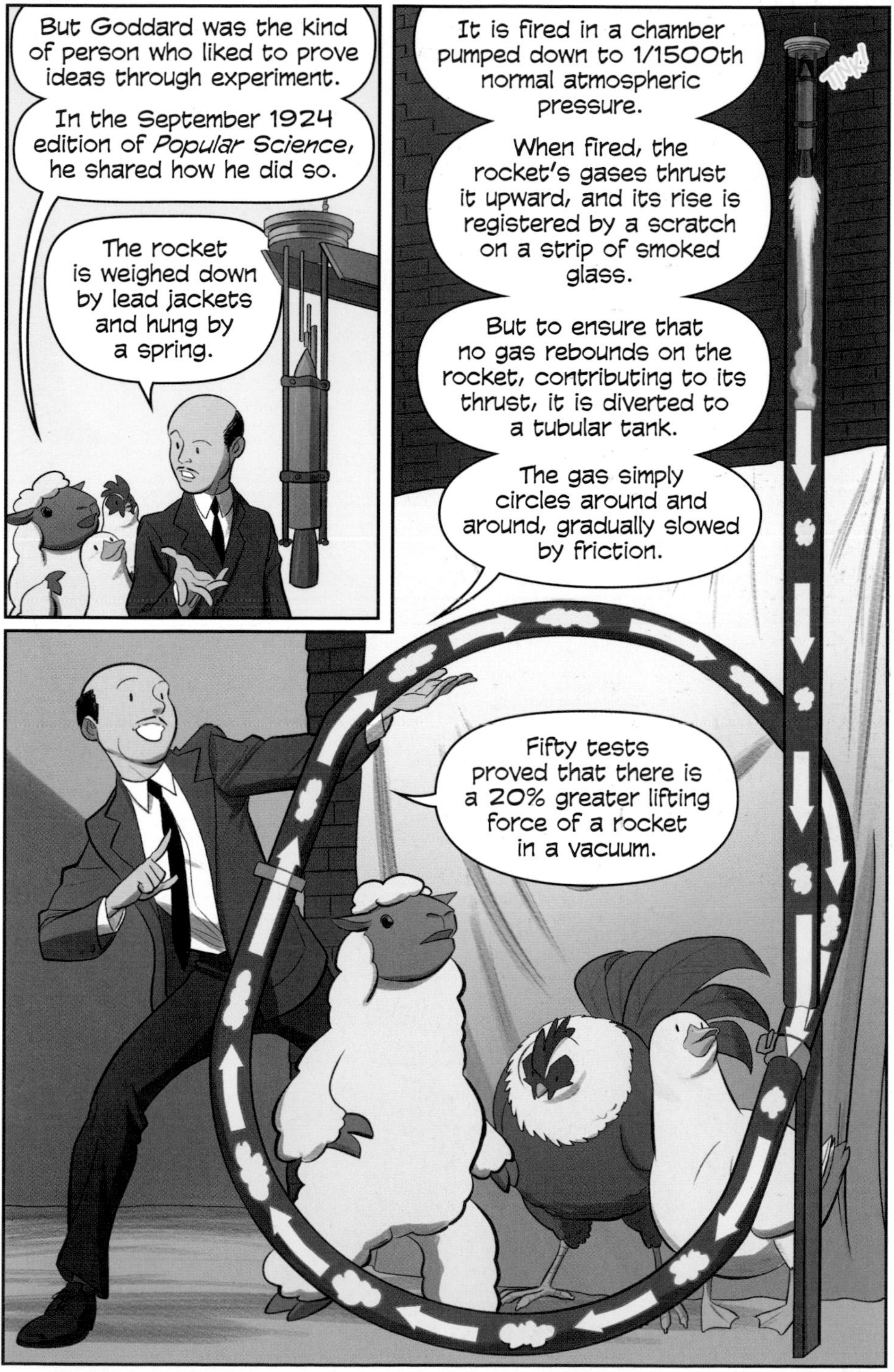
But Goddard was the kind of person who liked to prove ideas through experiment.
In the September 1924 edition of *Popular Science*, he shared how he did so.
The rocket is weighed down by lead jackets and hung by a spring.
It is fired in a chamber pumped down to 1/1500th normal atmospheric pressure.
When fired, the rocket's gases thrust it upward, and its rise is registered by a scratch on a strip of smoked glass.
But to ensure that no gas rebounds on the rocket, contributing to its thrust, it is diverted to a tubular tank.
The gas simply circles around and around, gradually slowed by friction.
TINK!
Fifty tests proved that there is a 20% greater lifting force of a rocket in a vacuum.

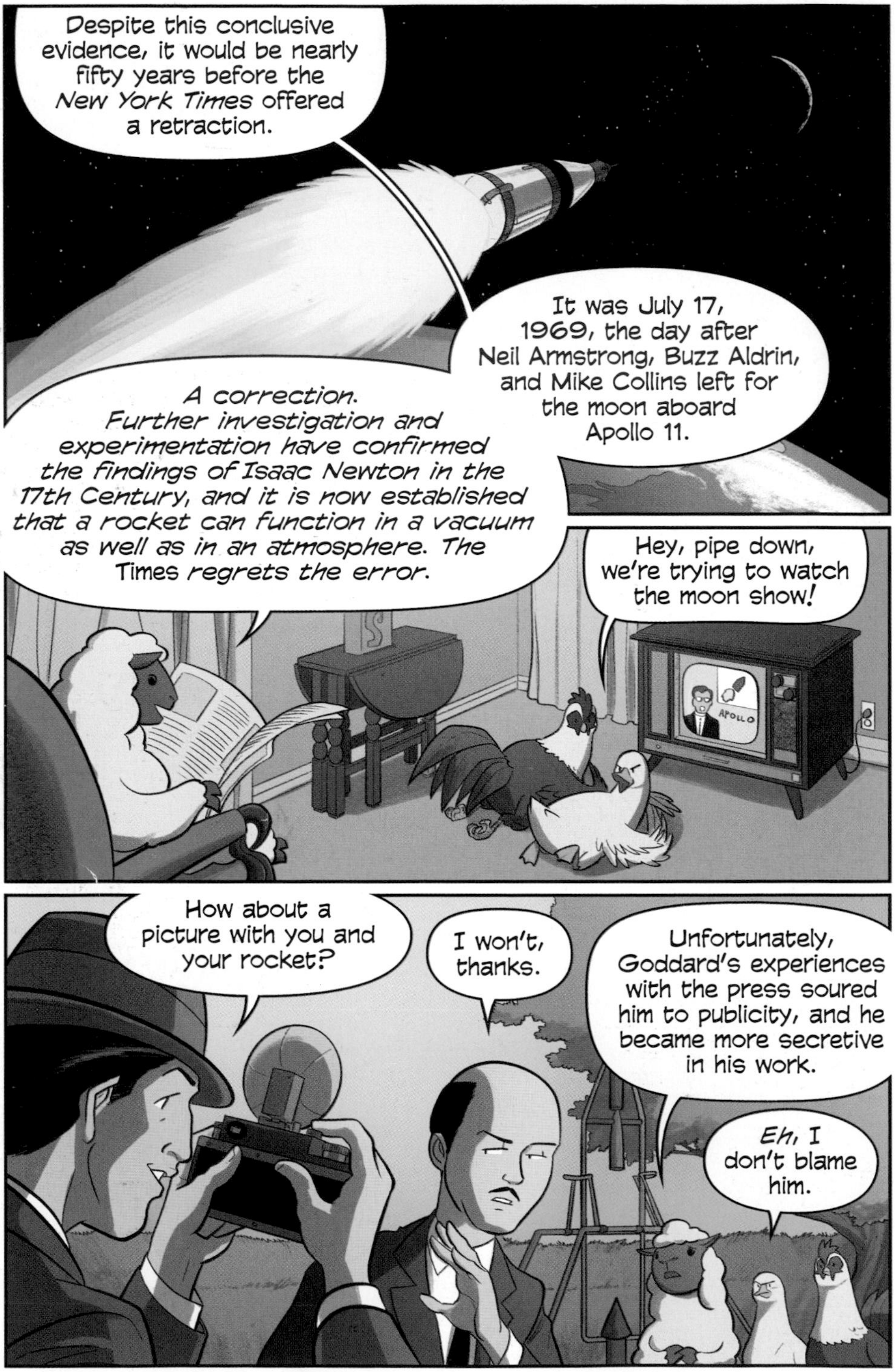
Despite this conclusive evidence, it would be nearly fifty years before the *New York Times* offered a retraction.
It was July 17, 1969, the day after Neil Armstrong, Buzz Aldrin, and Mike Collins left for the moon aboard Apollo 11.
A correction. Further investigation and experimentation have confirmed the findings of Isaac Newton in the 17th Century, and it is now established that a rocket can function in a vacuum as well as in an atmosphere. The Times *regrets the error.*
Hey, pipe down, we're trying to watch the moon show!
APOLLO
How about a picture with you and your rocket?
I won't, thanks.
Unfortunately, Goddard's experiences with the press soured him to publicity, and he became more secretive in his work.
Eh, I don't blame him.

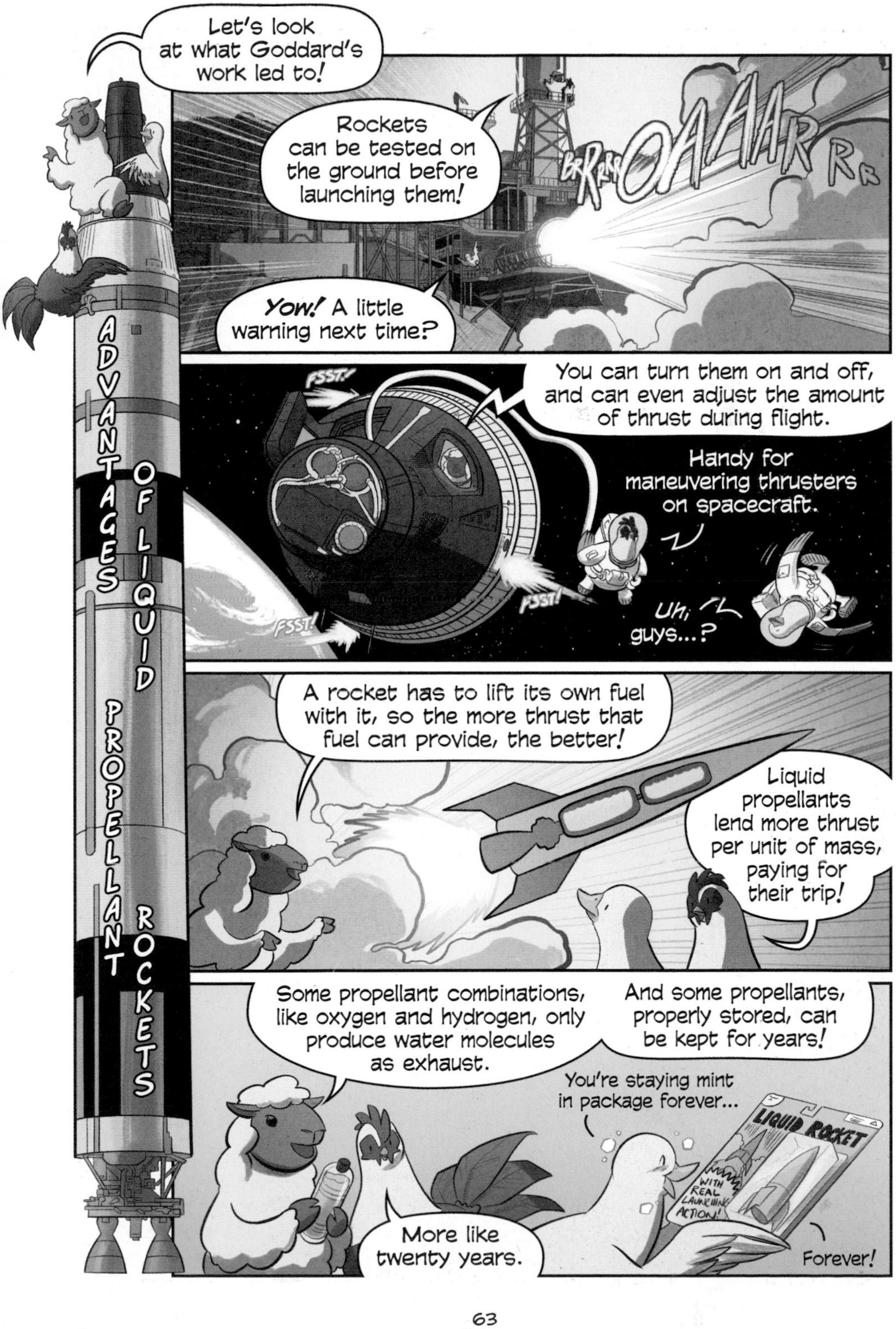
Let's look at what Goddard's work led to!
ADVANTAGES OF LIQUID PROPELLANT ROCKETS
Rockets can be tested on the ground before launching them!
BRRRRROAAAARRRR
Yow! A little warning next time?
FSST!
You can turn them on and off, and can even adjust the amount of thrust during flight.
Handy for maneuvering thrusters on spacecraft.
FSST!
FSST!
Uh, guys...?
A rocket has to lift its own fuel with it, so the more thrust that fuel can provide, the better!
Liquid propellants lend more thrust per unit of mass, paying for their trip!
Some propellant combinations, like oxygen and hydrogen, only produce water molecules as exhaust.
And some propellants, properly stored, can be kept for years!
You're staying mint in package forever...
LIQUID ROCKET
WITH REAL LAUNCHING ACTION!
More like twenty years.
Forever!

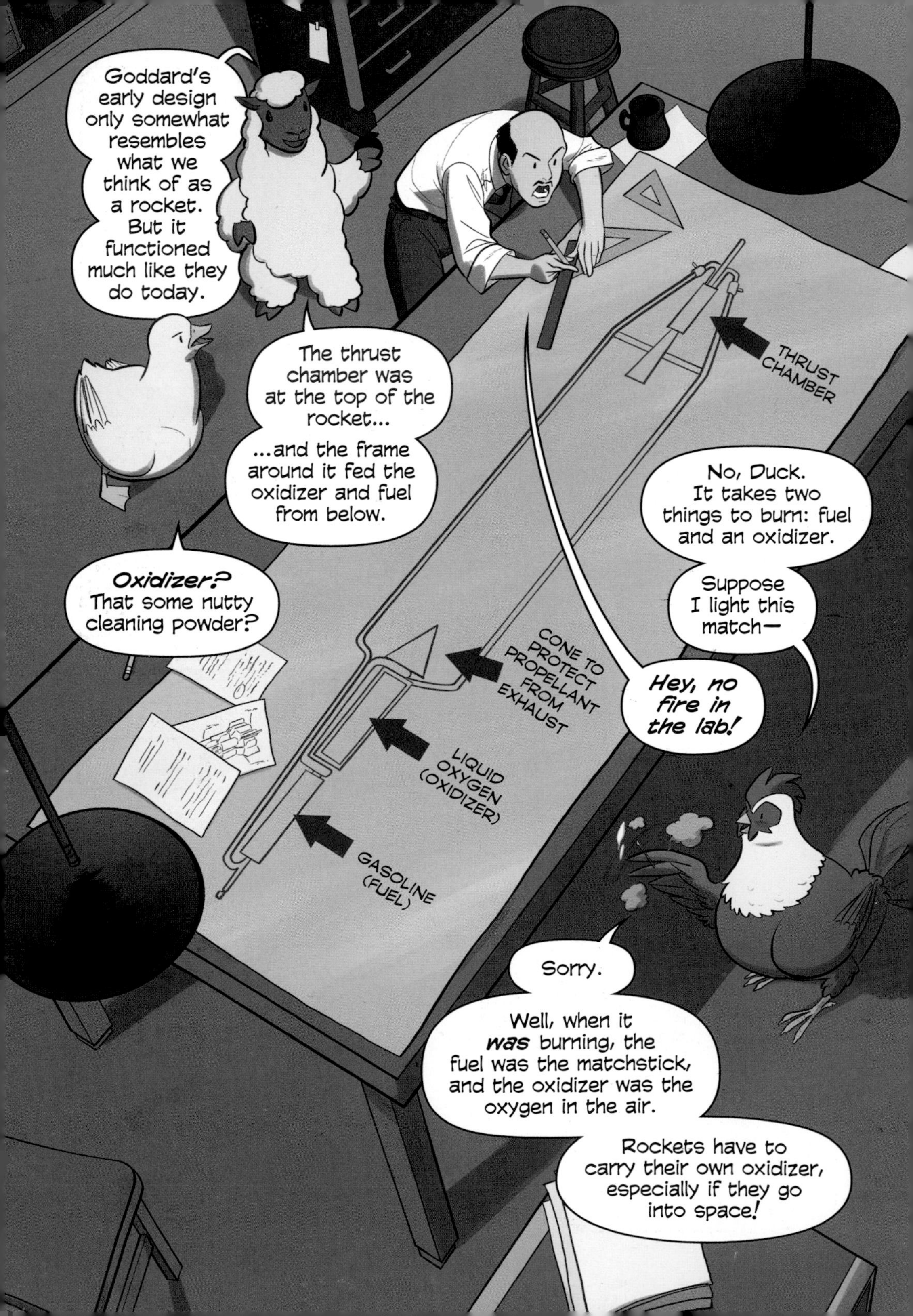
Goddard's early design only somewhat resembles what we think of as a rocket. But it functioned much like they do today.
The thrust chamber was at the top of the rocket...
...and the frame around it fed the oxidizer and fuel from below.
Oxidizer? That some nutty cleaning powder?
THRUST CHAMBER
CONE TO PROTECT PROPELLANT FROM EXHAUST
LIQUID OXYGEN (OXIDIZER)
GASOLINE (FUEL)
No, Duck. It takes two things to burn: fuel and an oxidizer.
Suppose I light this match—
Hey, no fire in the lab!
Sorry.
Well, when it was burning, the fuel was the matchstick, and the oxidizer was the oxygen in the air.
Rockets have to carry their own oxidizer, especially if they go into space!

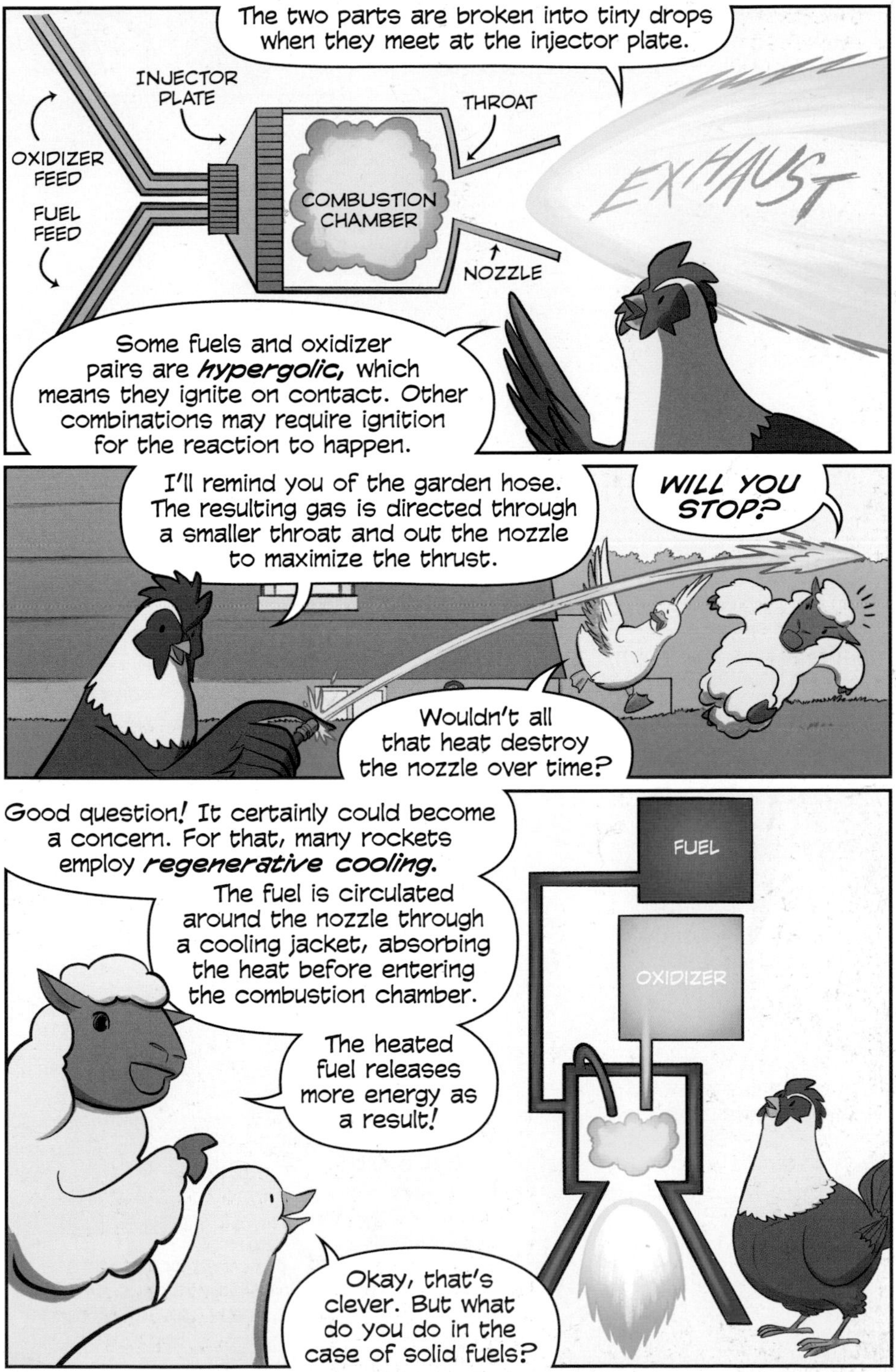
The two parts are broken into tiny drops when they meet at the injector plate.
INJECTOR PLATE
THROAT
OXIDIZER FEED
FUEL FEED
COMBUSTION CHAMBER
NOZZLE
EXHAUST
Some fuels and oxidizer pairs are ***hypergolic,*** which means they ignite on contact. Other combinations may require ignition for the reaction to happen.
I'll remind you of the garden hose. The resulting gas is directed through a smaller throat and out the nozzle to maximize the thrust.
WILL YOU STOP?
Wouldn't all that heat destroy the nozzle over time?
Good question! It certainly could become a concern. For that, many rockets employ ***regenerative cooling.***
The fuel is circulated around the nozzle through a cooling jacket, absorbing the heat before entering the combustion chamber.
The heated fuel releases more energy as a result!
FUEL
OXIDIZER
Okay, that's clever. But what do you do in the case of solid fuels?

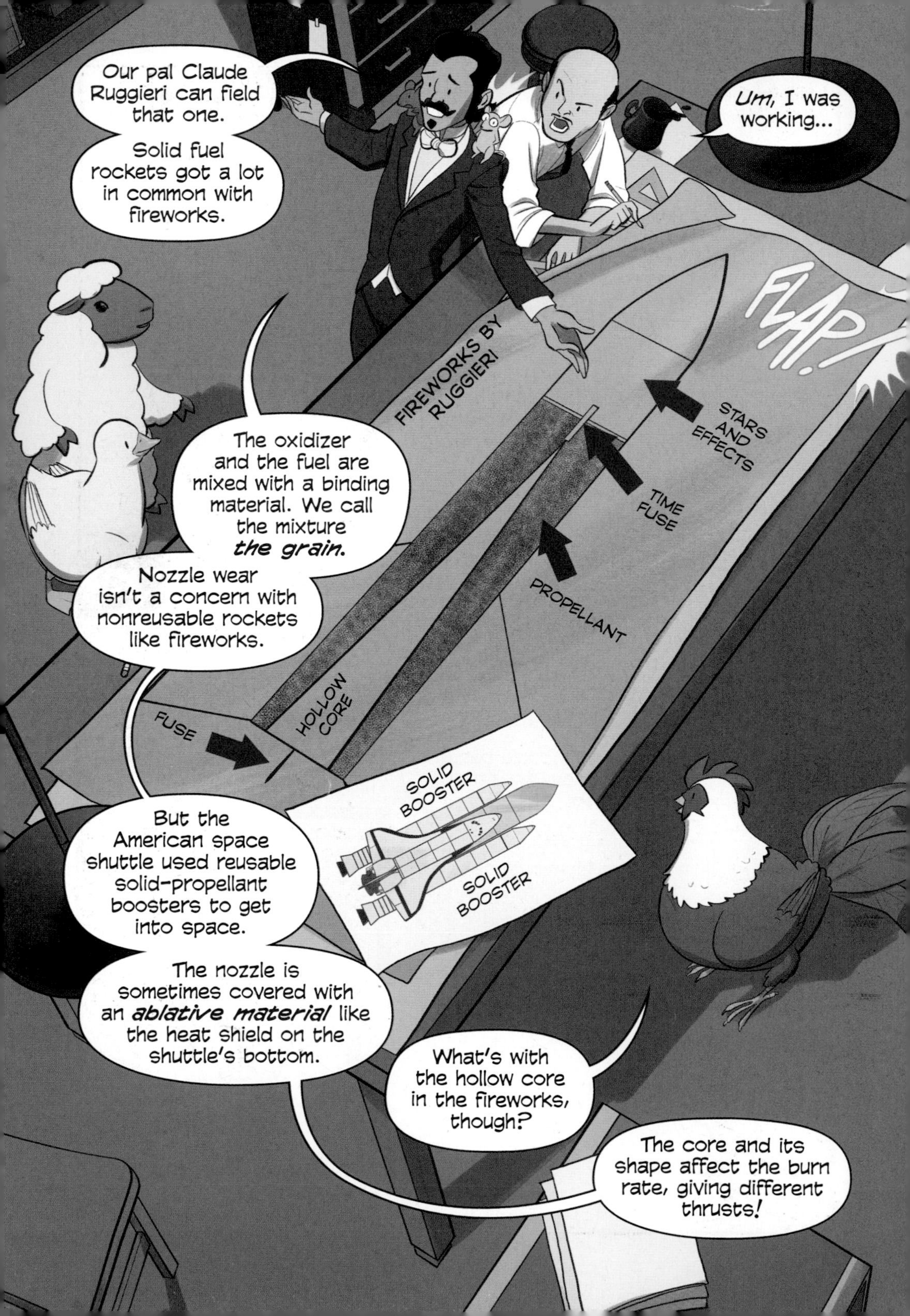
Our pal Claude Ruggieri can field that one.
Solid fuel rockets got a lot in common with fireworks.
Um, I was working...
FLAP!
FIREWORKS BY RUGGIERI
STARS AND EFFECTS
TIME FUSE
PROPELLANT
HOLLOW CORE
FUSE
The oxidizer and the fuel are mixed with a binding material. We call the mixture the grain.
Nozzle wear isn't a concern with nonreusable rockets like fireworks.
SOLID BOOSTER
SOLID BOOSTER
But the American space shuttle used reusable solid-propellant boosters to get into space.
The nozzle is sometimes covered with an ablative material like the heat shield on the shuttle's bottom.
What's with the hollow core in the fireworks, though?
The core and its shape affect the burn rate, giving different thrusts!

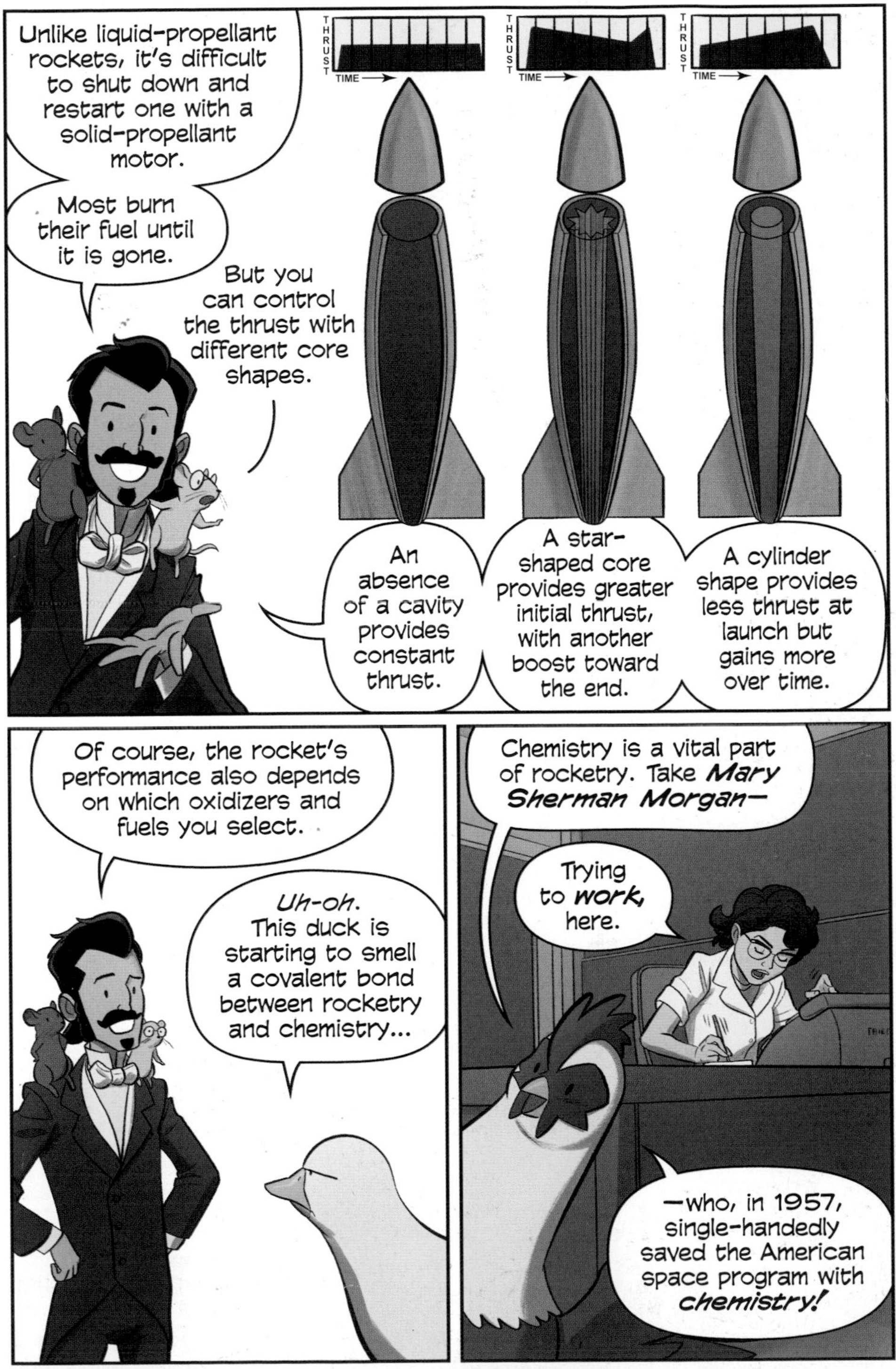
Unlike liquid-propellant rockets, it's difficult to shut down and restart one with a solid-propellant motor.
Most burn their fuel until it is gone.
But you can control the thrust with different core shapes.
THRUST
TIME
THRUST
TIME
THRUST
TIME
An absence of a cavity provides constant thrust.
A star-shaped core provides greater initial thrust, with another boost toward the end.
A cylinder shape provides less thrust at launch but gains more over time.
Of course, the rocket's performance also depends on which oxidizers and fuels you select.
Uh-oh. This duck is starting to smell a covalent bond between rocketry and chemistry...
Chemistry is a vital part of rocketry. Take ***Mary Sherman Morgan***—
Trying to ***work***, here.
—who, in 1957, single-handedly saved the American space program with ***chemistry!***

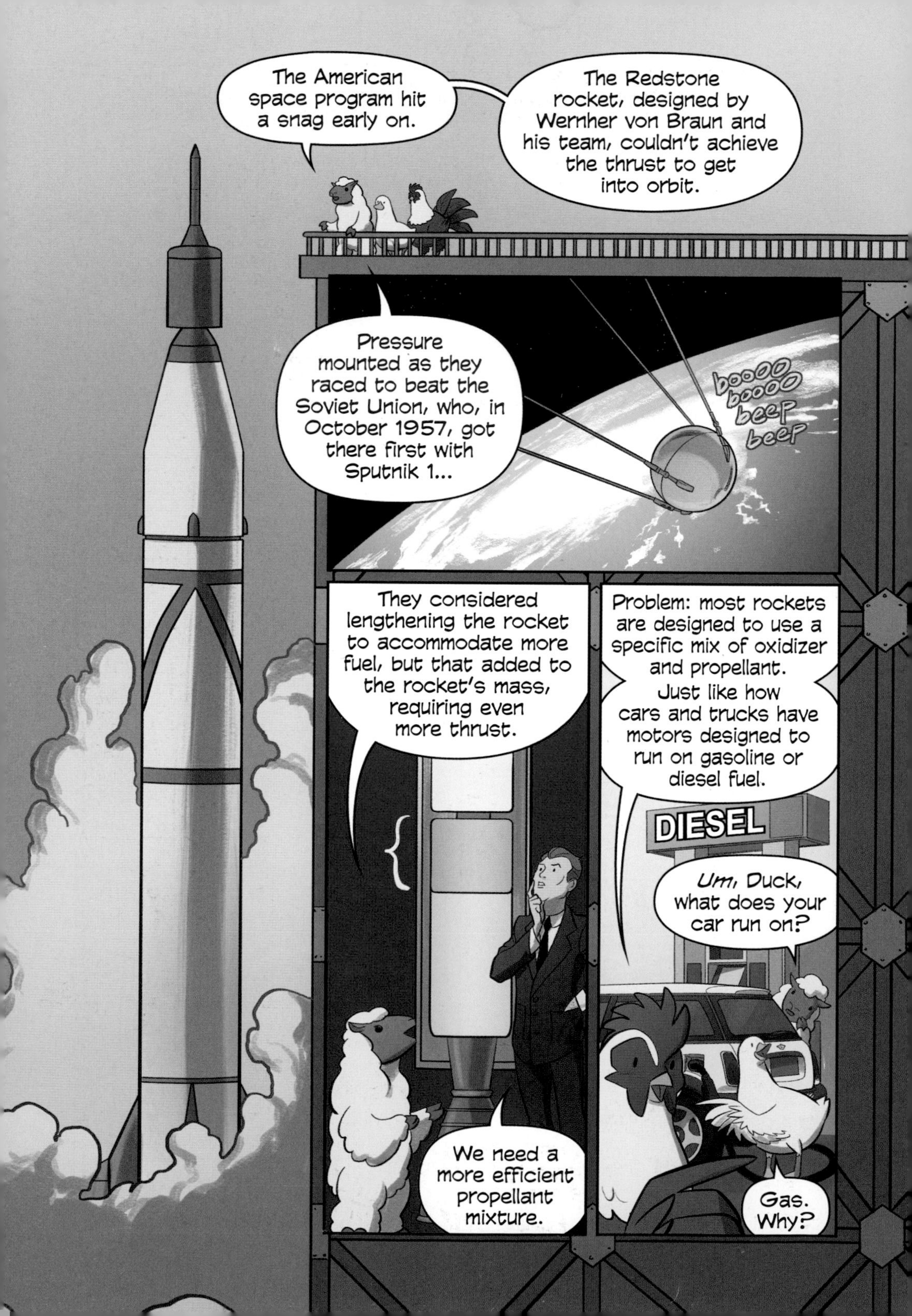

The American space program hit a snag early on.
The Redstone rocket, designed by Wernher von Braun and his team, couldn't achieve the thrust to get into orbit.
Pressure mounted as they raced to beat the Soviet Union, who, in October 1957, got there first with Sputnik 1...
boooo boooo beep beep
They considered lengthening the rocket to accommodate more fuel, but that added to the rocket's mass, requiring even more thrust.
We need a more efficient propellant mixture.
Problem: most rockets are designed to use a specific mix of oxidizer and propellant.
Just like how cars and trucks have motors designed to run on gasoline or diesel fuel.
DIESEL
Um, Duck, what does your car run on?
Gas. Why?

Mary Sherman Morgan worked at North American Aviation as a theoretical performance specialist.

Theoretical what now?

I calculate propellant performance. I've been charged with finding a new fuel for the Redstone.

The rocket, with its liquid oxygen and alcohol propellant mixture, yielded a *specific impulse* of 284. I need to find a mix that will lead to an impulse of 305.

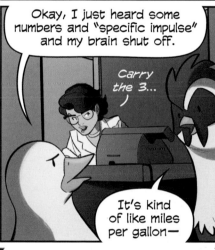

Okay, I just heard some numbers and "specific impulse" and my brain shut off.

Carry the 3...

It's kind of like miles per gallon—

Perhaps I can be of assistance!

Please, I'm in the middle of something important...

Specific impulse, or *ISP*, is the change in momentum delivered per unit of propellant consumed.

A rocket with a higher ISP uses less fuel to get more thrust, achieving a higher maximum change in velocity. I did the math on this!

EFFECTIVE EXHAUST VELOCITY

DELTA VELOCITY

$$\Delta V = V_e \ln \frac{m_0}{m_f}$$

TOTAL ROCKET MASS

NATURAL LOGARITHM

TOTAL MASS MINUS PROPELLANT

Wow, you oughta name this equation after yourself.

It's *called* the Tsiolkovsky rocket equation.

...

I'm Tsiolkovsky. Page 55.

Oh.

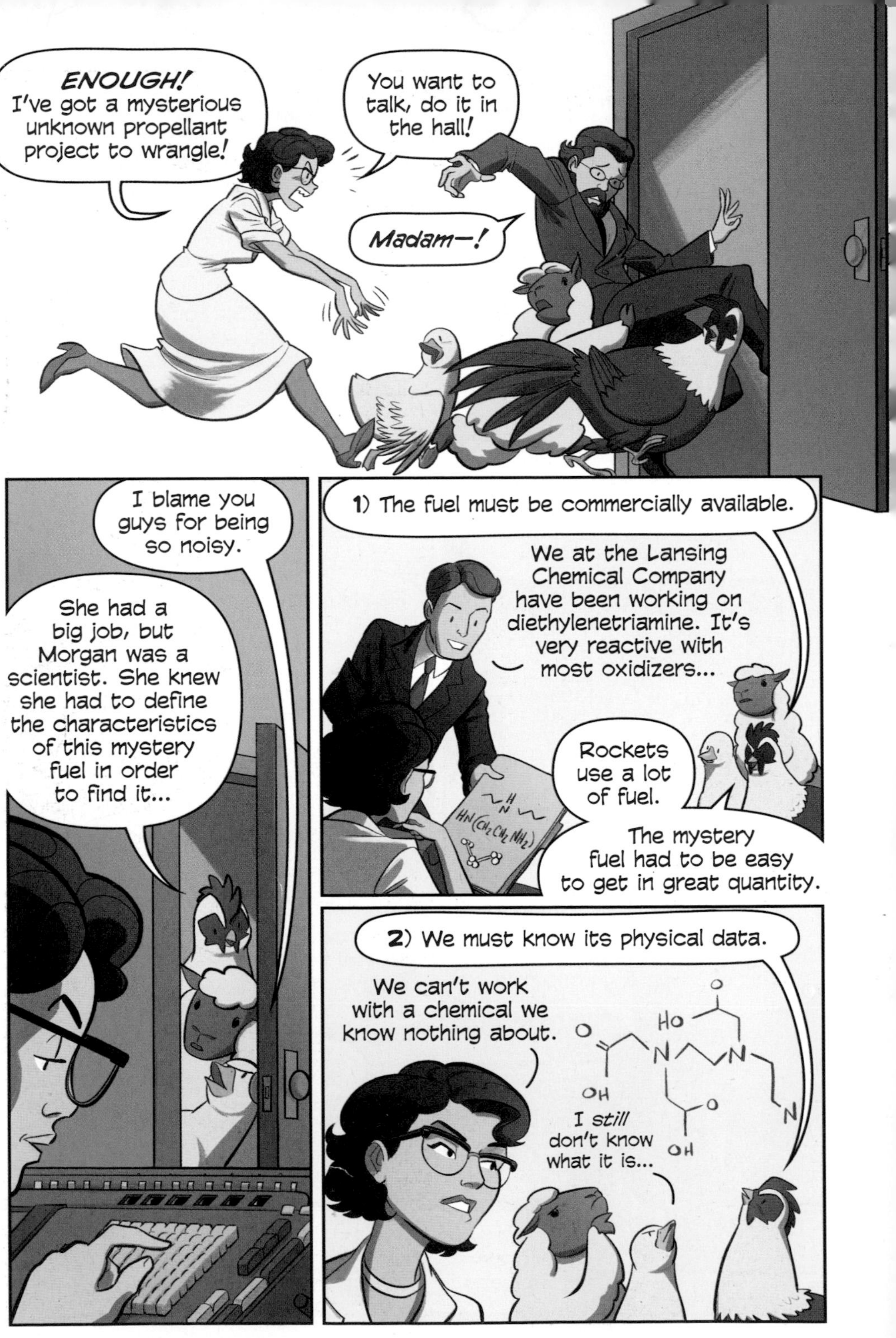

ENOUGH!
I've got a mysterious unknown propellant project to wrangle!
You want to talk, do it in the hall!
Madam—!
I blame you guys for being so noisy.
She had a big job, but Morgan was a scientist. She knew she had to define the characteristics of this mystery fuel in order to find it...
1) The fuel must be commercially available.
We at the Lansing Chemical Company have been working on diethylenetriamine. It's very reactive with most oxidizers...
Rockets use a lot of fuel.
The mystery fuel had to be easy to get in great quantity.
2) We must know its physical data.
We can't work with a chemical we know nothing about.
I *still* don't know what it is...

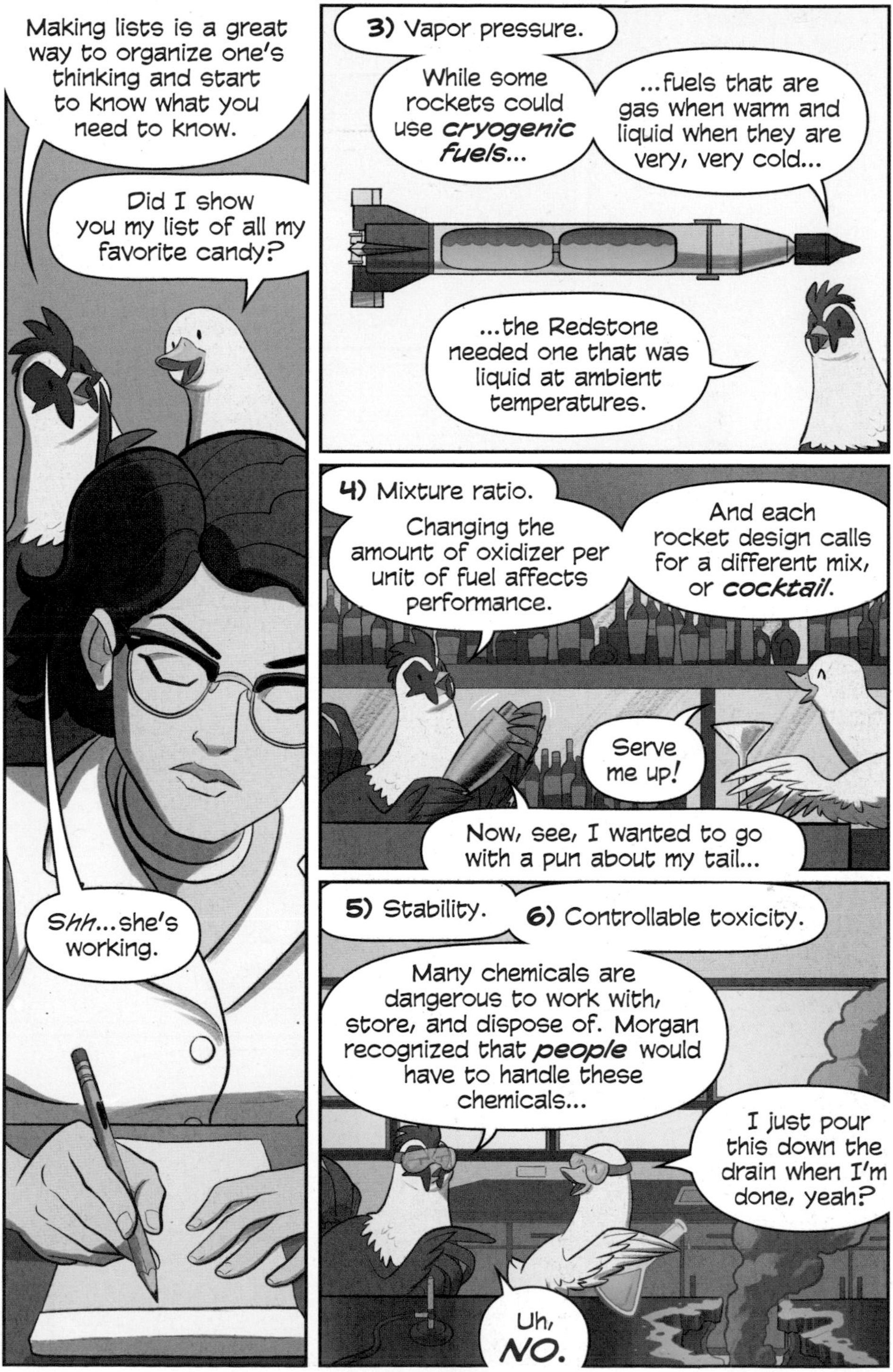
Making lists is a great way to organize one's thinking and start to know what you need to know.
Did I show you my list of all my favorite candy?
Shh...she's working.
3) Vapor pressure.
While some rockets could use *cryogenic fuels*...
...fuels that are gas when warm and liquid when they are very, very cold...
...the Redstone needed one that was liquid at ambient temperatures.
4) Mixture ratio.
Changing the amount of oxidizer per unit of fuel affects performance.
And each rocket design calls for a different mix, or *cocktail*.
Serve me up!
Now, see, I wanted to go with a pun about my tail...
5) Stability.
6) Controllable toxicity.
Many chemicals are dangerous to work with, store, and dispose of. Morgan recognized that *people* would have to handle these chemicals...
I just pour this down the drain when I'm done, yeah?
Uh, ***NO.***

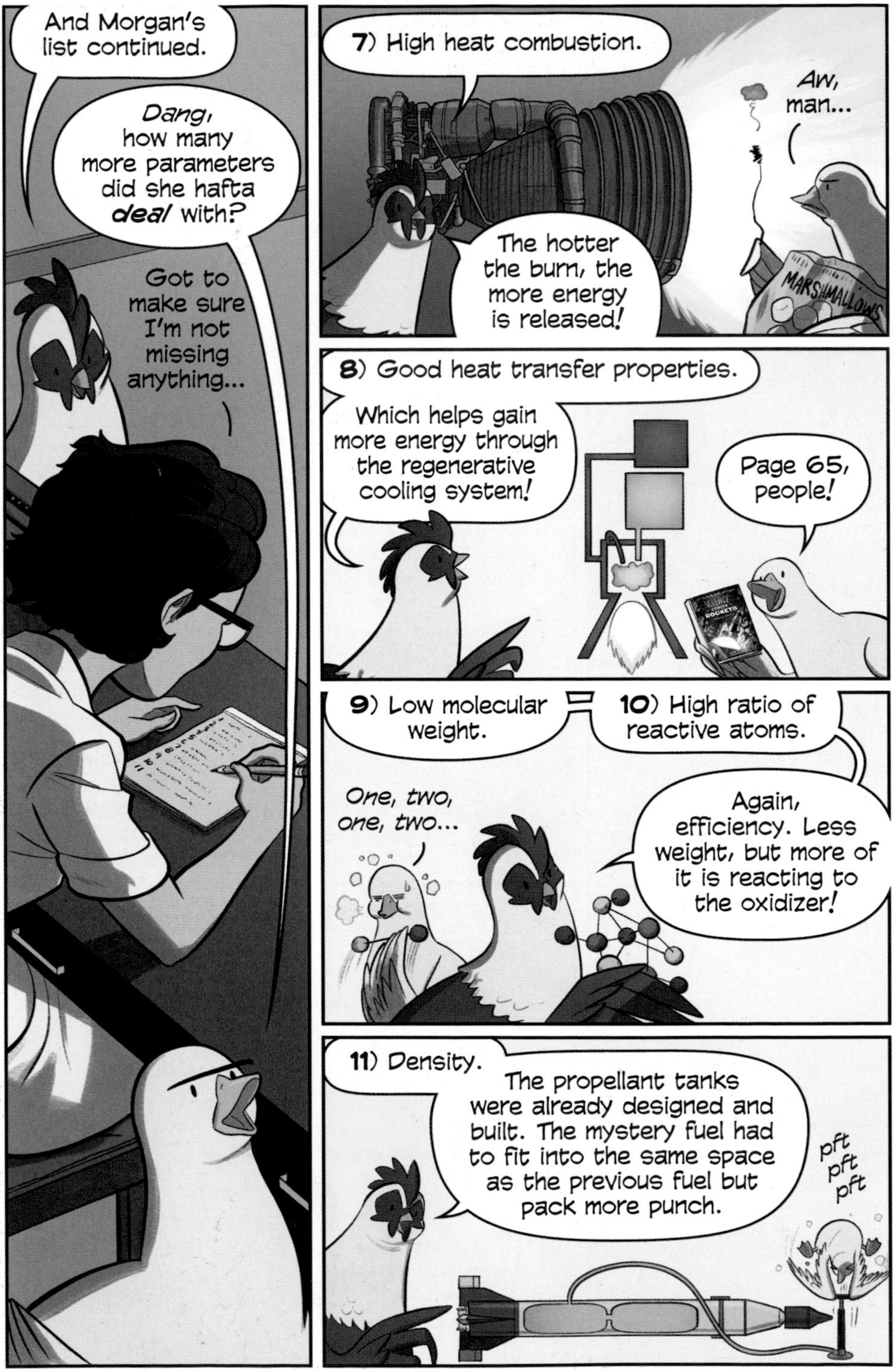
And Morgan's list continued.
Dang, how many more parameters did she hafta ***deal*** with?
Got to make sure I'm not missing anything...
7) High heat combustion.
Aw, man...
The hotter the burn, the more energy is released!
MARSHMALLOWS
8) Good heat transfer properties.
Which helps gain more energy through the regenerative cooling system!
Page 65, people!
ROCKETS
9) Low molecular weight.
10) High ratio of reactive atoms.
One, two, one, two...
Again, efficiency. Less weight, but more of it is reacting to the oxidizer!
11) Density.
The propellant tanks were already designed and built. The mystery fuel had to fit into the same space as the previous fuel but pack more punch.
pft pft pft

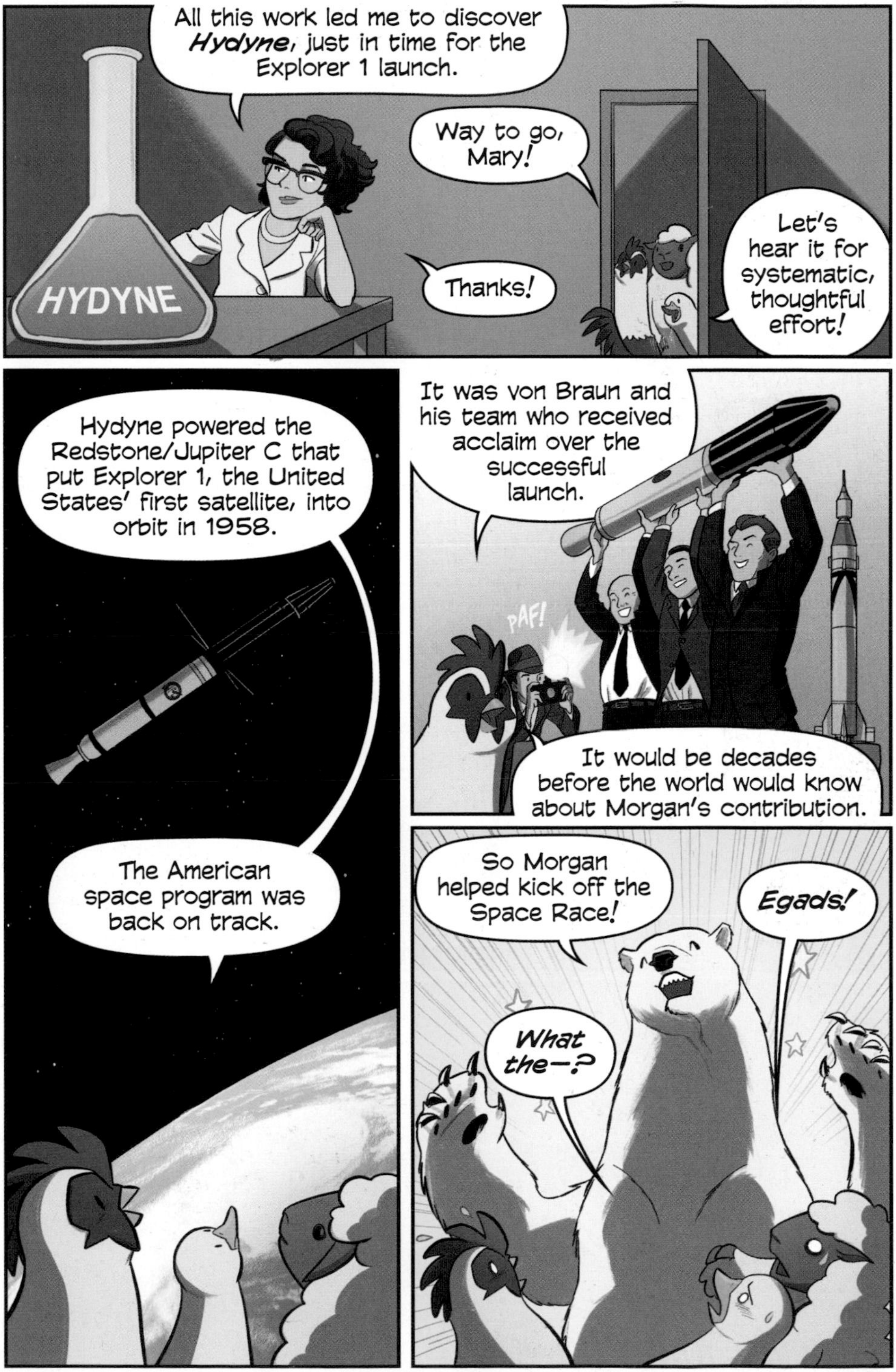

All this work led me to discover *Hydyne*, just in time for the Explorer 1 launch.
Way to go, Mary!
Thanks!
Let's hear it for systematic, thoughtful effort!
Hydyne powered the Redstone/Jupiter C that put Explorer 1, the United States' first satellite, into orbit in 1958.
The American space program was back on track.
It was von Braun and his team who received acclaim over the successful launch.
PAF!
It would be decades before the world would know about Morgan's contribution.
So Morgan helped kick off the Space Race!
Egads!
What the—?

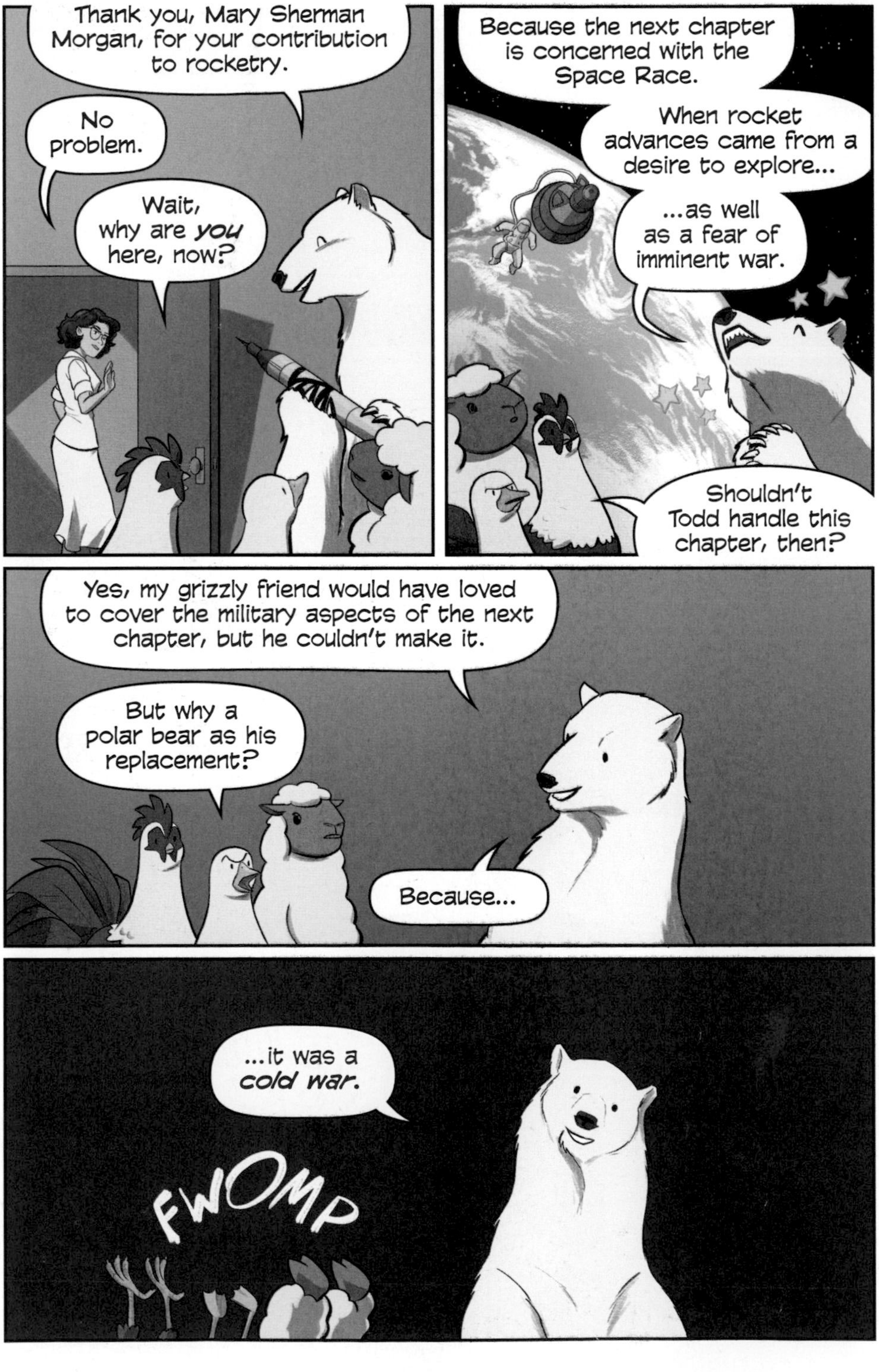
Thank you, Mary Sherman Morgan, for your contribution to rocketry.
No problem.
Wait, why are *you* here, now?
Because the next chapter is concerned with the Space Race.
When rocket advances came from a desire to explore...
...as well as a fear of imminent war.
Shouldn't Todd handle this chapter, then?
Yes, my grizzly friend would have loved to cover the military aspects of the next chapter, but he couldn't make it.
But why a polar bear as his replacement?
Because...
...it was a *cold war*.
FWOMP

CHAPTER 5: ROCKETS IN THE SPACE RACE

In March of 1950, as the United States and the Soviet Union engaged in the cold war, a group of scientists proposed a more cooperative global venture.

A year of international scientific study!

Let's get East and West scientists collaborating on big projects!

Big earth science projects, like studying geomagnetism, meteorology, global mapping, and solar activity.

1957 to 1958 would be a peak time of the solar cycle.

Rats, I'm breaking into sunspots again...

Perfect!

We lost so much science in the destruction of the world wars. Let's ensure not only cooperation but open sharing of data.

This is something that should benefit *all* nations.

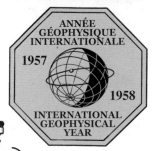

ANNÉE GÉOPHYSIQUE INTERNATIONALE
1957
1958
INTERNATIONAL GEOPHYSICAL YEAR

The IGY. A year of nations working together so we all might better understand our planet. Cool, huh?

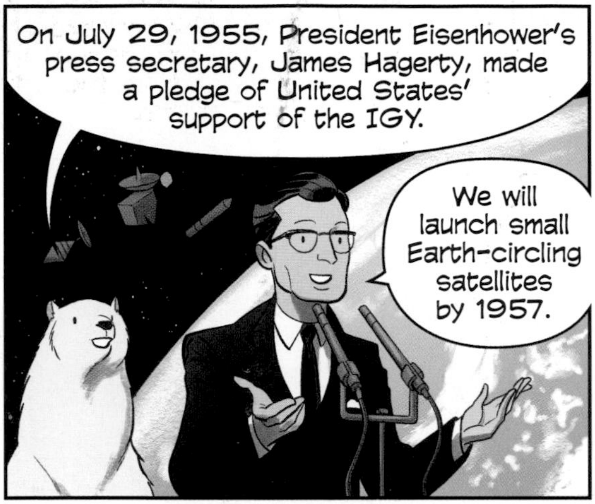
On July 29, 1955, President Eisenhower's press secretary, James Hagerty, made a pledge of United States' support of the IGY.
We will launch small Earth-circling satellites by 1957.

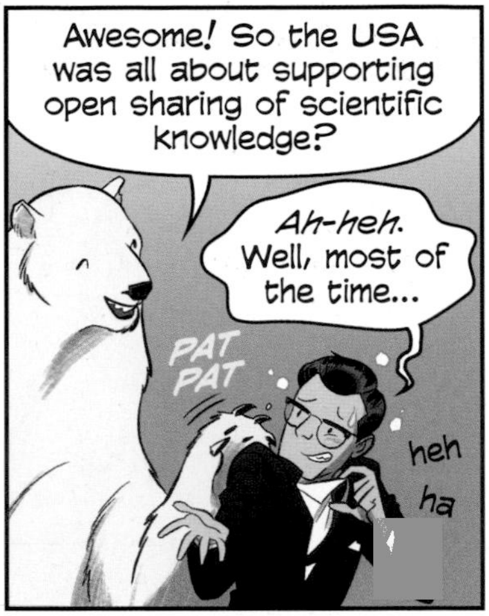
Awesome! So the USA was all about supporting open sharing of scientific knowledge?
Ah-heh. Well, most of the time...
PAT PAT
heh
ha

1945: OPERATION PAPERCLIP

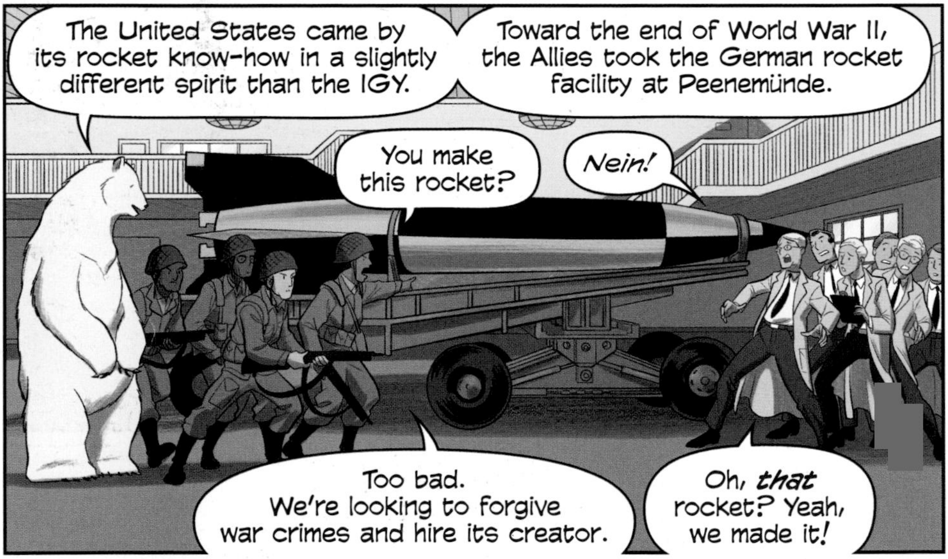
The United States came by its rocket know-how in a slightly different spirit than the IGY.
Toward the end of World War II, the Allies took the German rocket facility at Peenemünde.
You make this rocket?
Nein!
Too bad. We're looking to forgive war crimes and hire its creator.
Oh, *that* rocket? Yeah, we made it!

German rocketeers, once considered enemies of the Allied forces, had new personal and political histories "paperclipped" to their files.

This disinfecting was justified as a necessary measure to ***keep*** the Germans' rocket expertise ***from*** enemies of the United States.

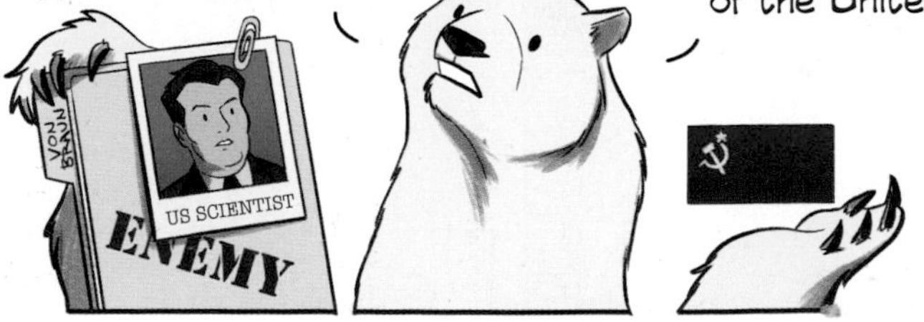
US SCIENTIST
ENEMY

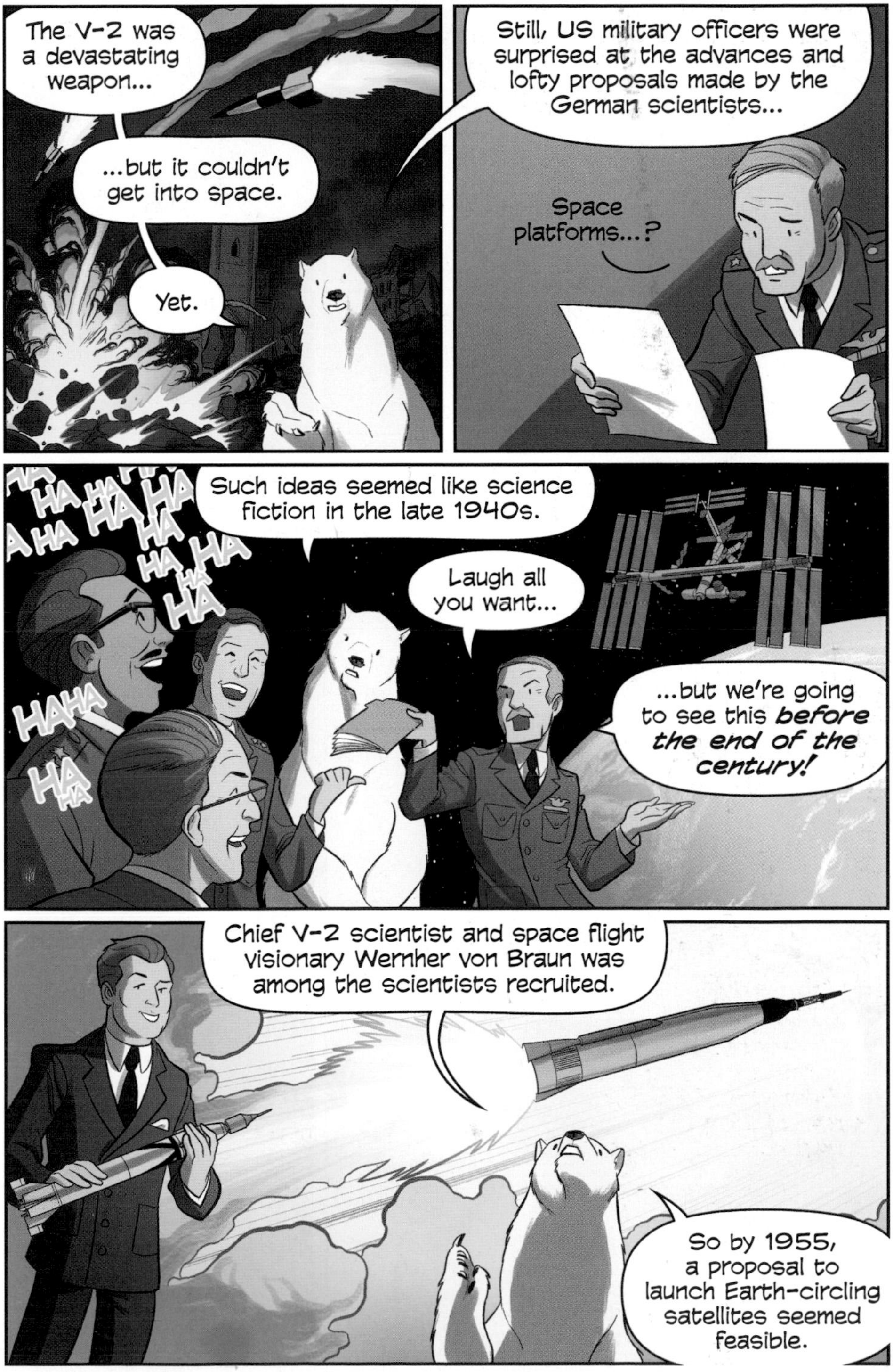

The V-2 was a devastating weapon...
...but it couldn't get into space.
Yet.
Still, US military officers were surprised at the advances and lofty proposals made by the German scientists...
Space platforms...?
HA HA HA HA HA HA HA HA HA HA HA
Such ideas seemed like science fiction in the late 1940s.
Laugh all you want...
...but we're going to see this ***before the end of the century!***
HAHA
HA HA
Chief V-2 scientist and space flight visionary Wernher von Braun was among the scientists recruited.
So by 1955, a proposal to launch Earth-circling satellites seemed feasible.

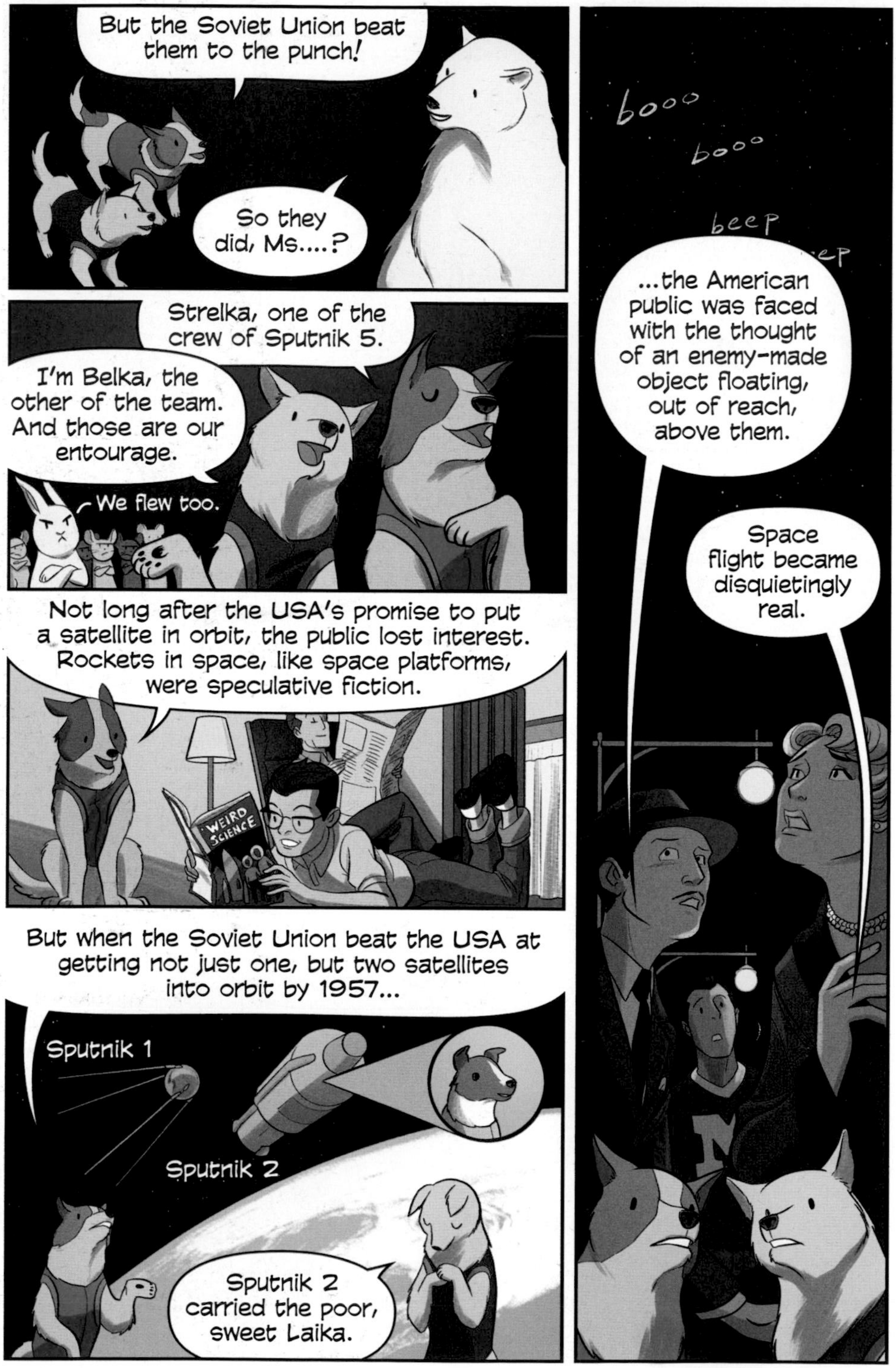
But the Soviet Union beat them to the punch!
So they did, Ms....?
Strelka, one of the crew of Sputnik 5.
I'm Belka, the other of the team. And those are our entourage.
We flew too.
Not long after the USA's promise to put a satellite in orbit, the public lost interest. Rockets in space, like space platforms, were speculative fiction.
WEIRD SCIENCE
But when the Soviet Union beat the USA at getting not just one, but two satellites into orbit by 1957...
Sputnik 1
Sputnik 2
Sputnik 2 carried the poor, sweet Laika.
booo
booo
beep
...the American public was faced with the thought of an enemy-made object floating, out of reach, above them.
Space flight became disquietingly real.

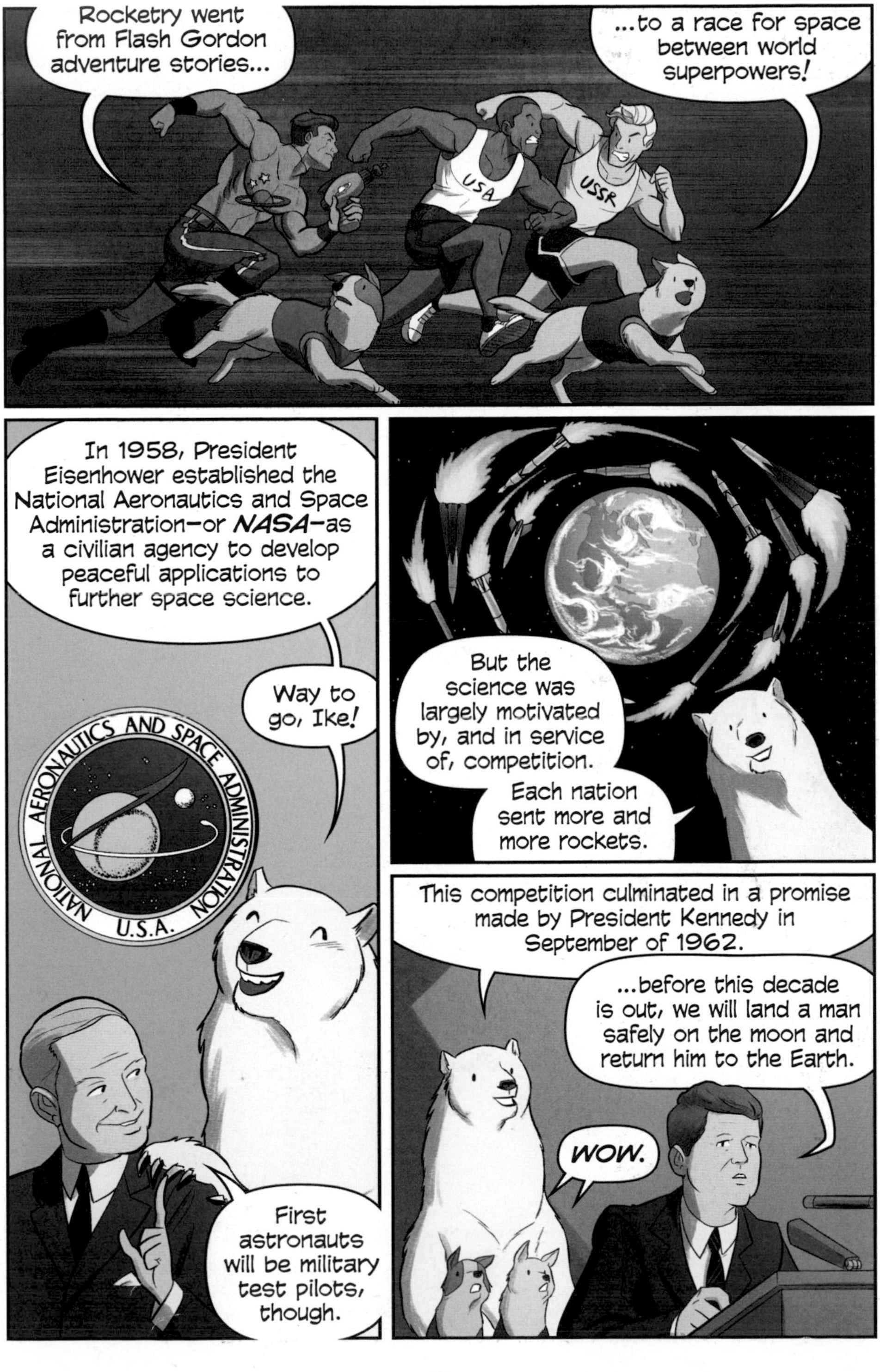

Rocketry went from Flash Gordon adventure stories...
...to a race for space between world superpowers!
USA
USSR
In 1958, President Eisenhower established the National Aeronautics and Space Administration—or *NASA*—as a civilian agency to develop peaceful applications to further space science.
Way to go, Ike!
NATIONAL AERONAUTICS AND SPACE ADMINISTRATION
U.S.A.
First astronauts will be military test pilots, though.
But the science was largely motivated by, and in service of, competition.
Each nation sent more and more rockets.
This competition culminated in a promise made by President Kennedy in September of 1962.
...before this decade is out, we will land a man safely on the moon and return him to the Earth.
WOW.

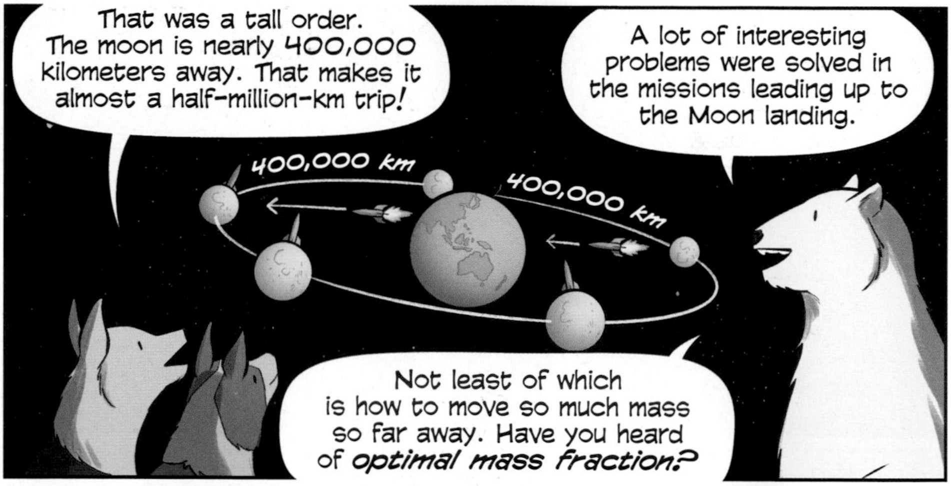
That was a tall order. The moon is nearly 400,000 kilometers away. That makes it almost a half-million-km trip!
A lot of interesting problems were solved in the missions leading up to the Moon landing.
400,000 km
400,000 km
Not least of which is how to move so much mass so far away. Have you heard of *optimal mass fraction?*

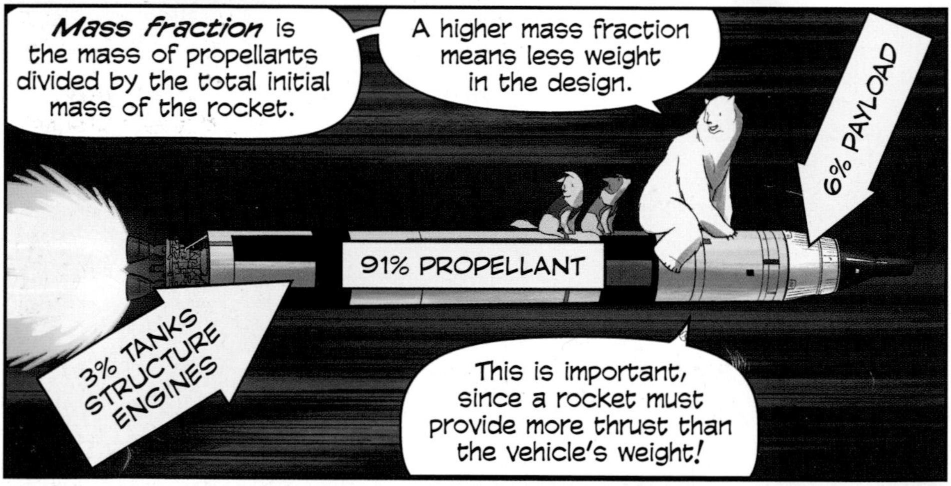
Mass fraction is the mass of propellants divided by the total initial mass of the rocket.
A higher mass fraction means less weight in the design.
6% PAYLOAD
91% PROPELLANT
3% TANKS STRUCTURE ENGINES
This is important, since a rocket must provide more thrust than the vehicle's weight!

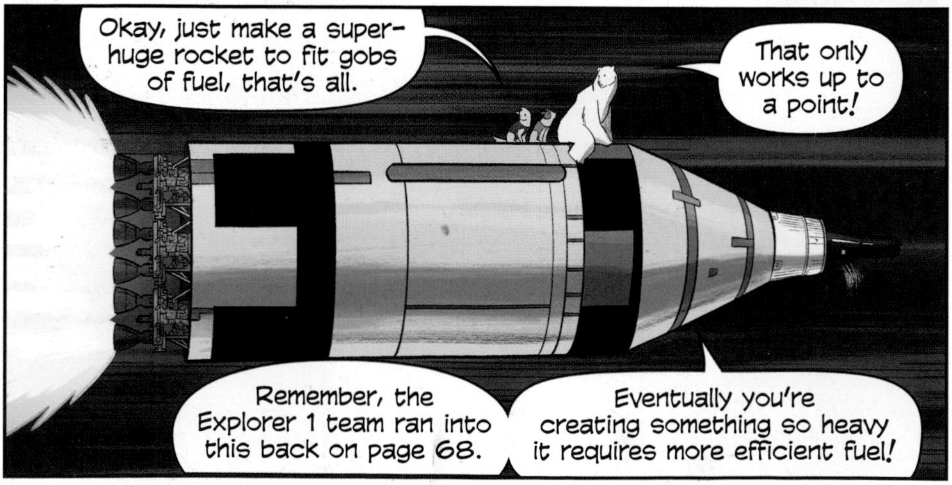
Okay, just make a super-huge rocket to fit gobs of fuel, that's all.
That only works up to a point!
Remember, the Explorer 1 team ran into this back on page 68.
Eventually you're creating something so heavy it requires more efficient fuel!

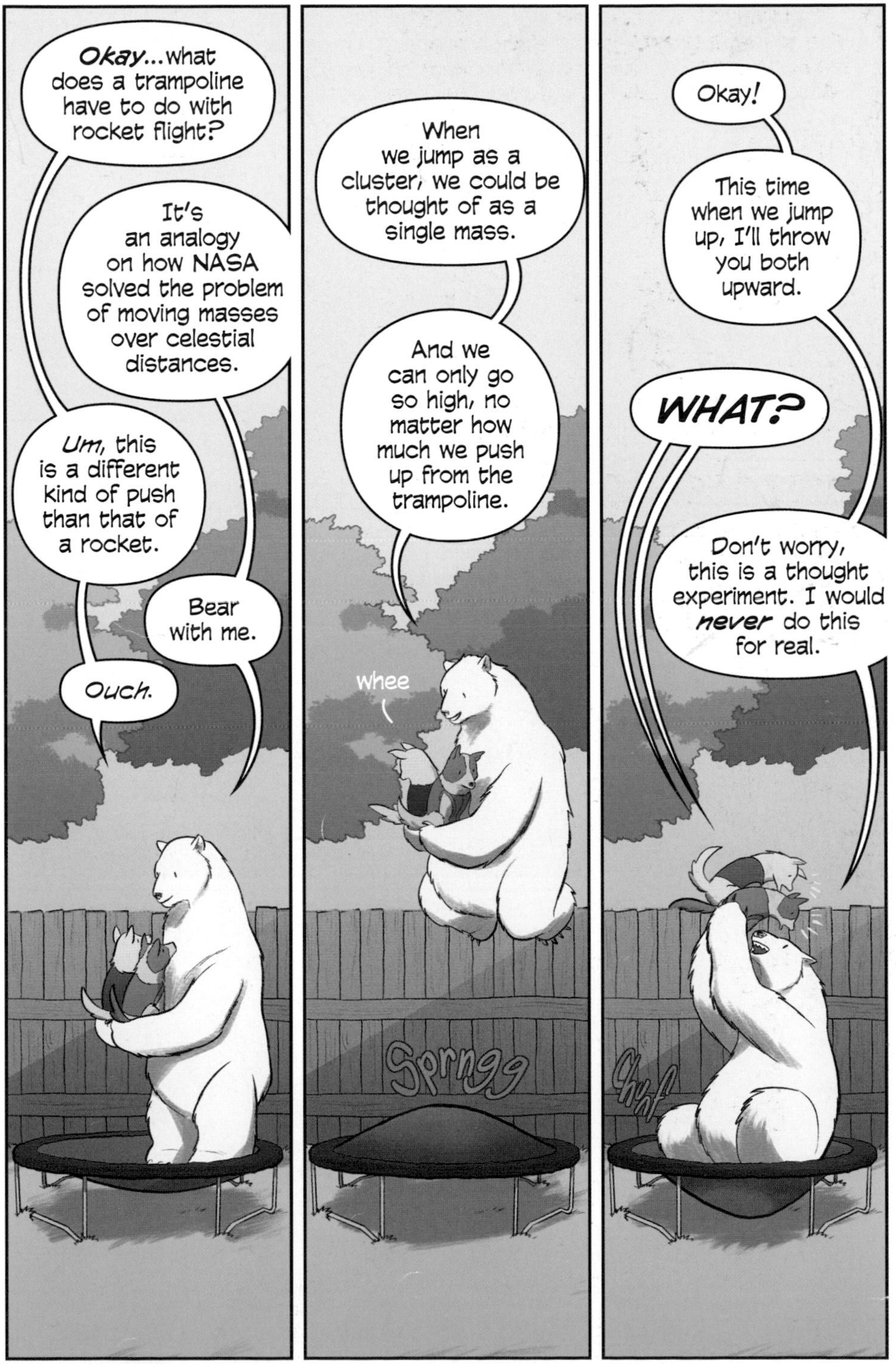

Okay...what does a trampoline have to do with rocket flight?
It's an analogy on how NASA solved the problem of moving masses over celestial distances.
Um, this is a different kind of push than that of a rocket.
Bear with me.
Ouch.
When we jump as a cluster, we could be thought of as a single mass.
And we can only go so high, no matter how much we push up from the trampoline.
whee
Sprngg
Okay!
This time when we jump up, I'll throw you both upward.
WHAT?
Don't worry, this is a thought experiment. I would ***never*** do this for real.

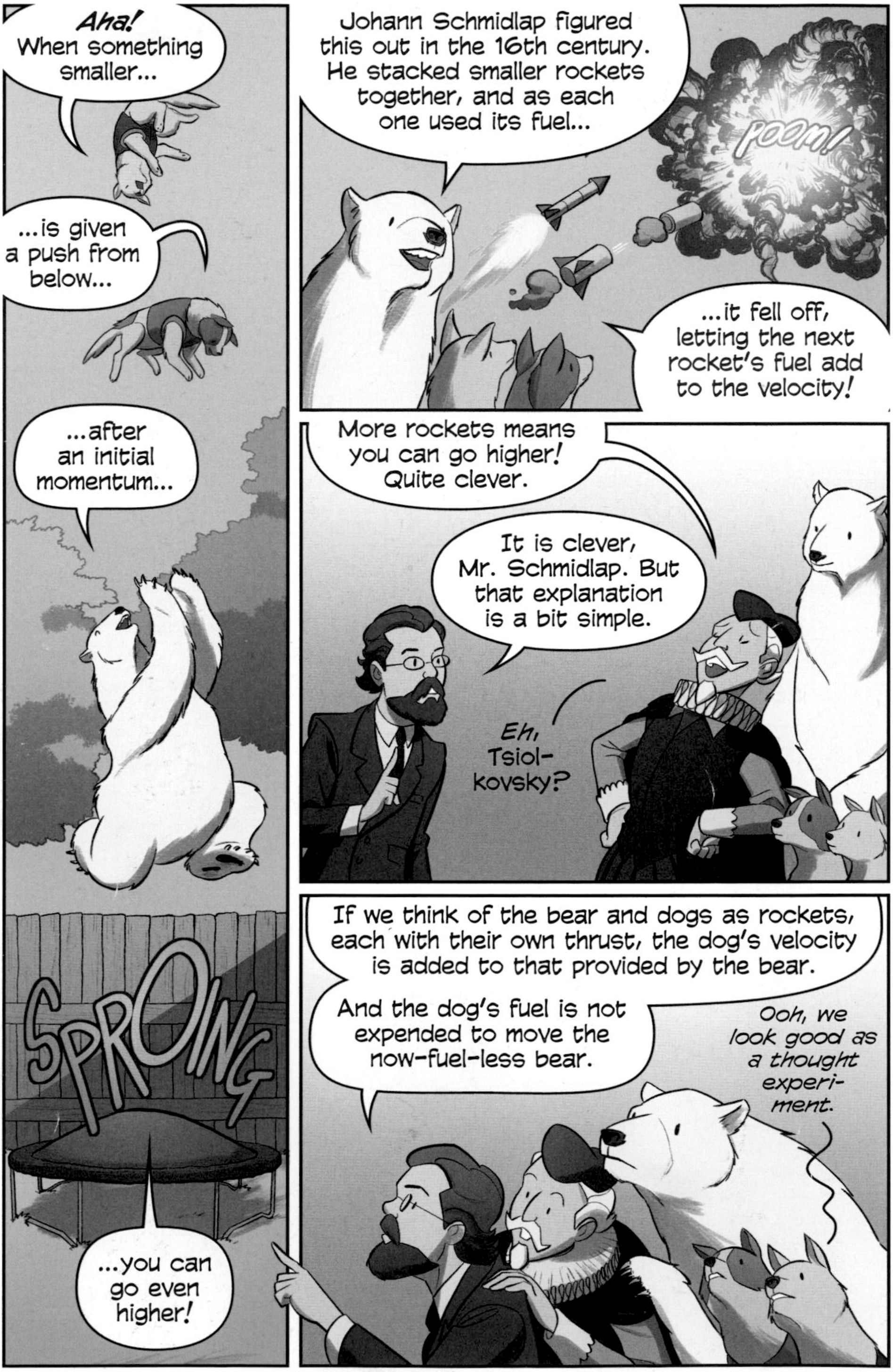

Aha! When something smaller...
...is given a push from below...
...after an initial momentum...
SPROING
...you can go even higher!
Johann Schmidlap figured this out in the 16th century. He stacked smaller rockets together, and as each one used its fuel...
POOM!
...it fell off, letting the next rocket's fuel add to the velocity!
More rockets means you can go higher! Quite clever.
It is clever, Mr. Schmidlap. But that explanation is a bit simple.
Eh, Tsiolkovsky?
If we think of the bear and dogs as rockets, each with their own thrust, the dog's velocity is added to that provided by the bear.
And the dog's fuel is not expended to move the now-fuel-less bear.
Ooh, we look good as a thought experiment.

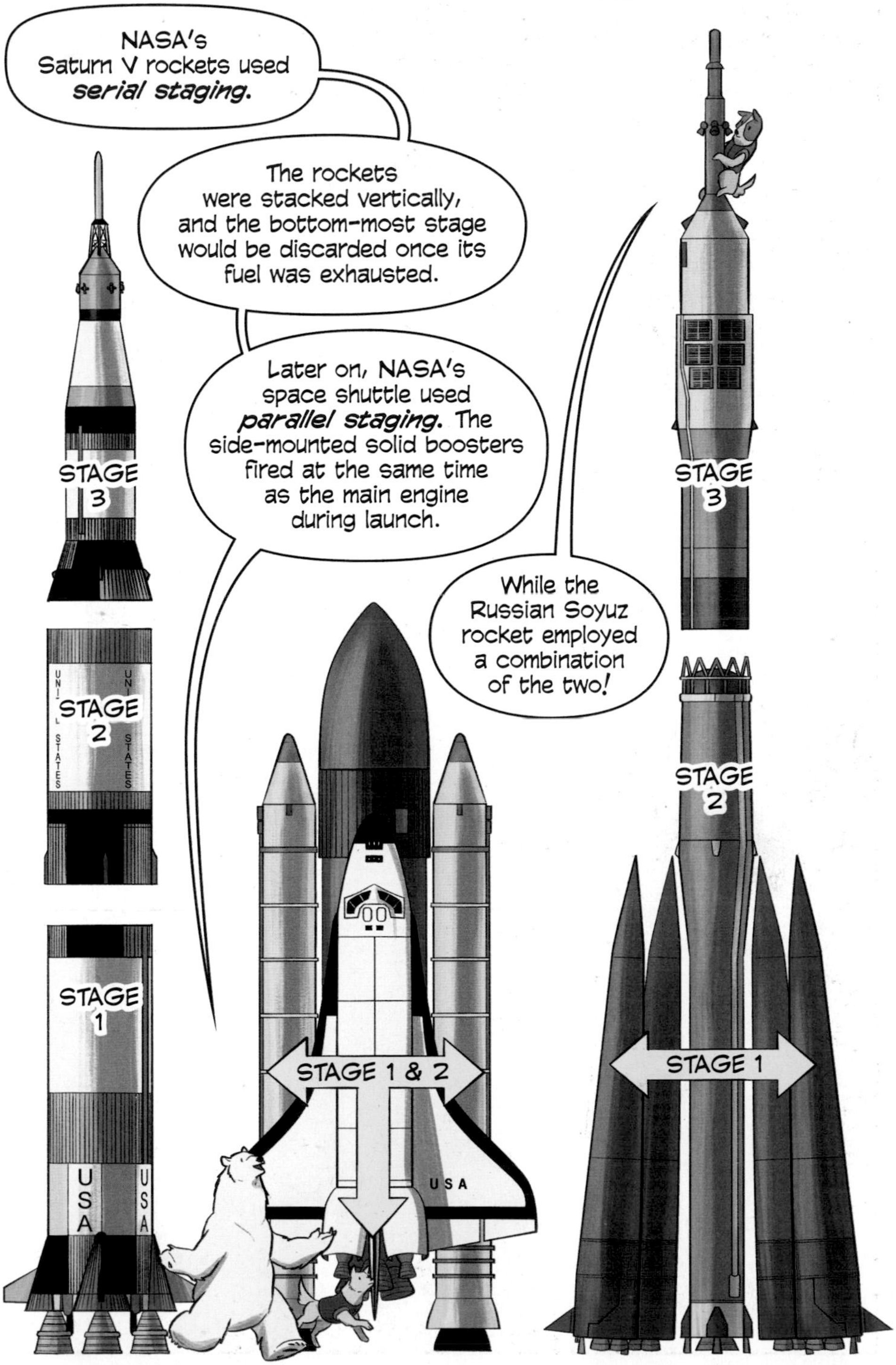
NASA's Saturn V rockets used ***serial staging.***
The rockets were stacked vertically, and the bottom-most stage would be discarded once its fuel was exhausted.
Later on, NASA's space shuttle used ***parallel staging.*** The side-mounted solid boosters fired at the same time as the main engine during launch.
While the Russian Soyuz rocket employed a combination of the two!
STAGE 3
STAGE 2
STAGE 1
USA
STAGE 1 & 2
USA
STAGE 3
STAGE 2
STAGE 1

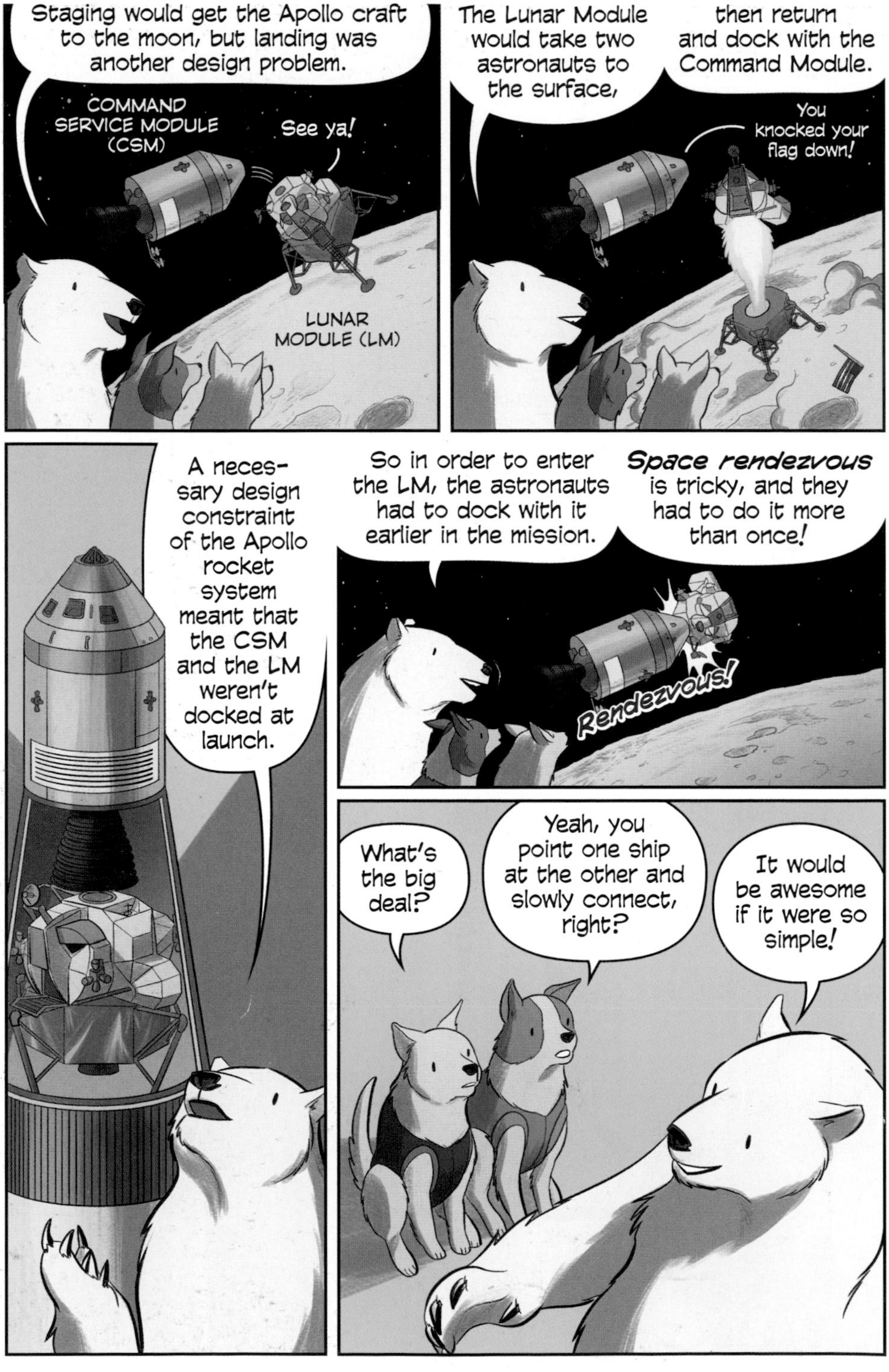
Staging would get the Apollo craft to the moon, but landing was another design problem.
COMMAND SERVICE MODULE (CSM)
See ya!
LUNAR MODULE (LM)
The Lunar Module would take two astronauts to the surface,
then return and dock with the Command Module.
You knocked your flag down!
A neces-sary design constraint of the Apollo rocket system meant that the CSM and the LM weren't docked at launch.
So in order to enter the LM, the astronauts had to dock with it earlier in the mission.
Space rendezvous is tricky, and they had to do it more than once!
Rendezvous!
What's the big deal?
Yeah, you point one ship at the other and slowly connect, right?
It would be awesome if it were so simple!

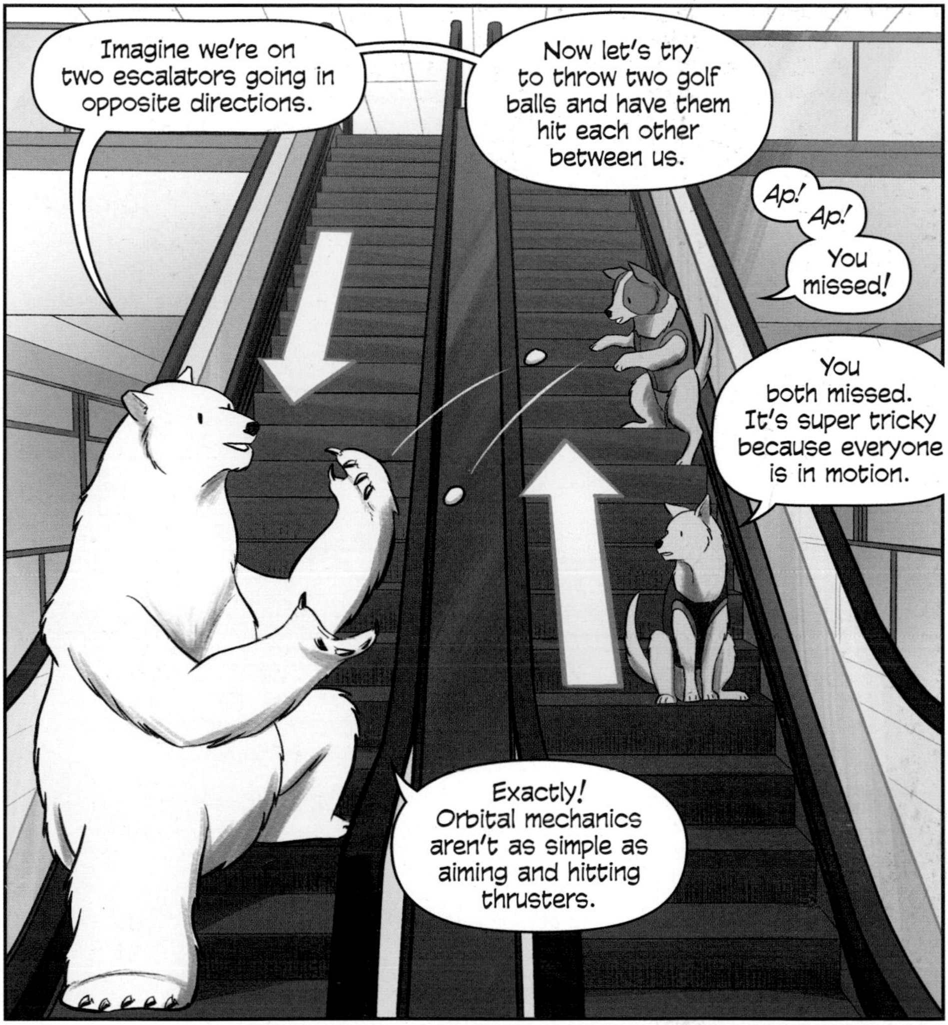
Imagine we're on two escalators going in opposite directions.
Now let's try to throw two golf balls and have them hit each other between us.
Ap! Ap!
You missed!
You both missed. It's super tricky because everyone is in motion.
Exactly! Orbital mechanics aren't as simple as aiming and hitting thrusters.

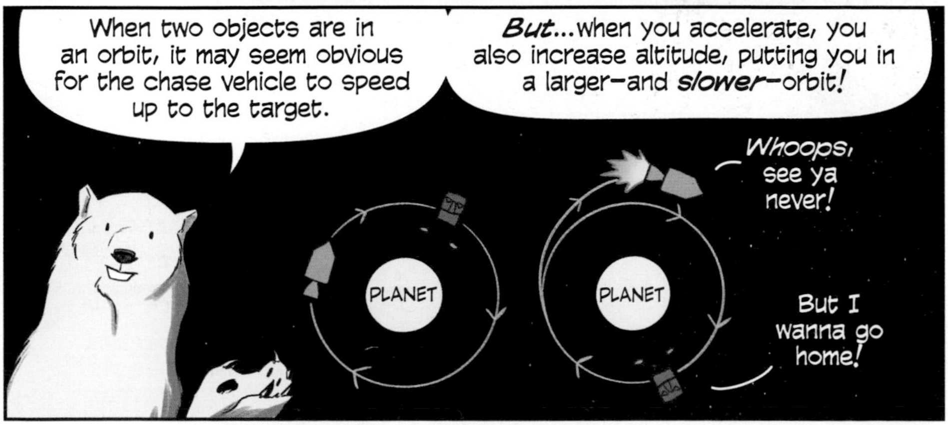
When two objects are in an orbit, it may seem obvious for the chase vehicle to speed up to the target.
But...when you accelerate, you also increase altitude, putting you in a larger–and *slower*–orbit!
Whoops, see ya never!
PLANET
PLANET
But I wanna go home!

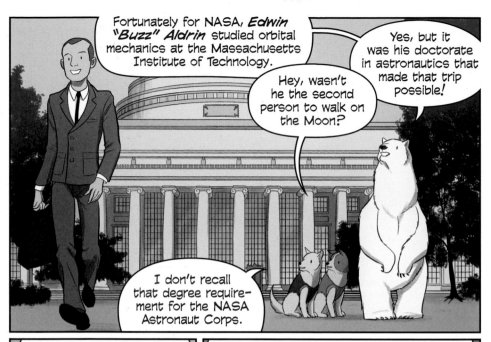

Fortunately for NASA, *Edwin "Buzz" Aldrin* studied orbital mechanics at the Massachusetts Institute of Technology.

Hey, wasn't he the second person to walk on the Moon?

Yes, but it was his doctorate in astronautics that made that trip possible!

I don't recall that degree requirement for the NASA Astronaut Corps.

It wasn't. Aldrin literally wrote the first book on space rendezvous in his doctoral thesis.

He helped his fellow astronauts understand the counterintuitive maneuvers required.

Line-of-Sight Guidance Techniques for Manned Orbital Rendezvous

...you speed up to get into an elliptical orbit, which slows you down. Then in two orbits, your path will intersect the target orbit here.

I wanna see too.

Quit pushing.

I get it now. Thanks, *Dr. Rendezvous!*

The nickname came from a playful form of respect.

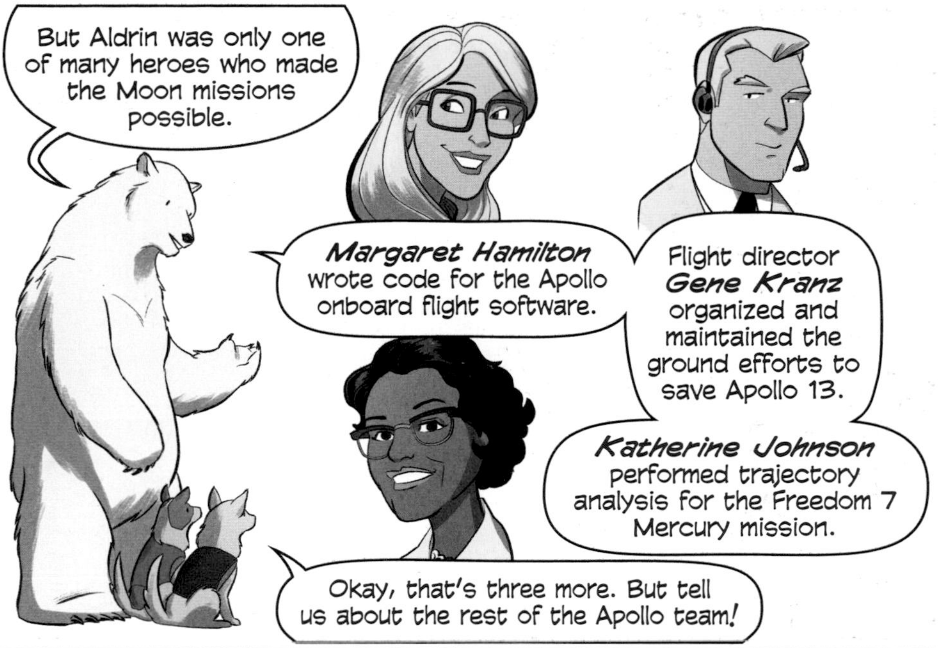
But Aldrin was only one of many heroes who made the Moon missions possible.
Margaret Hamilton wrote code for the Apollo onboard flight software.
Flight director Gene Kranz organized and maintained the ground efforts to save Apollo 13.
Katherine Johnson performed trajectory analysis for the Freedom 7 Mercury mission.
Okay, that's three more. But tell us about the rest of the Apollo team!

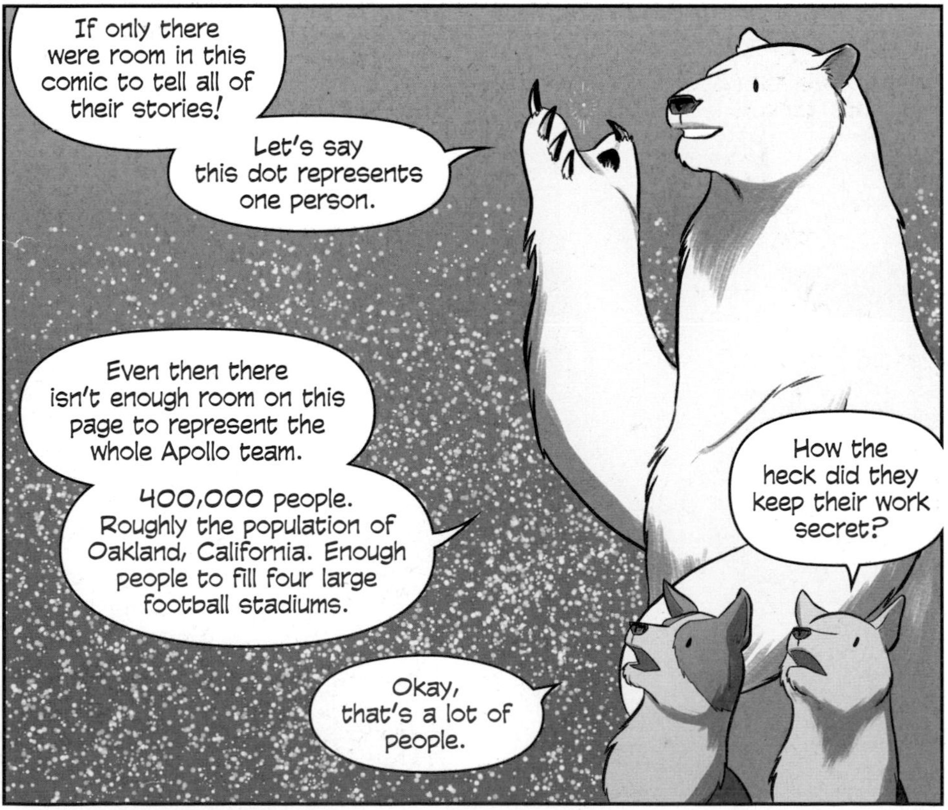
If only there were room in this comic to tell all of their stories!
Let's say this dot represents one person.
Even then there isn't enough room on this page to represent the whole Apollo team.
400,000 people. Roughly the population of Oakland, California. Enough people to fill four large football stadiums.
How the heck did they keep their work secret?
Okay, that's a lot of people.

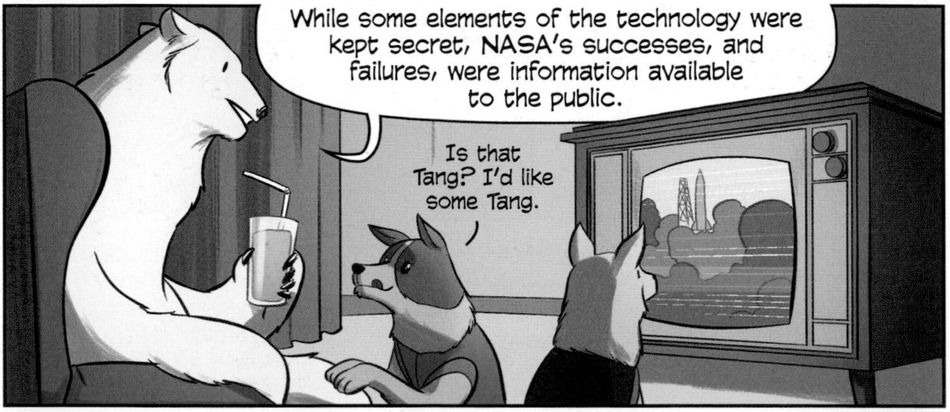
While some elements of the technology were kept secret, NASA's successes, and failures, were information available to the public.
Is that Tang? I'd like some Tang.

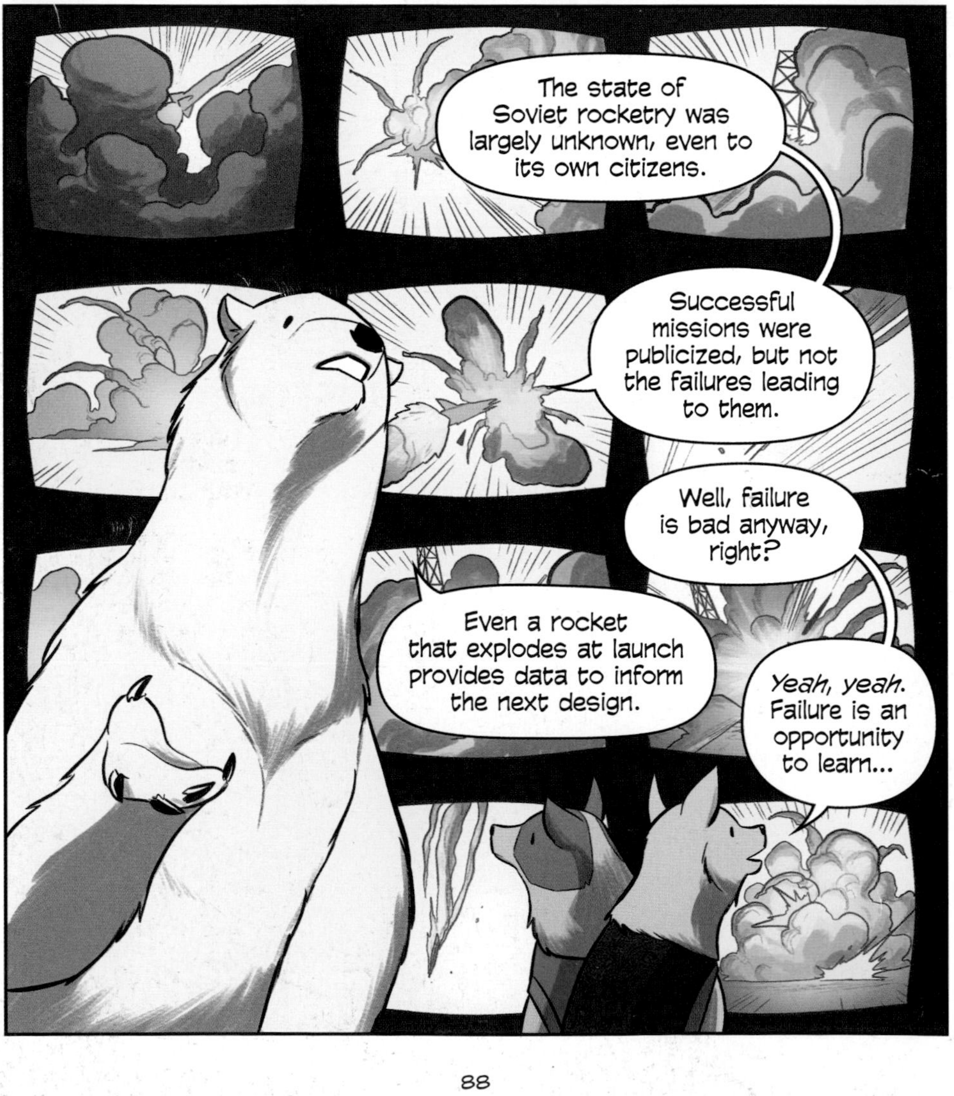
The state of Soviet rocketry was largely unknown, even to its own citizens.
Successful missions were publicized, but not the failures leading to them.
Well, failure is bad anyway, right?
Even a rocket that explodes at launch provides data to inform the next design.
Yeah, yeah. Failure is an opportunity to learn...

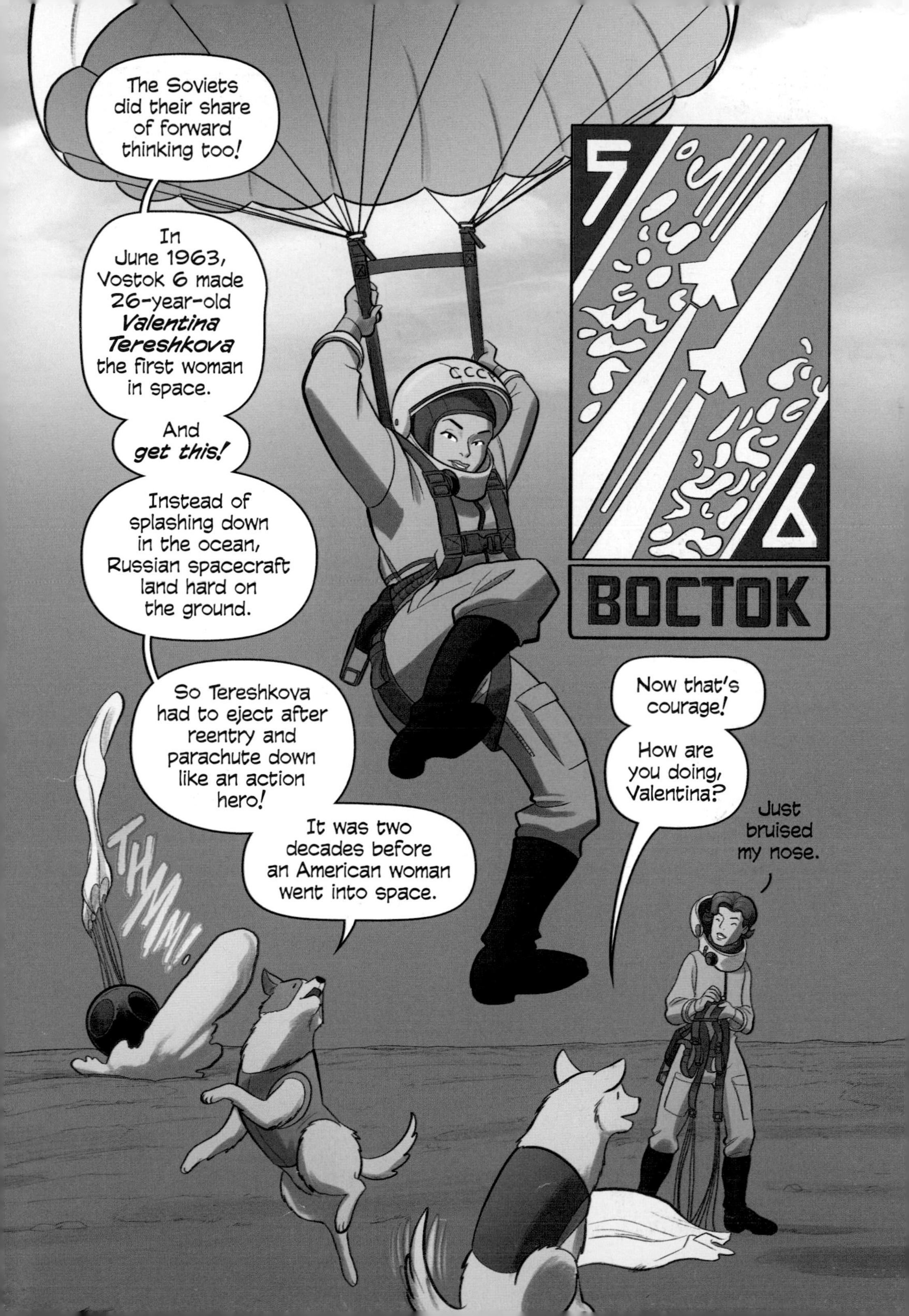
The Soviets did their share of forward thinking too!
In June 1963, Vostok 6 made 26-year-old *Valentina Tereshkova* the first woman in space.
And *get this!*
Instead of splashing down in the ocean, Russian spacecraft land hard on the ground.
So Tereshkova had to eject after reentry and parachute down like an action hero!
It was two decades before an American woman went into space.
5
6
ВОСТОК
CCCP
Now that's courage!
How are you doing, Valentina?
Just bruised my nose.
THMM!

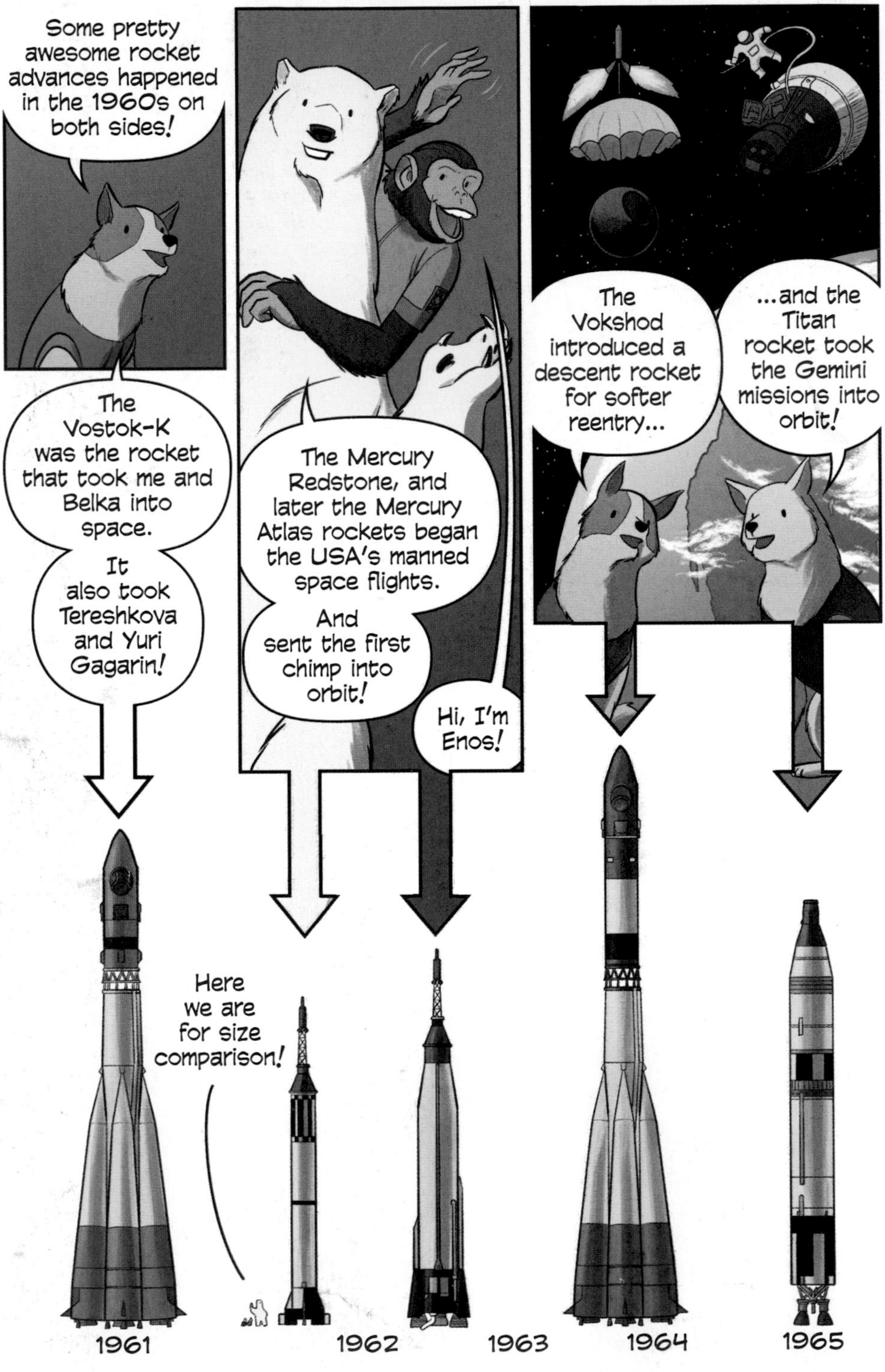

Some pretty awesome rocket advances happened in the 1960s on both sides!
The Vostok-K was the rocket that took me and Belka into space.
It also took Tereshkova and Yuri Gagarin!
The Mercury Redstone, and later the Mercury Atlas rockets began the USA's manned space flights.
And sent the first chimp into orbit!
Hi, I'm Enos!
The Vokshod introduced a descent rocket for softer reentry...
...and the Titan rocket took the Gemini missions into orbit!
Here we are for size comparison!
1961
1962
1963
1964
1965

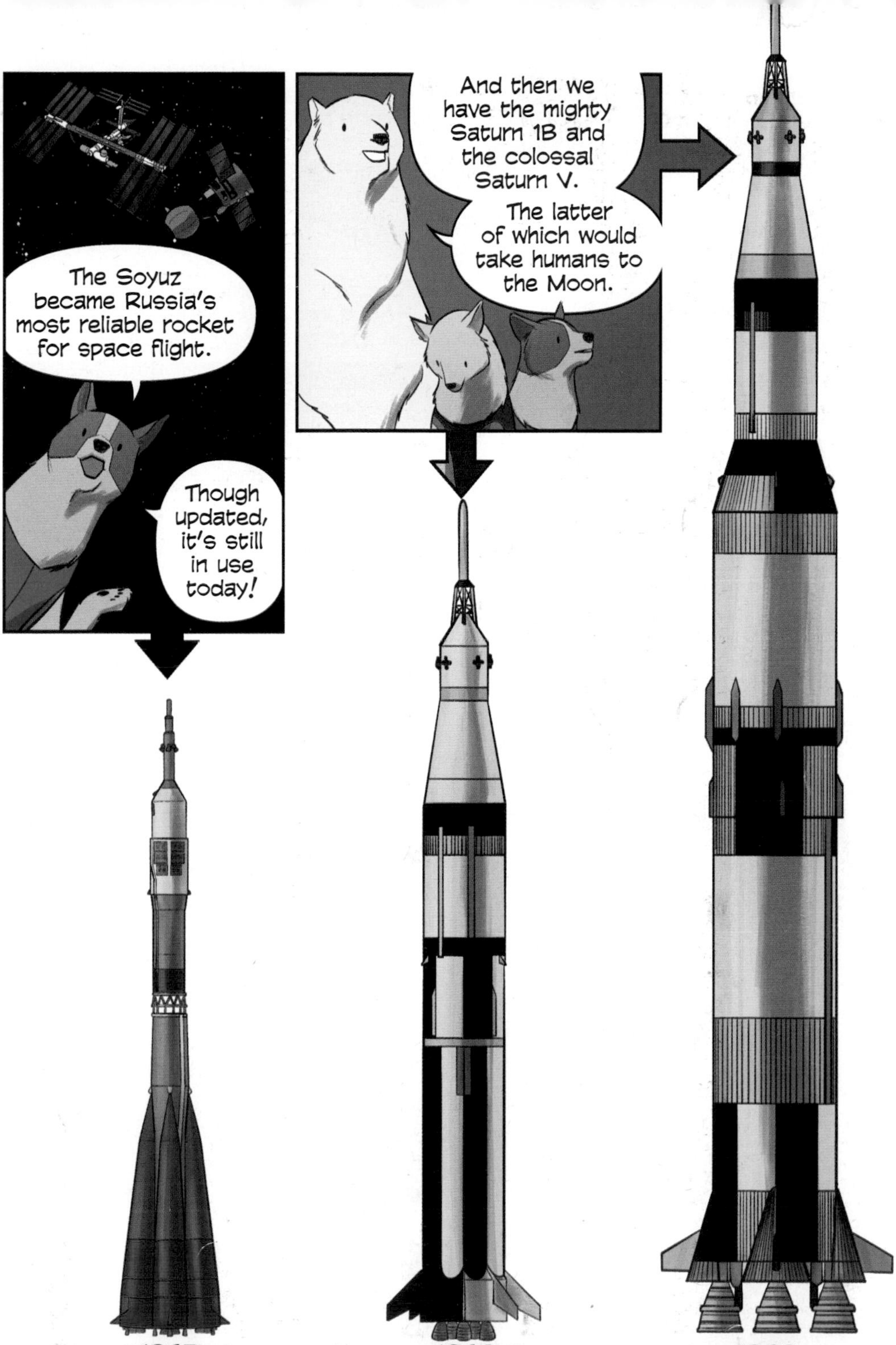
The Soyuz became Russia's most reliable rocket for space flight.
Though updated, it's still in use today!
And then we have the mighty Saturn 1B and the colossal Saturn V.
The latter of which would take humans to the Moon.
1967
1968
1969

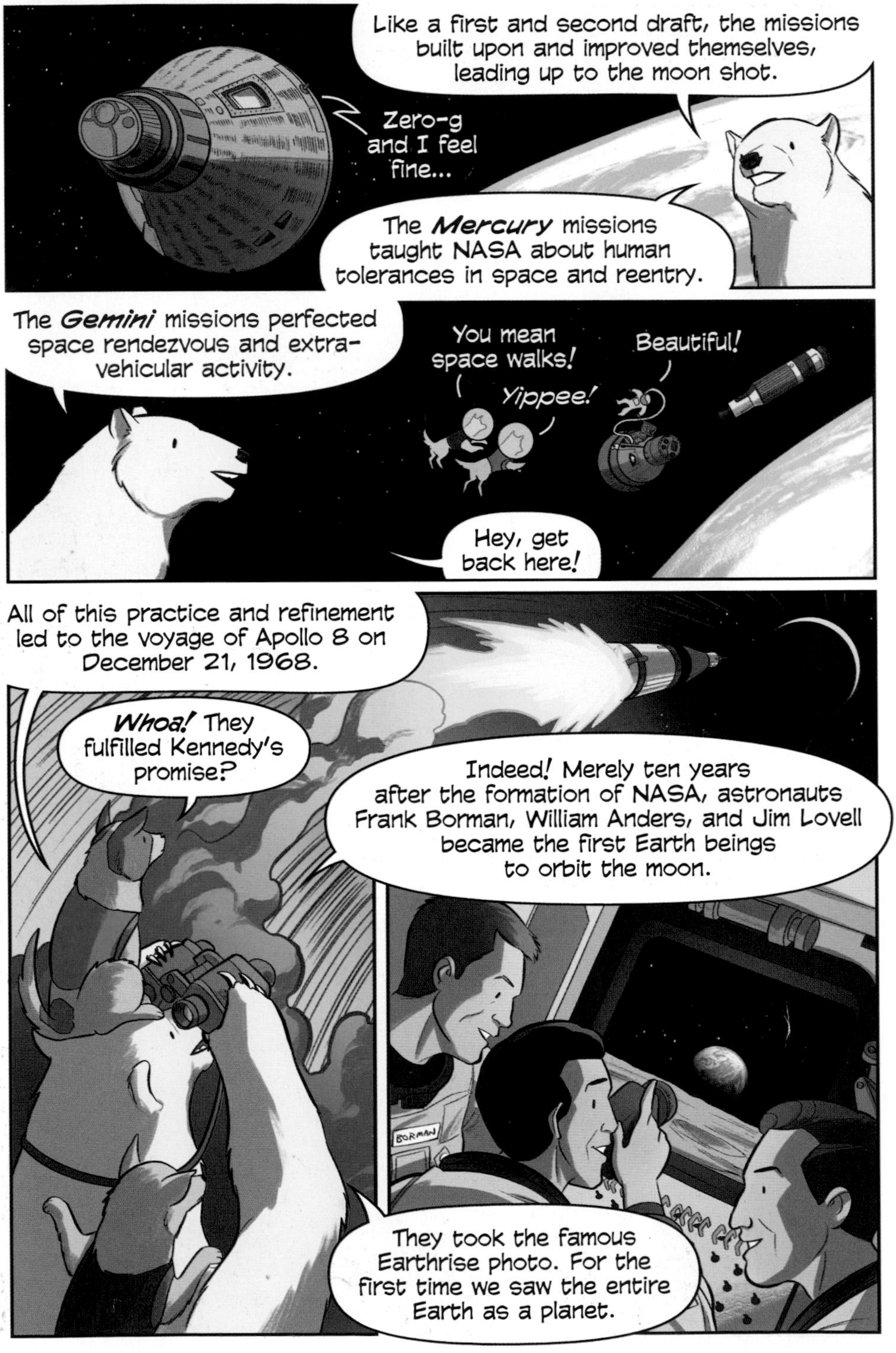
Like a first and second draft, the missions built upon and improved themselves, leading up to the moon shot.
Zero-g and I feel fine...
The *Mercury* missions taught NASA about human tolerances in space and reentry.
The *Gemini* missions perfected space rendezvous and extra-vehicular activity.
You mean space walks!
Yippee!
Beautiful!
Hey, get back here!
All of this practice and refinement led to the voyage of Apollo 8 on December 21, 1968.
Whoa! They fulfilled Kennedy's promise?
Indeed! Merely ten years after the formation of NASA, astronauts Frank Borman, William Anders, and Jim Lovell became the first Earth beings to orbit the moon.
BORMAN
They took the famous Earthrise photo. For the first time we saw the entire Earth as a planet.

Ak-hem.

Hold up, buddy.

?

They might've been the first *humans*, but me an' my buddy here were the first Earth *beings* to orbit the moon.

You said it, buddy.

Whaat?

It's true! We were selected by the Soviet space program for a series of moon orbit test flights.

An' lemme tell ya, they were really lookin' for the right stuff!

Go, buddy, go!

TOO FAST!

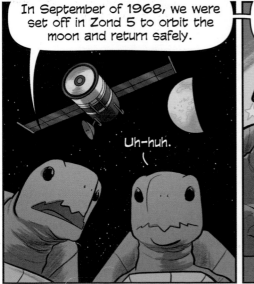

In September of 1968, we were set off in Zond 5 to orbit the moon and return safely.

Uh-huh.

An' it was *us* who saw the Earthrise first, but they forgot to pack us a camera!

HIGH FIVE!

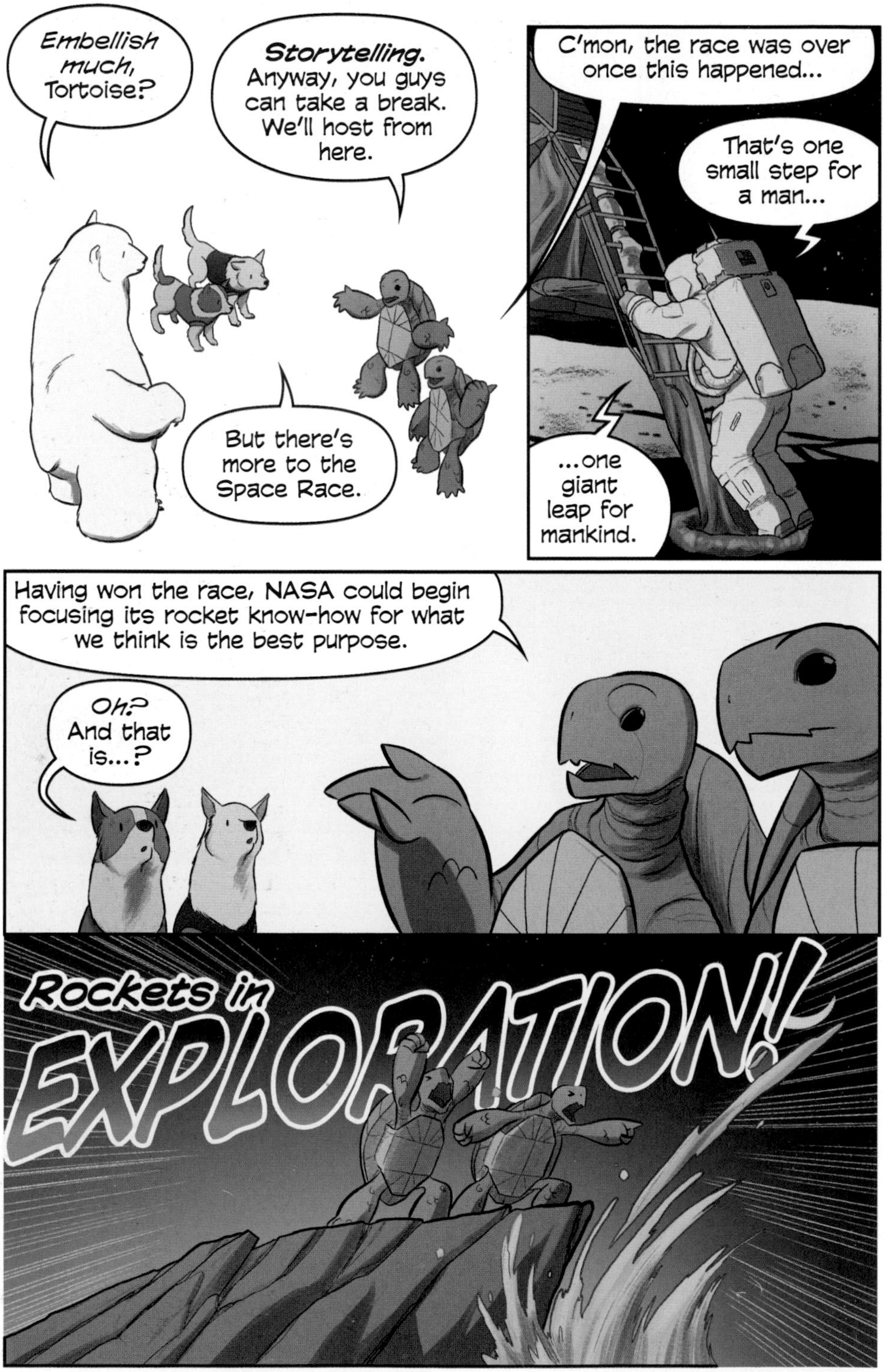
Embellish much, Tortoise?
Storytelling. Anyway, you guys can take a break. We'll host from here.
But there's more to the Space Race.
C'mon, the race was over once this happened...
That's one small step for a man...
...one giant leap for mankind.
Having won the race, NASA could begin focusing its rocket know-how for what we think is the best purpose.
Oh? And that is...?
Rockets in EXPLORATION!

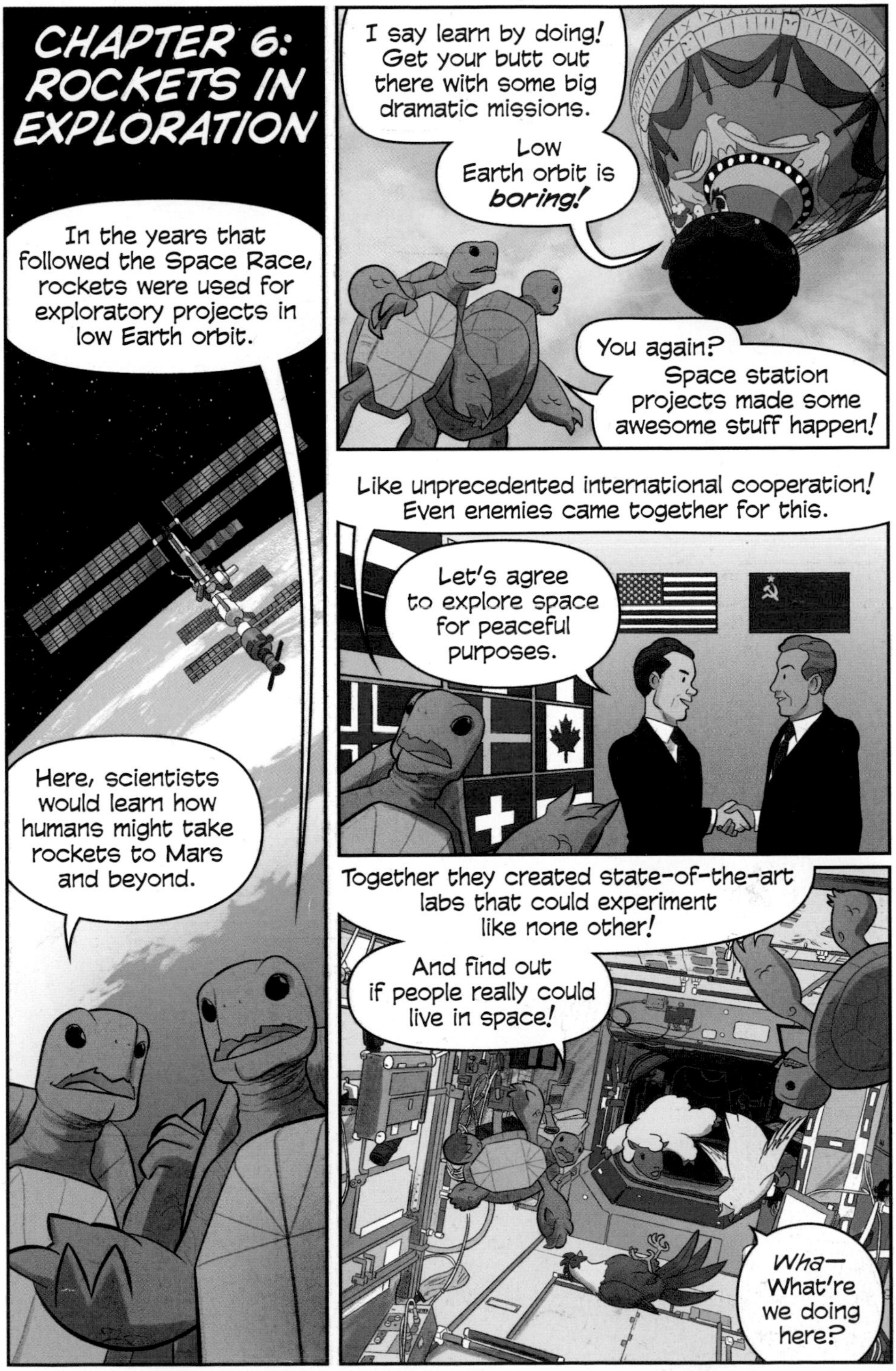
CHAPTER 6: ROCKETS IN EXPLORATION
In the years that followed the Space Race, rockets were used for exploratory projects in low Earth orbit.
Here, scientists would learn how humans might take rockets to Mars and beyond.
I say learn by doing! Get your butt out there with some big dramatic missions.
Low Earth orbit is *boring!*
You again? Space station projects made some awesome stuff happen!
Like unprecedented international cooperation! Even enemies came together for this.
Let's agree to explore space for peaceful purposes.
Together they created state-of-the-art labs that could experiment like none other!
And find out if people really could live in space!
Wha— What're we doing here?

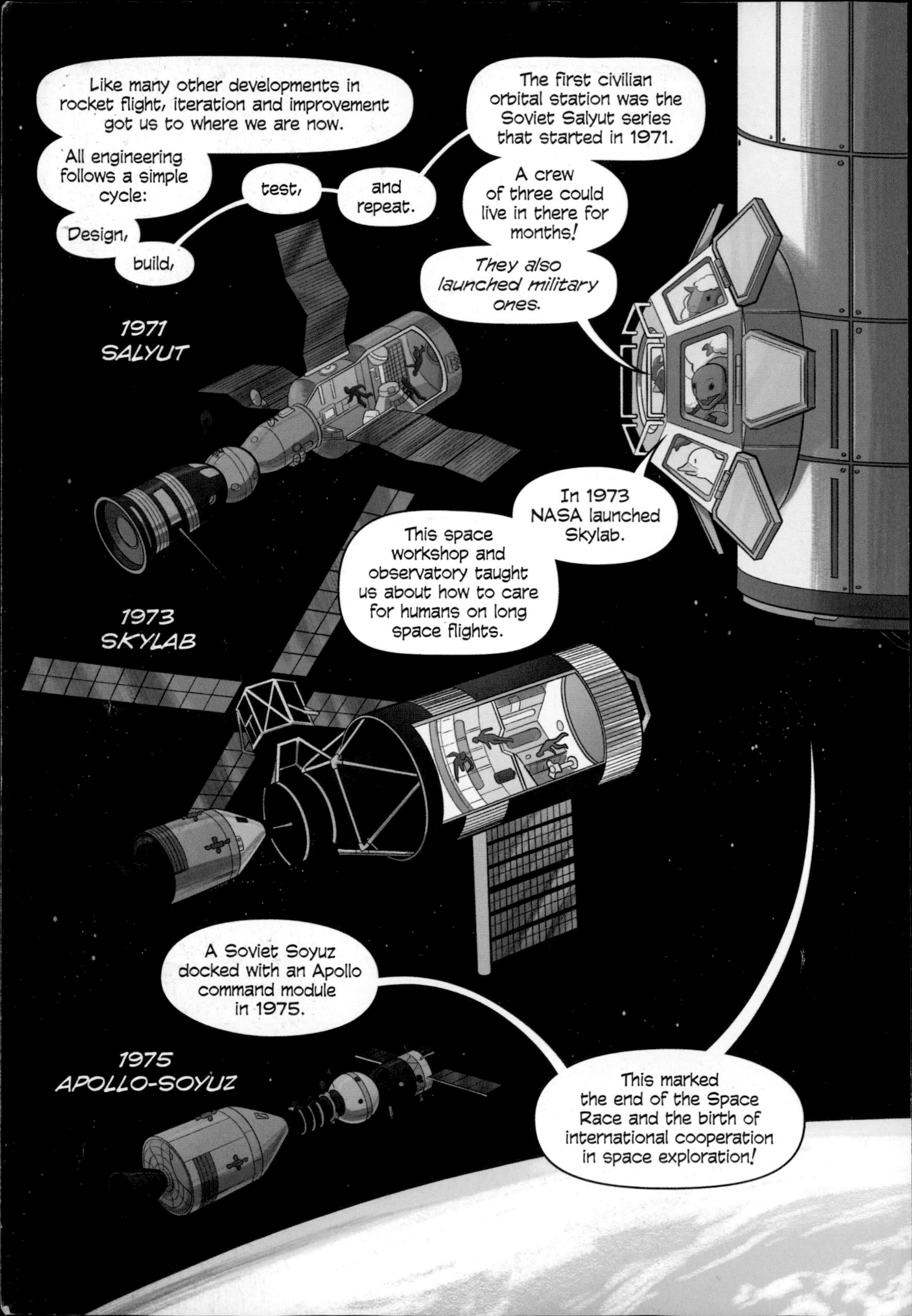
Like many other developments in rocket flight, iteration and improvement got us to where we are now.
All engineering follows a simple cycle:
Design,
build,
test,
and repeat.
The first civilian orbital station was the Soviet Salyut series that started in 1971.
A crew of three could live in there for months!
They also launched military ones.
1971 SALYUT
In 1973 NASA launched Skylab.
This space workshop and observatory taught us about how to care for humans on long space flights.
1973 SKYLAB
A Soviet Soyuz docked with an Apollo command module in 1975.
1975 APOLLO-SOYUZ
This marked the end of the Space Race and the birth of international cooperation in space exploration!

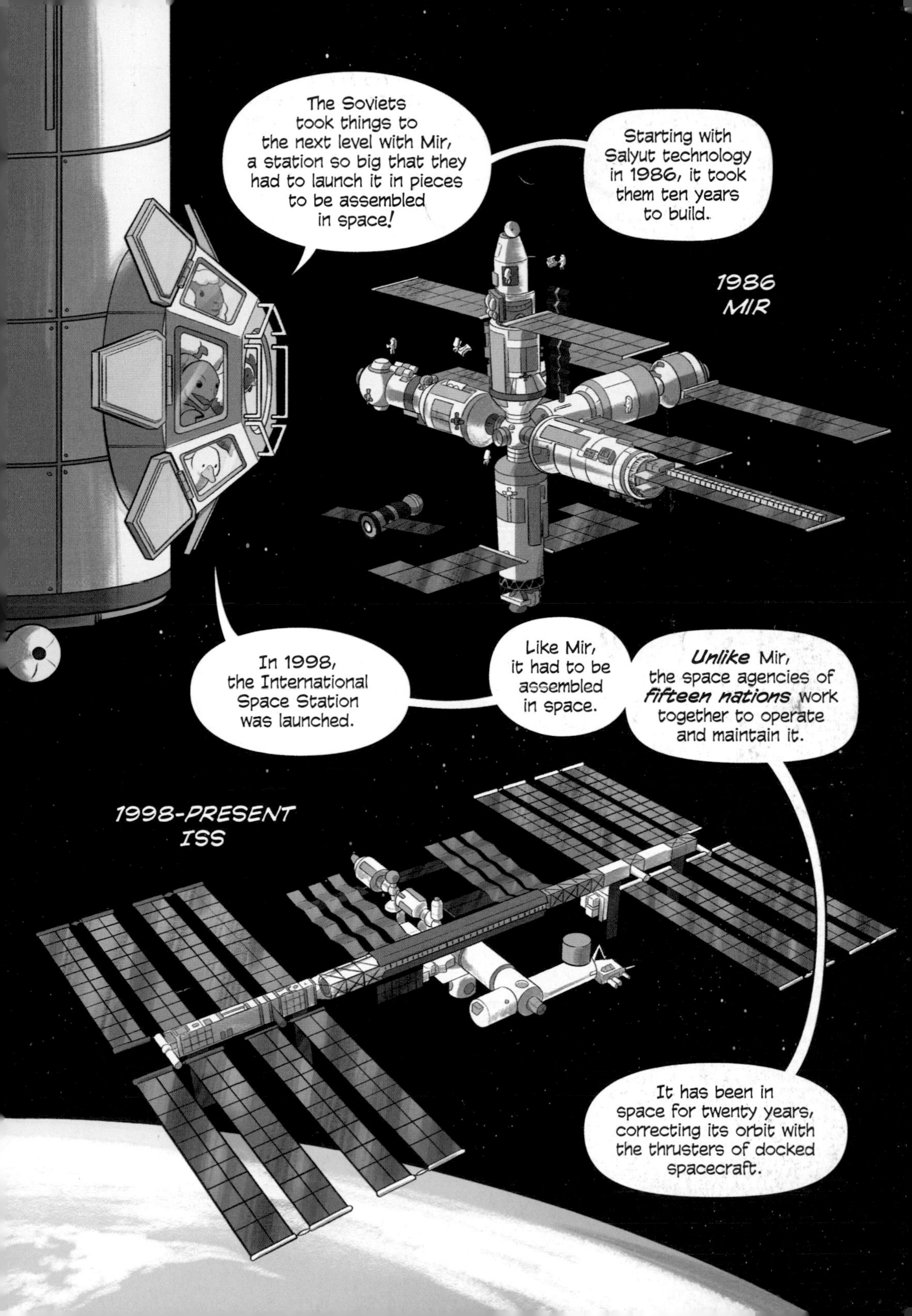
The Soviets took things to the next level with Mir, a station so big that they had to launch it in pieces to be assembled in space!
Starting with Salyut technology in 1986, it took them ten years to build.
1986 MIR
In 1998, the International Space Station was launched.
Like Mir, it had to be assembled in space.
Unlike Mir, the space agencies of ***fifteen nations*** work together to operate and maintain it.
1998-PRESENT ISS
It has been in space for twenty years, correcting its orbit with the thrusters of docked spacecraft.

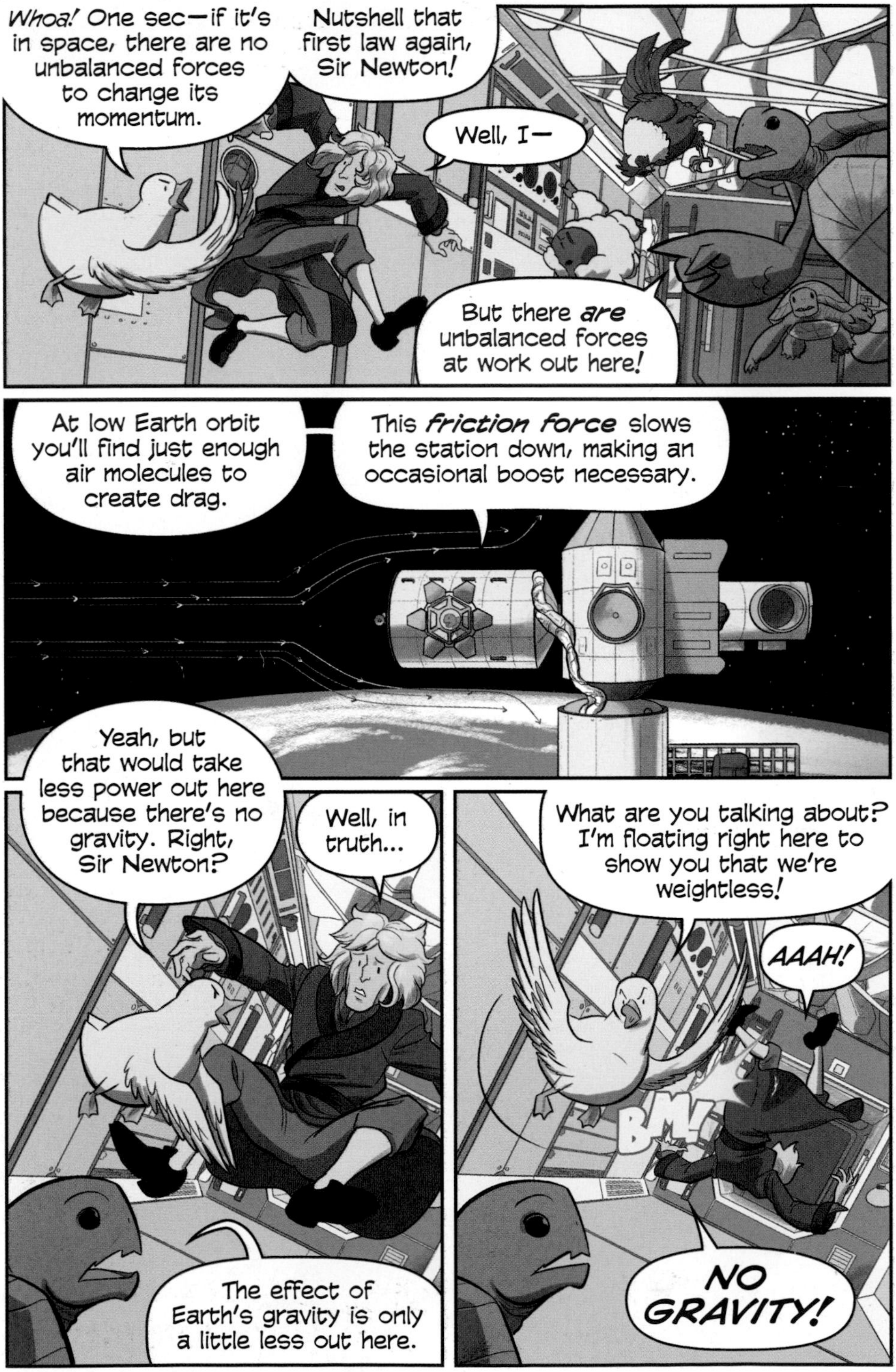
Whoa! One sec—if it's in space, there are no unbalanced forces to change its momentum.
Nutshell that first law again, Sir Newton!
Well, I—
But there are unbalanced forces at work out here!
At low Earth orbit you'll find just enough air molecules to create drag.
This friction force slows the station down, making an occasional boost necessary.
Yeah, but that would take less power out here because there's no gravity. Right, Sir Newton?
Well, in truth...
The effect of Earth's gravity is only a little less out here.
What are you talking about? I'm floating right here to show you that we're weightless!
AAAH!
BAM!
NO GRAVITY!

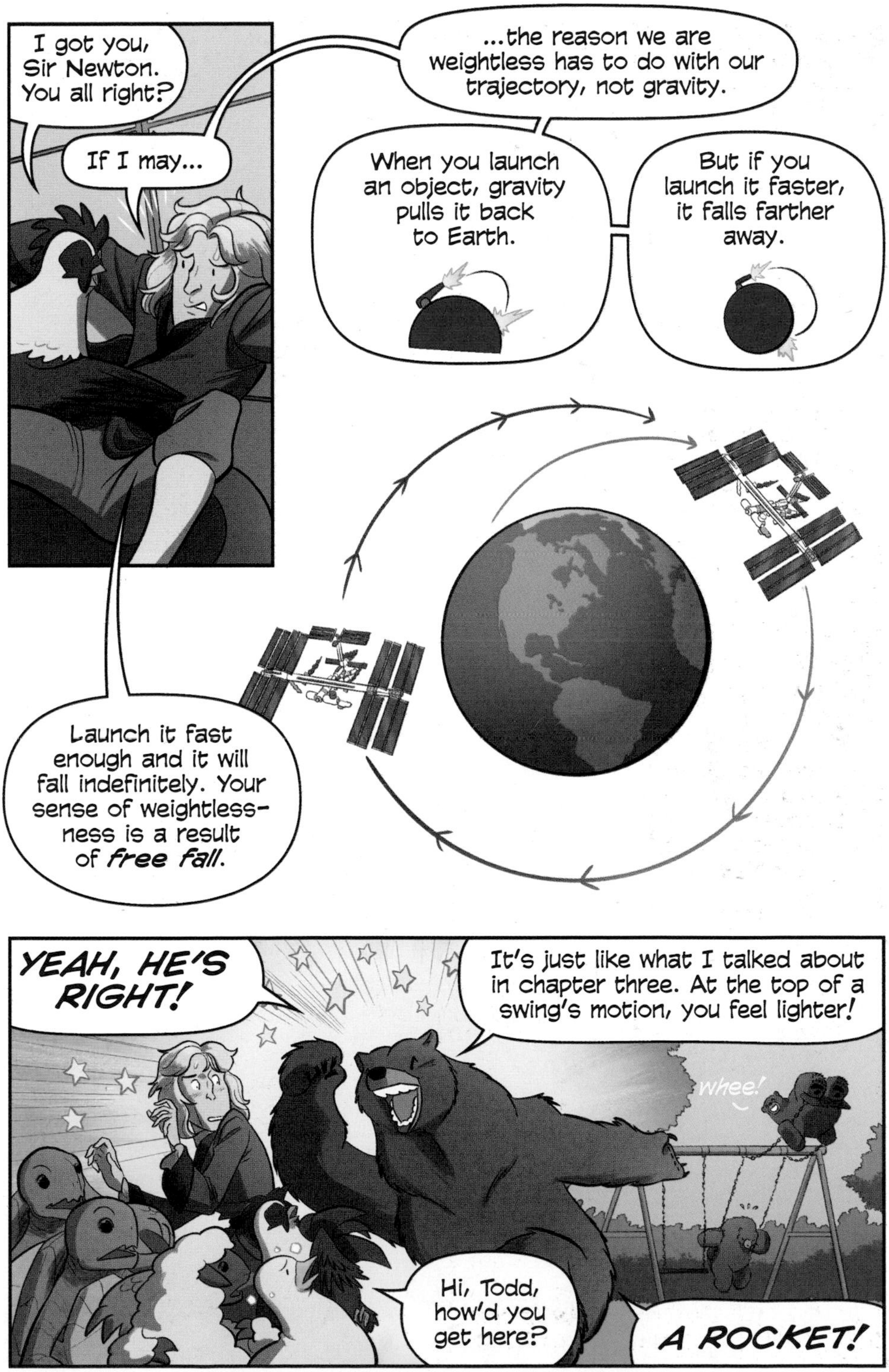

I got you, Sir Newton. You all right?
If I may...
...the reason we are weightless has to do with our trajectory, not gravity.
When you launch an object, gravity pulls it back to Earth.
But if you launch it faster, it falls farther away.
Launch it fast enough and it will fall indefinitely. Your sense of weightlessness is a result of *free fall*.
YEAH, HE'S RIGHT!
It's just like what I talked about in chapter three. At the top of a swing's motion, you feel lighter!
whee!
Hi, Todd, how'd you get here?
A ROCKET!

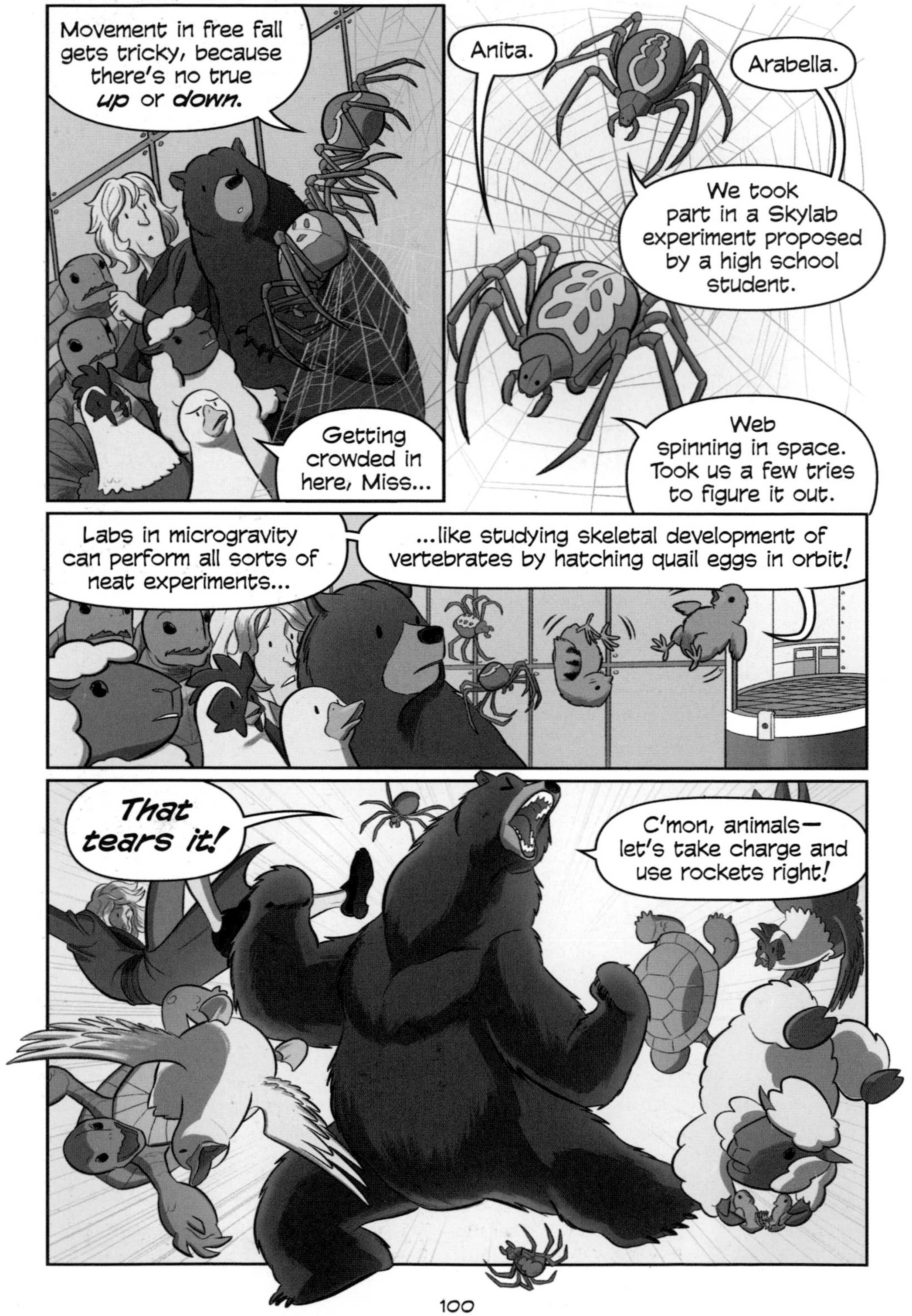
Movement in free fall gets tricky, because there's no true *up* or *down*.
Anita.
Arabella.
We took part in a Skylab experiment proposed by a high school student.
Getting crowded in here, Miss...
Web spinning in space. Took us a few tries to figure it out.
Labs in microgravity can perform all sorts of neat experiments...
...like studying skeletal development of vertebrates by hatching quail eggs in orbit!
That tears it!
C'mon, animals—let's take charge and use rockets right!

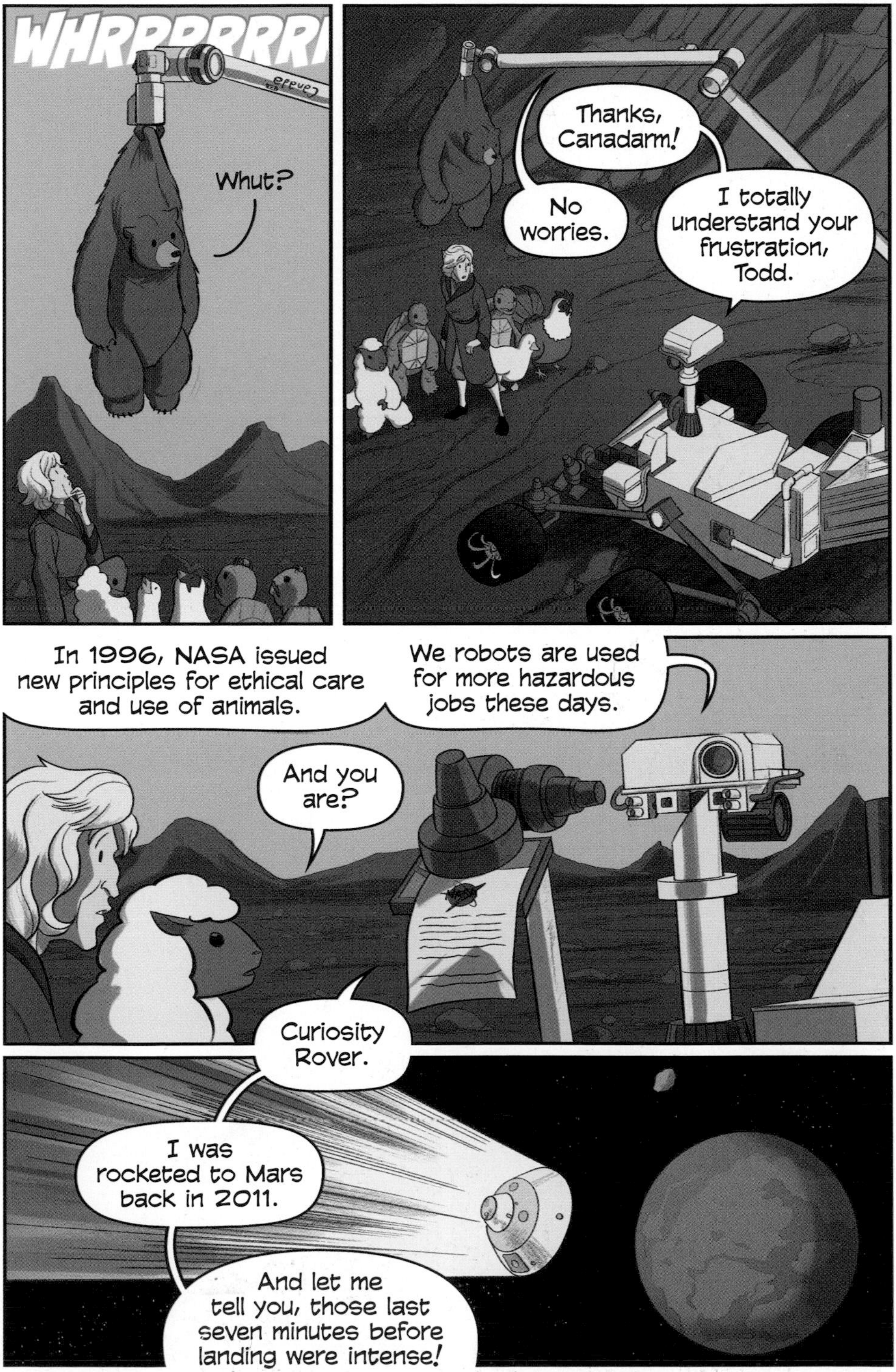
WHRRRRRR!
Whut?
Thanks, Canadarm!
No worries.
I totally understand your frustration, Todd.
In 1996, NASA issued new principles for ethical care and use of animals.
We robots are used for more hazardous jobs these days.
And you are?
Curiosity Rover.
I was rocketed to Mars back in 2011.
And let me tell you, those last seven minutes before landing were intense!

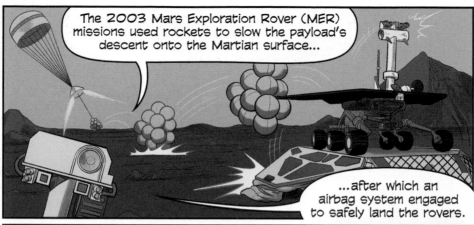

The 2003 Mars Exploration Rover (MER) missions used rockets to slow the payload's descent onto the Martian surface...

...after which an airbag system engaged to safely land the rovers.

Airbags weren't a reliable solution for me, though.

I'm a much larger laboratory than the MER, weighing in at one ton on Earth.

Getting me safely to the surface of Mars was an engineering puzzle.

The folks at the Jet Propulsion Laboratory considered putting me on top of a descent rocket like the previous Viking missions.

Hey, Viking!

Yo.

However, *unlike* Viking, I was meant to move about. And working out such a steep ramp system was tricky.

Watch your step, kid!

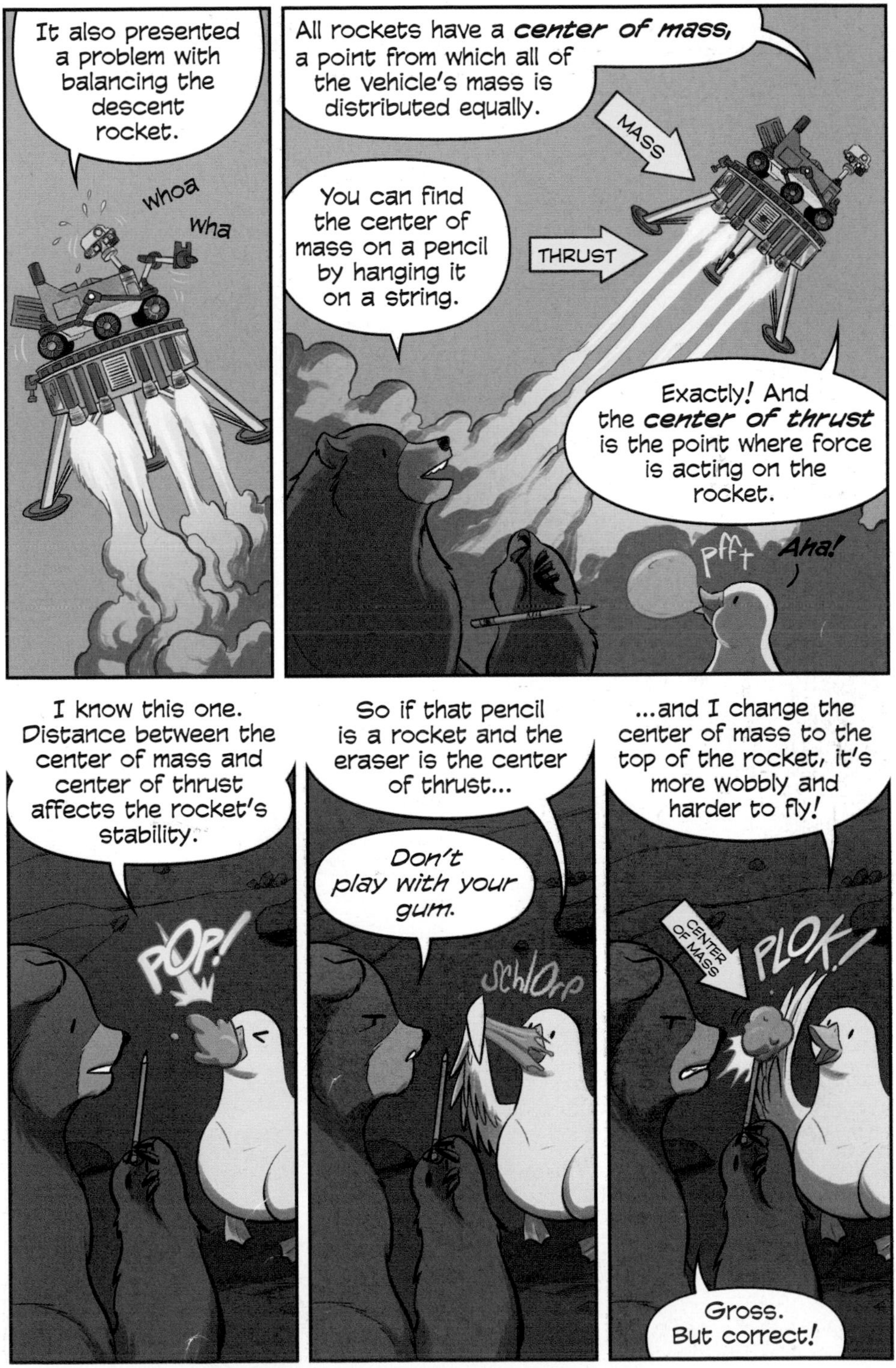
It also presented a problem with balancing the descent rocket.
whoa
wha
All rockets have a **center of mass,** a point from which all of the vehicle's mass is distributed equally.
MASS
You can find the center of mass on a pencil by hanging it on a string.
THRUST
Exactly! And the **center of thrust** is the point where force is acting on the rocket.
pfft
Aha!
I know this one. Distance between the center of mass and center of thrust affects the rocket's stability.
POP!
So if that pencil is a rocket and the eraser is the center of thrust...
Don't play with your gum.
schlorp
...and I change the center of mass to the top of the rocket, it's more wobbly and harder to fly!
CENTER OF MASS
PLOK!
Gross. But correct!

After entering the atmosphere...

...the Sky Crane would use rockets to slow our descent...

The people at JPL figured they could solve this by putting me *under* the rocket.

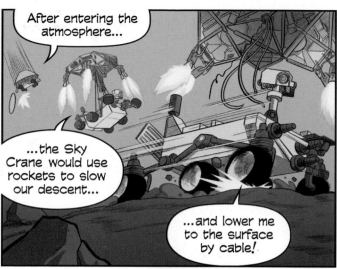

...and lower me to the surface by cable!

Extraterrestrial probes and robots began with the 1977 launch of Voyager 1. It's the first human-made object to enter interstellar space!

See ya never, gang!

1973's Mariner 10 mission featured the first use of a *gravity assist*, where the vehicle uses a close flyby of a larger celestial body to add to its velocity.

Sorry, Venus, Mercury ain't gonna take pictures of itself!

You can't even stay for tea?

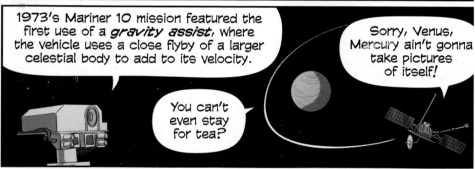

The Mariner series evolved into the Cassini-Huygens probe, from which we've learned a lot about Saturn.

It took *seven years* to get there. That would be an exceedingly long trip for a human!

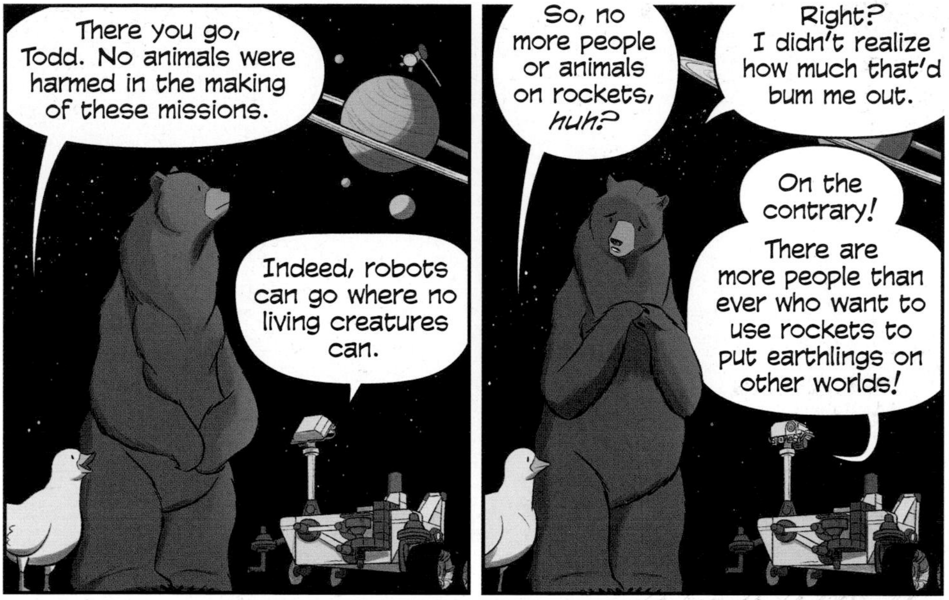
There you go, Todd. No animals were harmed in the making of these missions.
Indeed, robots can go where no living creatures can.
So, no more people or animals on rockets, *huh?*
Right? I didn't realize how much that'd bum me out.
On the contrary!
There are more people than ever who want to use rockets to put earthlings on other worlds!

CHAPTER 7: THE FUTURE OF ROCKETS

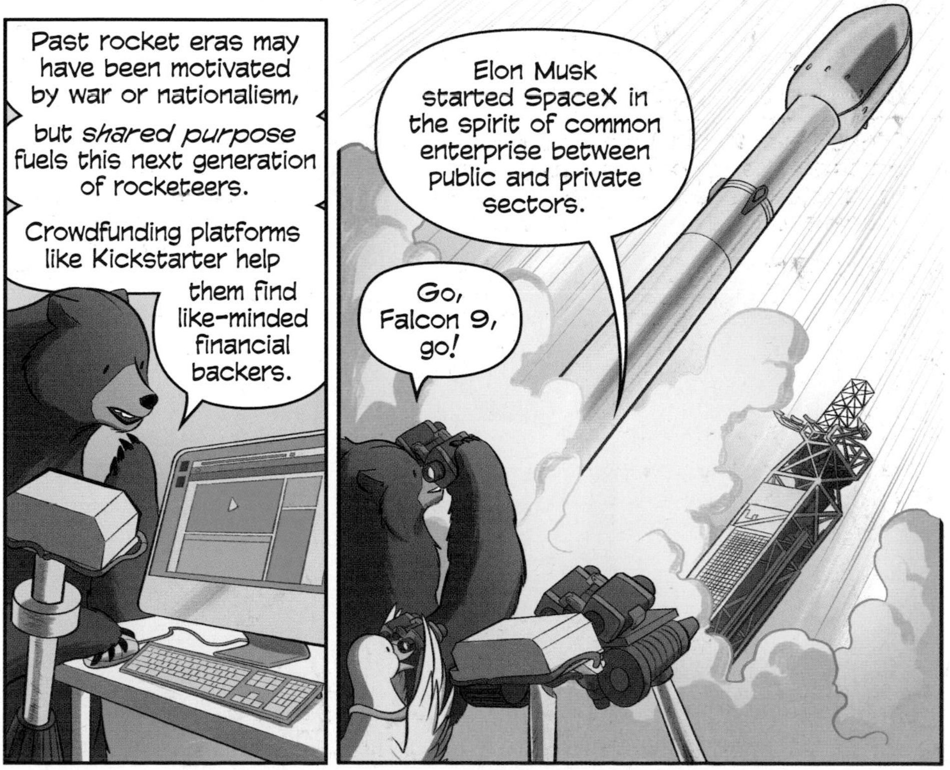
Past rocket eras may have been motivated by war or nationalism,
but *shared purpose* fuels this next generation of rocketeers.
Crowdfunding platforms like Kickstarter help them find like-minded financial backers.
Elon Musk started SpaceX in the spirit of common enterprise between public and private sectors.
Go, Falcon 9, go!

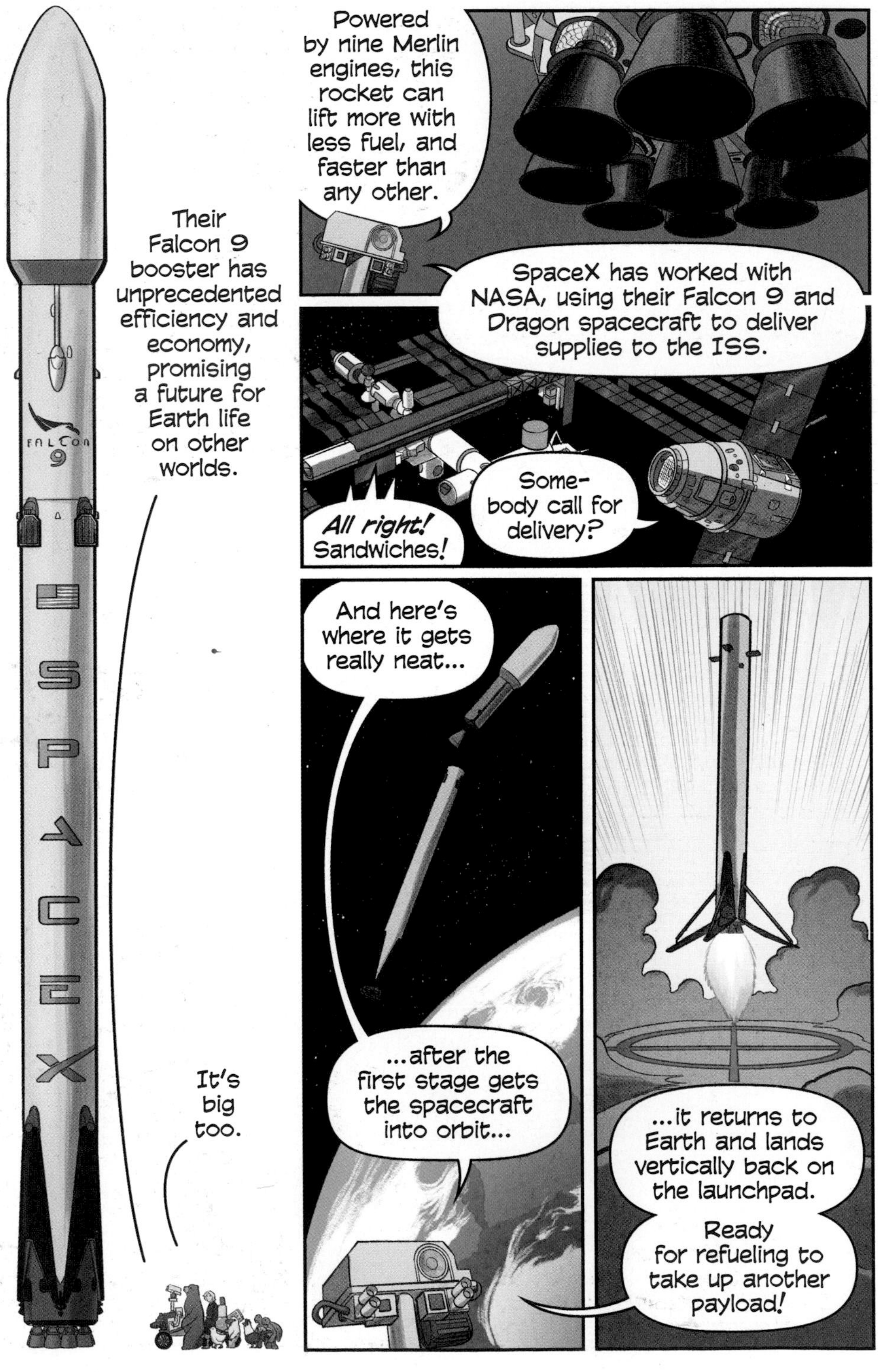
Their Falcon 9 booster has unprecedented efficiency and economy, promising a future for Earth life on other worlds.
It's big too.
FALCON 9
SPACEX
Powered by nine Merlin engines, this rocket can lift more with less fuel, and faster than any other.
SpaceX has worked with NASA, using their Falcon 9 and Dragon spacecraft to deliver supplies to the ISS.
Some-body call for delivery?
All right! Sandwiches!
And here's where it gets really neat...
...after the first stage gets the spacecraft into orbit...
...it returns to Earth and lands vertically back on the launchpad.
Ready for refueling to take up another payload!

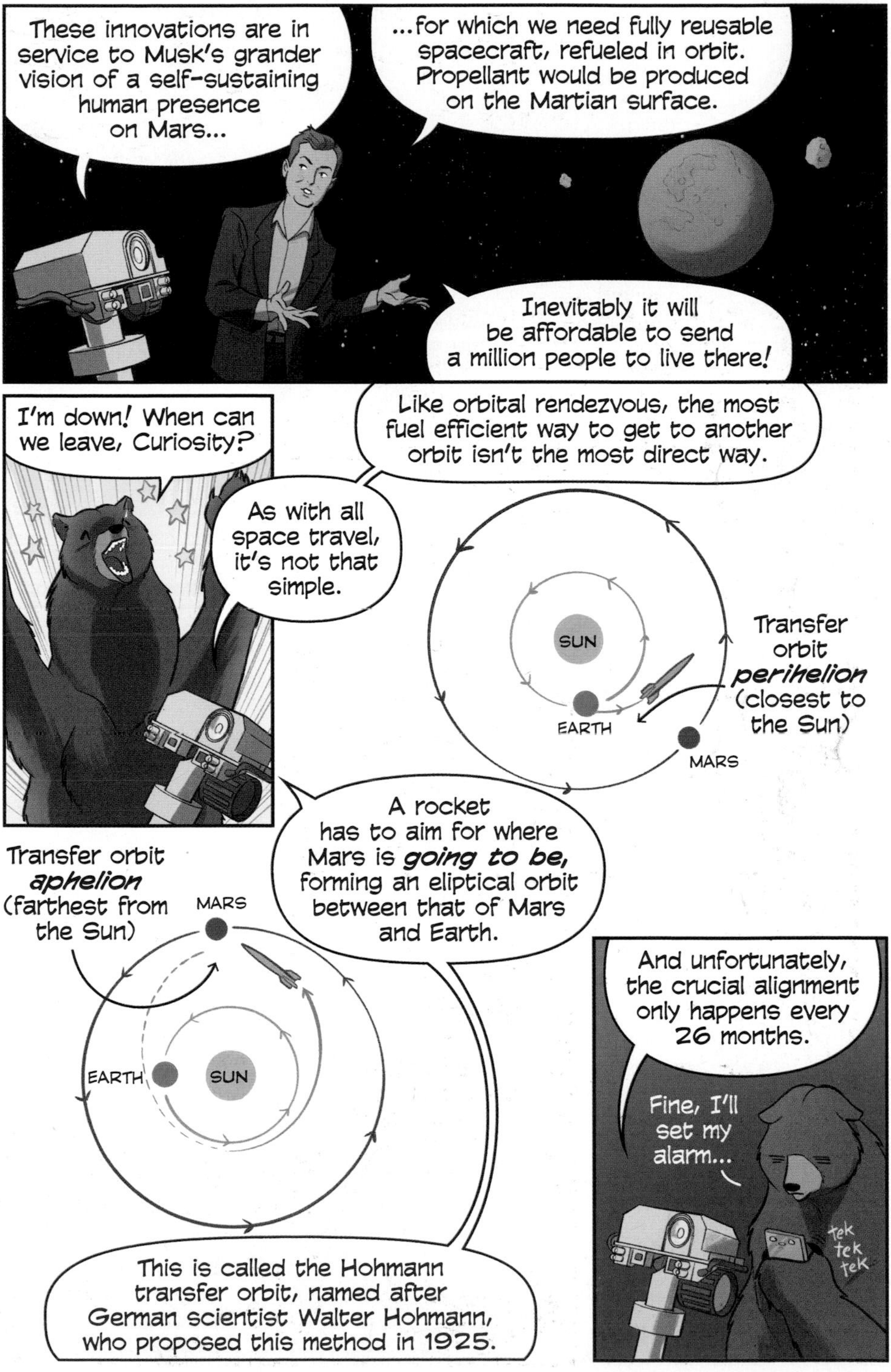
These innovations are in service to Musk's grander vision of a self-sustaining human presence on Mars...
...for which we need fully reusable spacecraft, refueled in orbit. Propellant would be produced on the Martian surface.
Inevitably it will be affordable to send a million people to live there!
I'm down! When can we leave, Curiosity?
As with all space travel, it's not that simple.
Like orbital rendezvous, the most fuel efficient way to get to another orbit isn't the most direct way.
SUN
EARTH
MARS
Transfer orbit *perihelion* (closest to the Sun)
A rocket has to aim for where Mars is *going to be,* forming an eliptical orbit between that of Mars and Earth.
Transfer orbit *aphelion* (farthest from the Sun)
MARS
EARTH
SUN
This is called the Hohmann transfer orbit, named after German scientist Walter Hohmann, who proposed this method in 1925.
And unfortunately, the crucial alignment only happens every 26 months.
Fine, I'll set my alarm...
tek tek tek

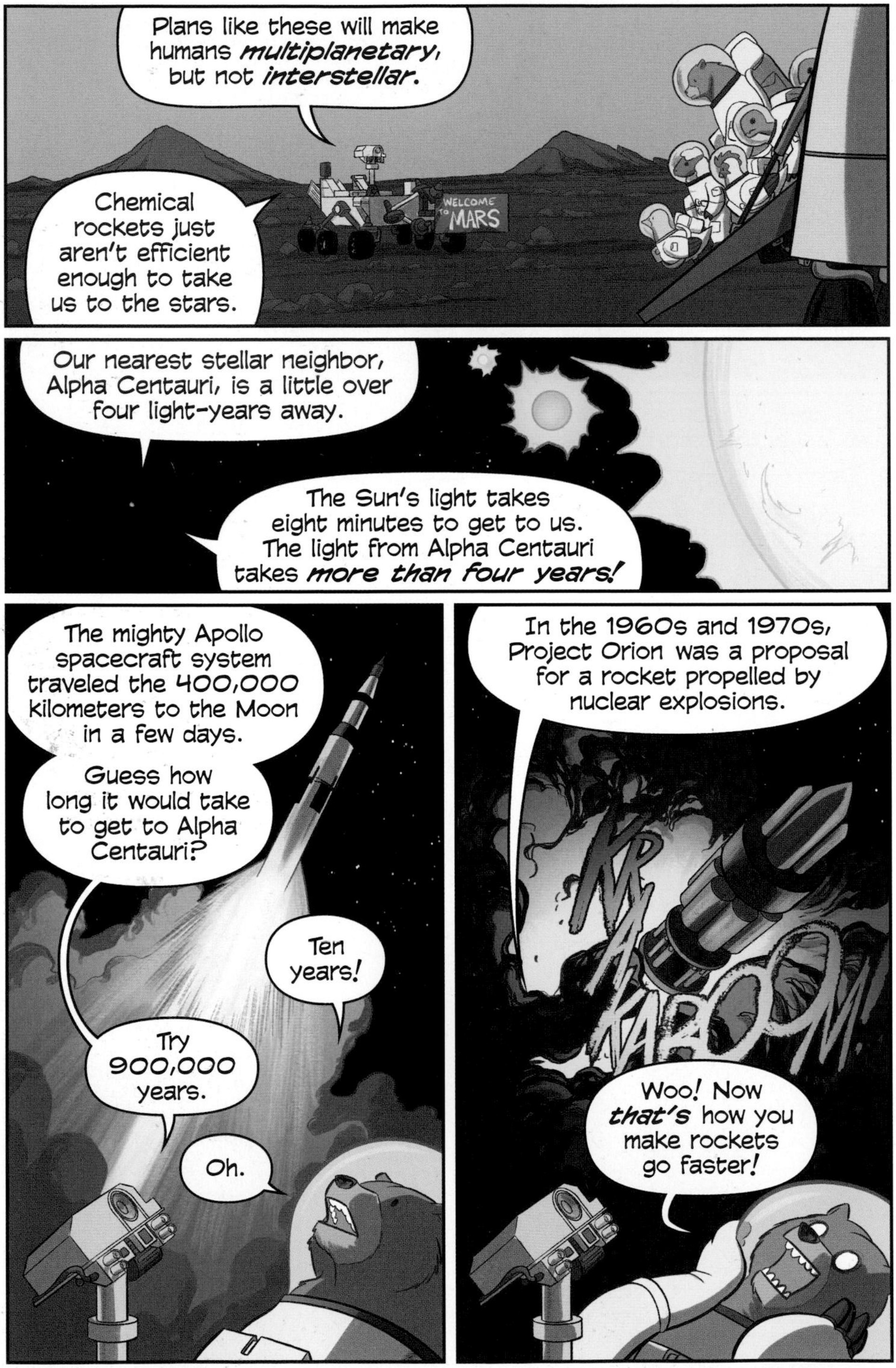

Plans like these will make humans *multiplanetary*, but not *interstellar*.
WELCOME TO MARS
Chemical rockets just aren't efficient enough to take us to the stars.
Our nearest stellar neighbor, Alpha Centauri, is a little over four light-years away.
The Sun's light takes eight minutes to get to us. The light from Alpha Centauri takes ***more than four years!***
The mighty Apollo spacecraft system traveled the 400,000 kilometers to the Moon in a few days.
Guess how long it would take to get to Alpha Centauri?
Ten years!
Try 900,000 years.
Oh.
In the 1960s and 1970s, Project Orion was a proposal for a rocket propelled by nuclear explosions.
KRAKABOOM
Woo! Now ***that's*** how you make rockets go faster!

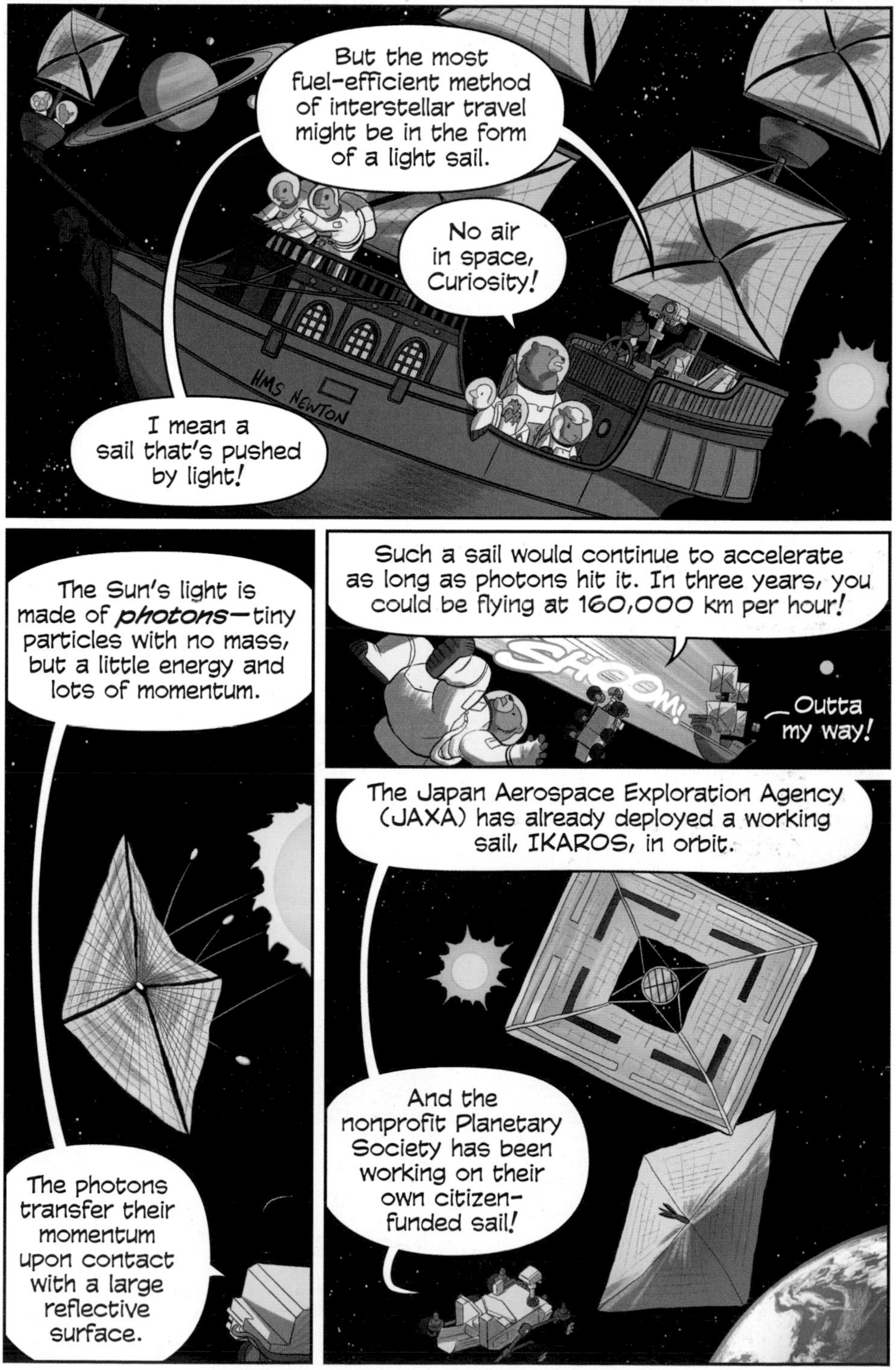

But the most fuel-efficient method of interstellar travel might be in the form of a light sail.
No air in space, Curiosity!
HMS NEWTON
I mean a sail that's pushed by light!
The Sun's light is made of *photons*—tiny particles with no mass, but a little energy and lots of momentum.
The photons transfer their momentum upon contact with a large reflective surface.
Such a sail would continue to accelerate as long as photons hit it. In three years, you could be flying at 160,000 km per hour!
SHOOM!
Outta my way!
The Japan Aerospace Exploration Agency (JAXA) has already deployed a working sail, IKAROS, in orbit.
And the nonprofit Planetary Society has been working on their own citizen-funded sail!

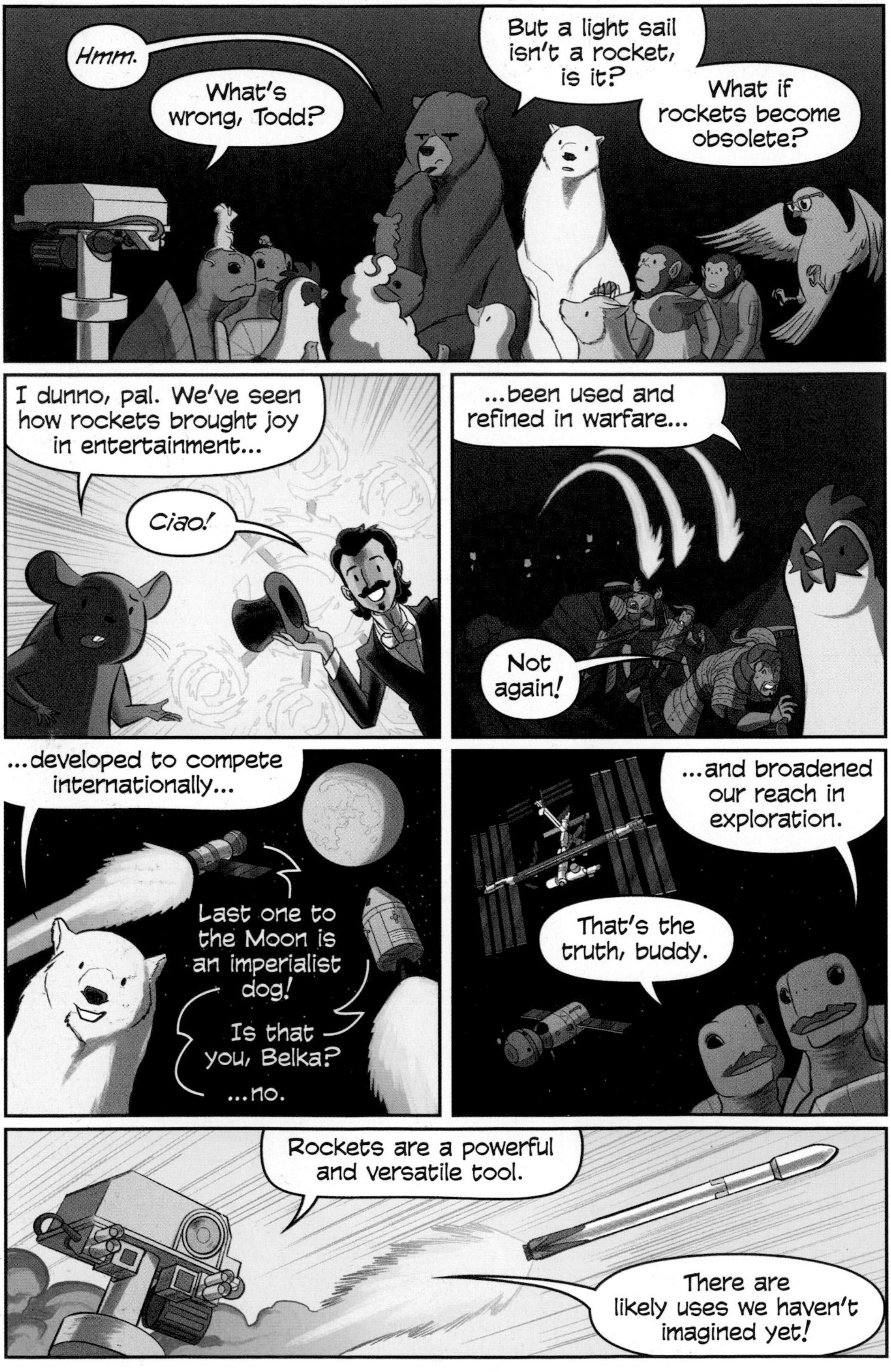
Hmm.
What's wrong, Todd?
But a light sail isn't a rocket, is it?
What if rockets become obsolete?
I dunno, pal. We've seen how rockets brought joy in entertainment...
Ciao!
...been used and refined in warfare...
Not again!
...developed to compete internationally...
Last one to the Moon is an imperialist dog!
Is that you, Belka?
...no.
...and broadened our reach in exploration.
That's the truth, buddy.
Rockets are a powerful and versatile tool.
There are likely uses we haven't imagined yet!

Okay, but I still need to know when bears are gonna ride rockets and go to other worlds and stuff!

You're doing it again.

Sorry.

That's a question for the young people reading this comic right now.

They are the ones who will decide how to work with animals and machines to take rockets into the future.

They're the ones who will start or join a rocket club at their library or school...

...they're the ones who will study math, science, and engineering. Together with them, you can make a future for rockets.

Cool! You hear that? We bears are counting on you!

Meet me at rocket cluuuuuuub!

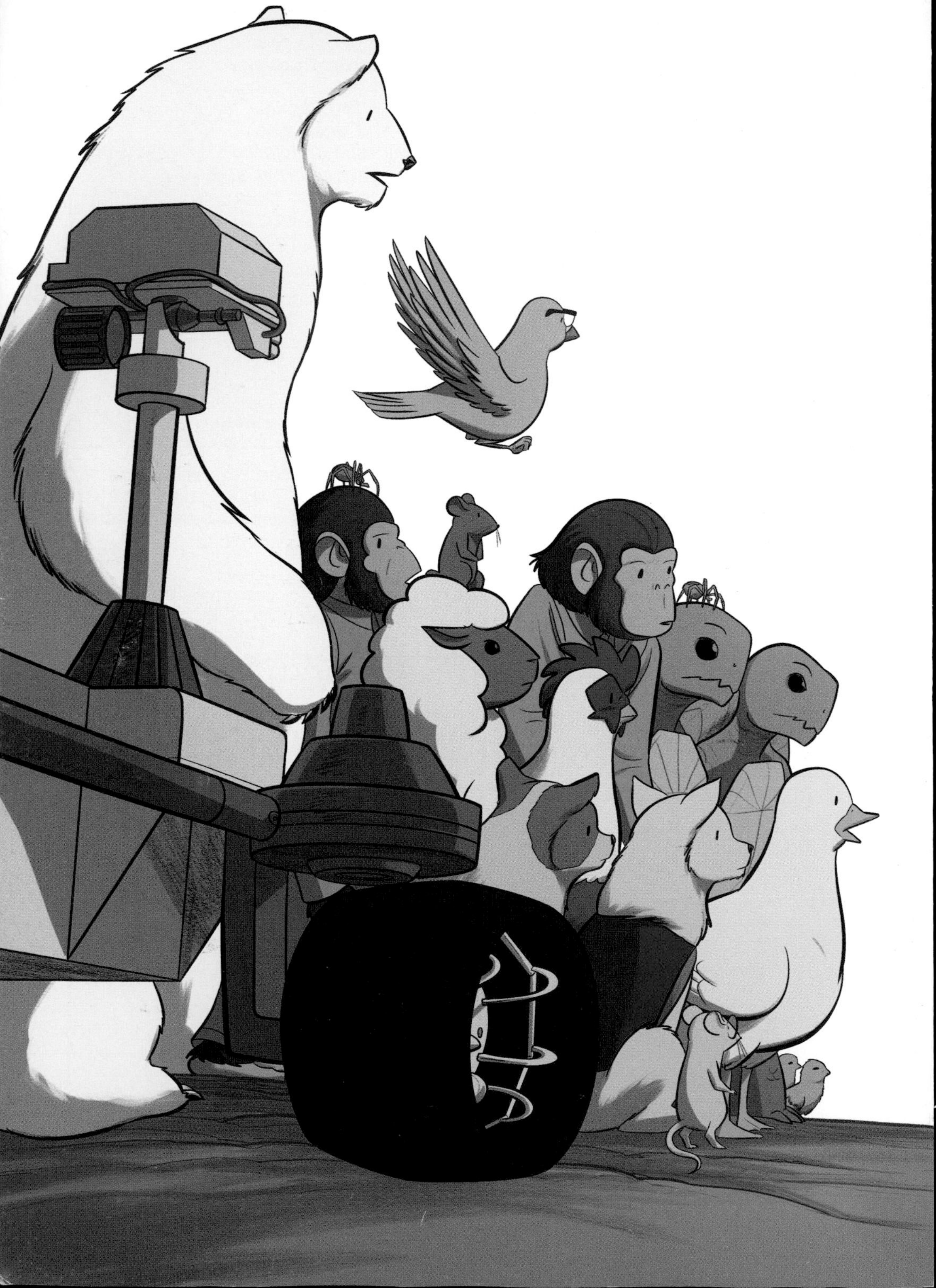

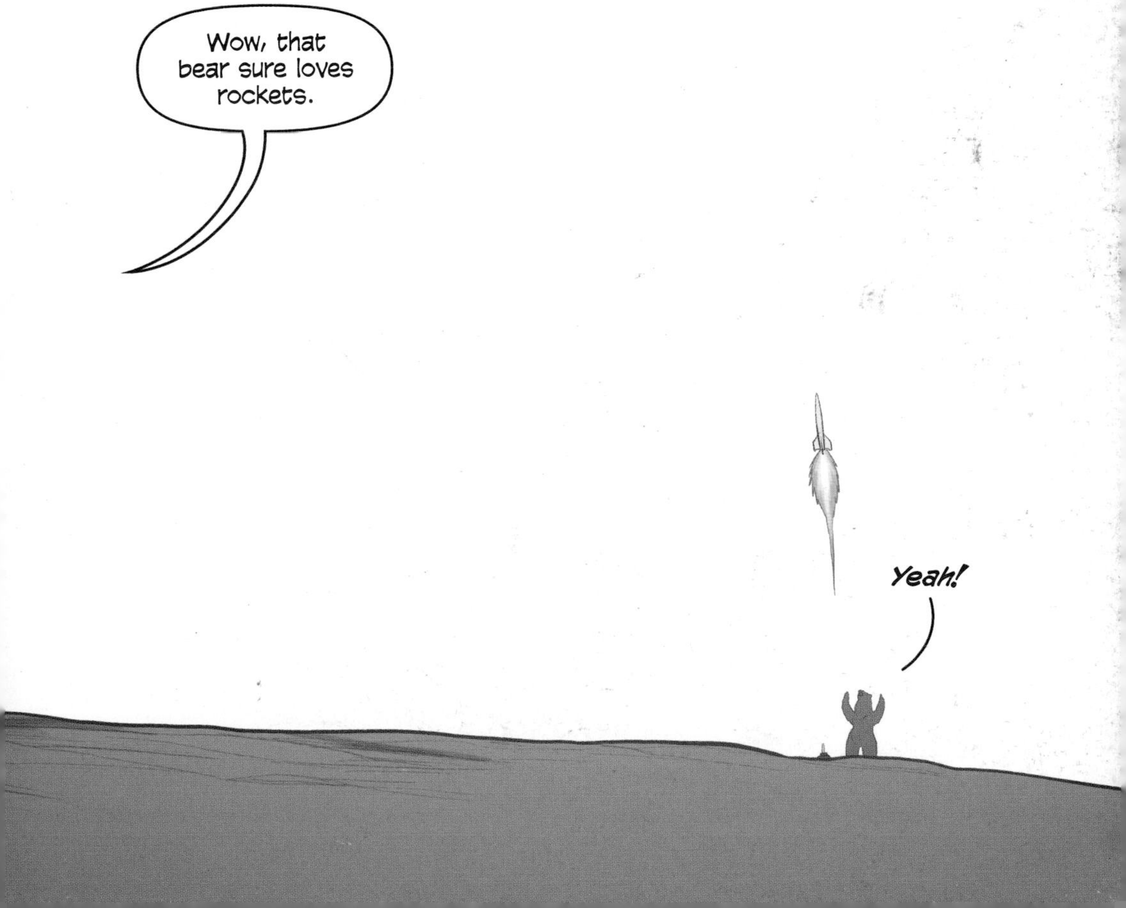
Wow, that bear sure loves rockets.
Yeah!

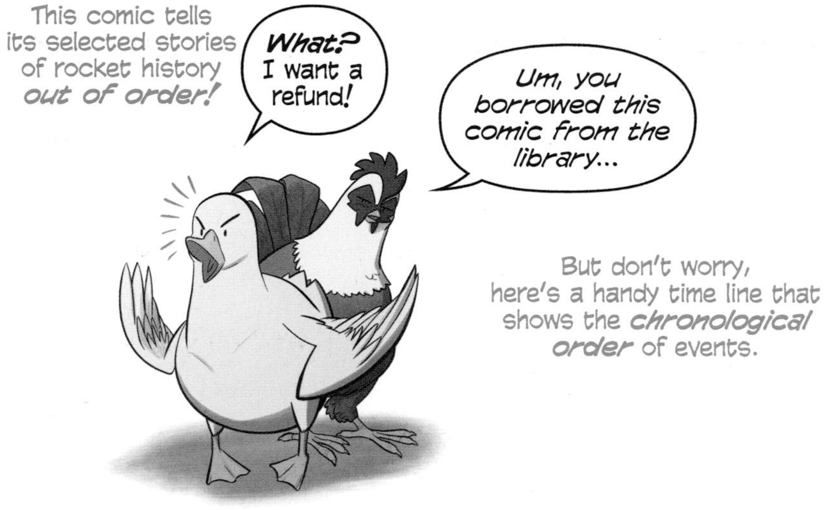
This comic tells its selected stories of rocket history *out of order!*
What? I want a refund!
Um, you borrowed this comic from the library...
But don't worry, here's a handy time line that shows the ***chronological order*** of events.

400 BCE — Archytas makes a steam-powered wooden pigeon — pages 2–3

1st Century CE — Gunpowder-filled bamboo sticks are used in Chinese religious festivals — page 24

Hero of Alexandria makes the aeolipile — page 4

1232 — Fire arrows turn the tide at the Battle of Kai-Keng — page 33

1379 — A rocket dove dazzles the crowds during an Italian mystery play — page 26

1564 — Johann Schmidlap's *Knüstliche und rechtschaffene Feuerwerk* is published — page 32

1687 — Isaac Newton's *Philosophiæ Naturalis Principia Mathematica* is published — page 6

1743 — The Ruggieris debut the spectacles pyrriques — page 28–29

1783 — The Montgolfier brothers launch their balloon with Sheep, Duck, and Rooster — page 21

1806 — Claude Ruggieri launches rocket full of rats with parachutes — page 21

1810 — Claude Ruggieri's *Élémens de pyrotechnie* is published — page 32

1865 — Jules Verne's *From the Earth to the Moon* is published — page 57

1873 — Konstantin Tsiolkovsky begins his formative years at the Russian State Library — page 56

1883 — Konstantin Tsiolkovsky writes *Free Space* — page 55

1903 — Konstantin Tsiolkovsky writes "Research into Interplanetary Space by Means of Rocket Power" — page 55

1926 — Robert Goddard launches the first successful liquid-propellant rocket — page 58

1930 — Robert Goddard begins setting up his lab in Roswell, New Mexico — page 52

1936 — The Suicide Squad is formed, soon followed by the creation of the Jet Propulsion Laboratory (JPL) — pages 42–43

1937 — Walter Dornberger and Wernher von Braun begin development of the A-4 rocket (later called the V-2) — page 39

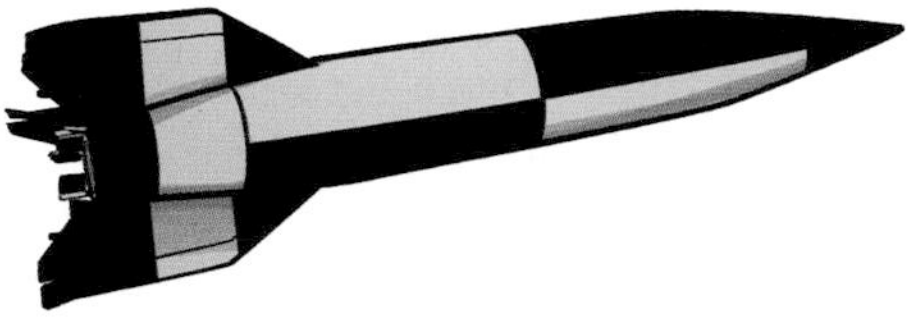

1940 — Project Pigeon — page 38

1944 — Wernher von Braun and his team are arrested by the Gestapo for talking about space too much — page 50

1945 — The United States military hires former Nazi sceintists and forgives their war crimes in Operation Paperclip — page 76

1947 — John Paul Stapp arrives at Project MX-981 and begins work on the Gee Whiz — page 47

1950 — JPL launches the Bumper WAC — page 43

A general suggests awarding one of Stapp's rocket chimps a medal for bravery — page 48

Bears are used to test ejector seat technology — page 49

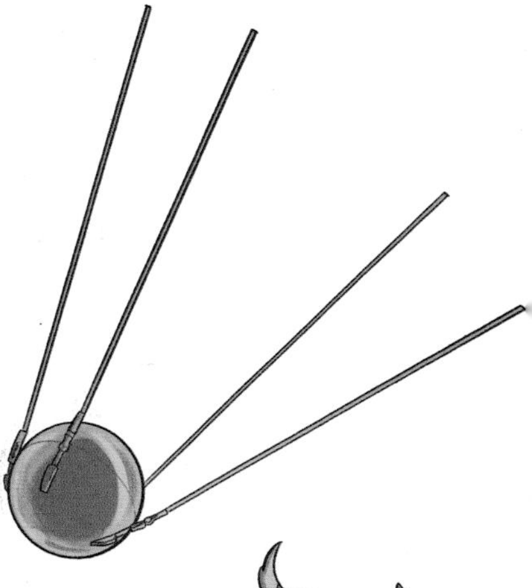

1955 — James Hagerty pledges the USA will launch Earth circling satellites by 1957 — page 76

1957 — Sputnik 1 launches — page 68

Mary Sherman Morgan invents Hydyne and saves the US space program — page 67–73

1958 — Explorer 1 launches — page 73

President Eisenhower establishes the National Aeronautics and Space Administration (NASA) — page 79

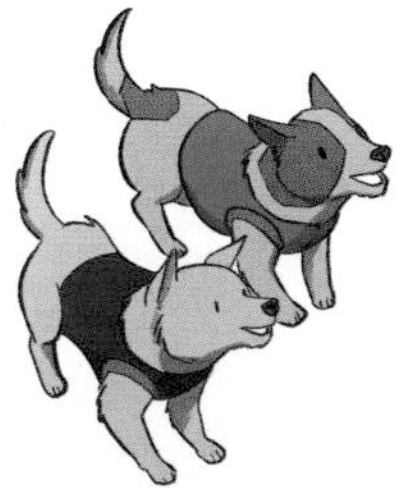

1960 — Belka and Strelka go to space on Sputnik 5 — page 78

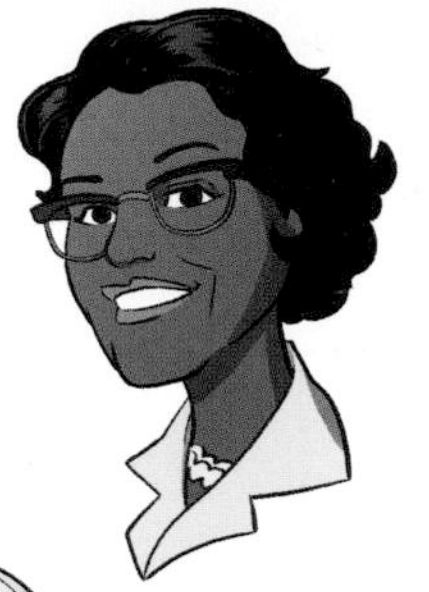

1961 Katherine Johnson peforms trajectory analysis for the Freedom 7 launch — page 87

1962 President Kennedy pledges to put humans on the Moon before 1970 — page 79

1963 Edwin "Buzz" Aldrin writes his thesis *Line-of-Sight Guidance Techniques for Manned Orbital Rendezvous* — page 86

Margaret Hamilton develops software for Apollo vehicles — page 87

Valentina Tereshkova flies in Vostok 6 — page 89

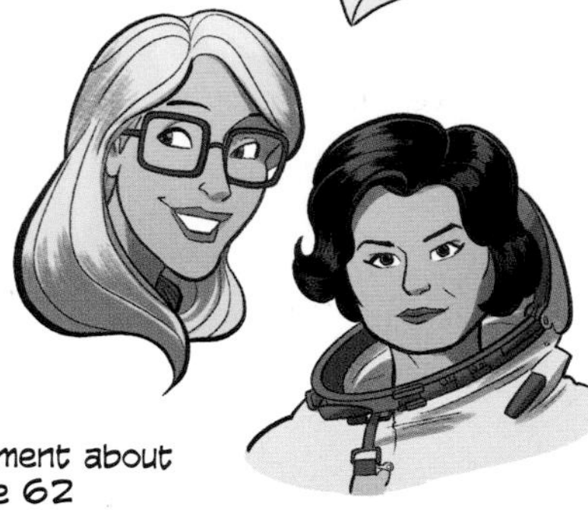

1968 Zond 5 orbits the Moon — page 93

Apollo 8 orbits the Moon — page 92

1969 Apollo 11 launches — page 62

The *New York Times* retracts its statement about rockets not working in a vacuum — page 62

1971 The Salyut series begins — page 96

1973 Skylab launches — page 96

Anita and Arabella spin webs on Skylab — page 100

Mariner 10 launches — page 104

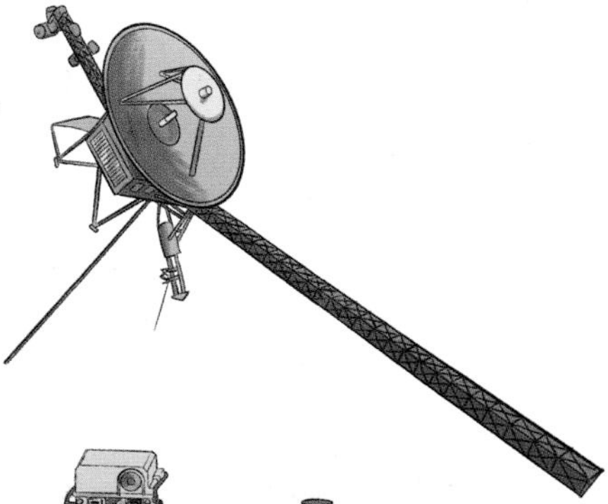

1975 Viking probe launches — page 102

Apollo-Soyuz becomes the first international docking in space — page 96

1977 Voyager 1 launches — page 104

1986 The Soviet Union begins work on their Mir space station - pg 97

1996 NASA issues updated guidelines for the ethical treatment of animals — page 101

1998 The International Space Station (ISS) is launched— page 97

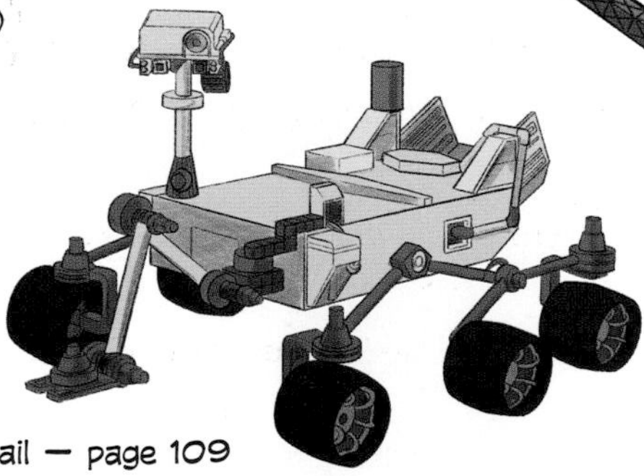

2002 SpaceX is founded — page 105

2003 The Mars Exploration Rover (MER) missions begin — page 102

2010 The Japan Aerospace Exploration Agency (JAXA) launches the IKAROS solar sail — page 109

2011 Curiosity Rover launches - pg 101

2017 The Planetary Society launches LightSail — page 109

—GLOSSARY—

Acceleration — To change the speed of an object over time.

Center of mass (cm) — The point on an object where its mass is equally balanced on both sides.

Center of pressure (cp) — The point on an airborne object where the drag and lift forces acting on it are equal.

Center of thrust (cot) — The midpoint where thrust from a craft's reaction engines balances and the direction in which a craft's thrust is acting.

Drag — The resistance air exerts on a body moving through it.

Escape velocity — The velocity at which an object would escape the gravitational attraction of a given astronomical body. The escape velocity of the Earth is 11.2 kilometers per second.

Euthanize — To put to death without pain.

Exhaust velocity — The speed at which gas escapes from a rocket.

Fins — Fixed rudders on a rocket to help give it direction.

Flaps — Movable rudders, either attached to the fins or placed in the jet of a rocket, to direct the flight.

Force — A push or pull that changes the speed or direction of an object.

Friction — The resistance that one surface or object encounters when moving over another.

Fuel — The combustible component of a rocket propellant.

g (lowercase) — The symbol for gravity, the unit of acceleration, equal to 9.81 meters per second every second.

Gimbal — A pivoted support mechanism that allows attached objects to rotate around a central axis.

G-force — The force of gravity or acceleration on a body.

Gravity assist — The technique of using the energy of a gravitational field and the orbital velocity of a planet to change the speed and trajectory of a spacecraft.

Gyroscope — A device with a spinning disc used to stabilize, guide, or measure rotational movement.

Inertia — The tendency of matter to stay at rest or stay in motion unless acted upon by an outside force.

Initial mass — The mass of a rocket at the beginning of flight.

—GLOSSARY CONTINUED—

Initial velocity — The velocity of a rocket at the start of the firing period.

Mass — The amount of matter in an object.

Nozzle — A narrow opening at the base of a rocket that controls the flow of exhaust gases from its engine.

Orbit — The curved path an object or spacecraft around a star, planet, or moon.

Orientation — The determination of the relative position of something.

Oxidizer — A chemical needed by a fuel in order to burn. Most fuels use the oxygen in our atmosphere as their oxidizer, but a rocket must carry its own oxidizer when traveling into the vacuum of space.

Payload — The useful load carried by the rocket, in addition to its necessary structural weight and fuel.

Physics — The science of matter, motion, force, and energy.

Pitch — How a rocket is rotated on the y-axis. It describes whether the rocket's nose is up or down.

Propellant — A combination of fuel and oxidizer that burns to produce thrust in a rocket.

Rest — The state of an object when there are no unbalanced forces acting on it.

Rocket — An enclosed chamber with gas under pressure.

Roll — How a rocket is rotated on the x-axis. It describes the rotation of the rocket around an axis running from nose to tail.

Serial staging — A rocket consisting of several sections or "steps" fired successively, each step being jettisoned when its fuel is exhausted.

Space rendezvous — A series of orbital maneuvers to bring two spacecraft in close proximity.

Throat — The narrowest part of a rocket motor nozzle.

Thrust — The push produced by a jet or rocket motor.

Trajectory — The path followed by a projectile flying or an object moving under the action of given forces.

Vacuum — A space in which there is no air.

Yaw — How a rocket is rotated on the z-axis. It describes whether the nose is left or right.

—FURTHER READING—

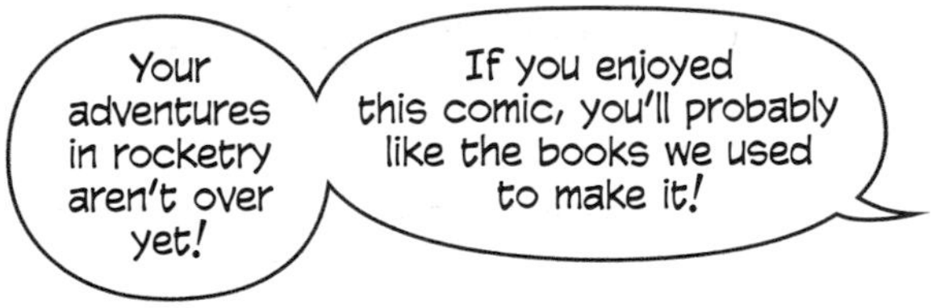
Your adventures in rocketry aren't over yet!
If you enjoyed this comic, you'll probably like the books we used to make it!

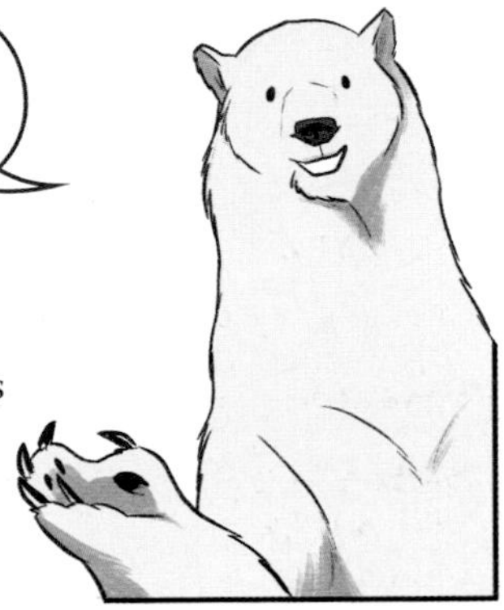

Gruntman, Mike. *Blazing the Trail: The Early History of Spacecraft and Rocketry*. American Institute of Aeronautics and Astronautics, 2004.

The History of Rocket Technology: Essays on Research, Development, and Utility, edited by Eugene M. Emme. Wayne State University Press, 1964.

Jet Propulsion: Journal of the American Rocket Society, v. 14–17. American Rocket Society, 1944–1947.

Morgan, George D. *Rocket Girl: The Story of Mary Sherman Morgan, America's First Female Rocket Scientist*. Prometheus Books, 2013.

Pyle, Rod. *Curiosity: An Inside Look at the Mars Rover Mission and the People Who Made It Happen*. Prometheus Books, 2014.

Rogers, Lucy. *It's ONLY Rocket Science: An Introduction in Plain English*. Springer, 2008.

Ryan, Craig. *Sonic Wind: The Story of John Paul Stapp and How a Renegade Doctor Became the Fastest Man on Earth*. W.W. Norton & Company, 2015.

Shetterly, Margot Lee. *Hidden Figures: The American Dream and the Untold Story of the Black Women Mathmeticians Who Helped Win the Space Race*. HarperCollins, 2016.

Vogt, Gregory L. *Rockets, information and activities for elementary teachers to use in preparing students for a unit on model rocketry*. NASA, 1992.

Werrett, Simon. *Fireworks: Pyrotechnic Arts & Sciences in European History*. The University of Chicago Press, 2010.

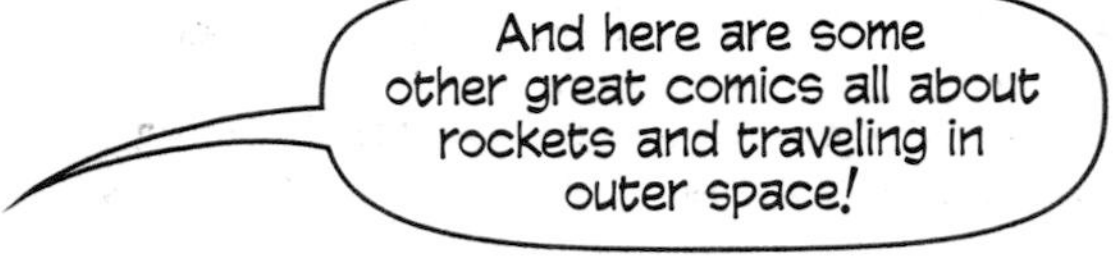
And here are some other great comics all about rockets and traveling in outer space!

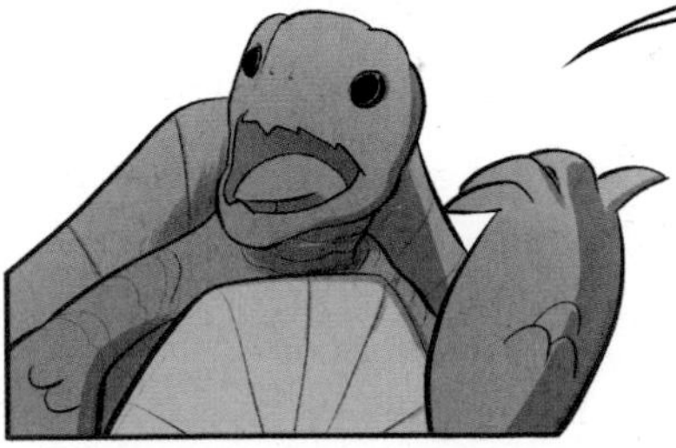

Abadzis, Nick. *Laika*. First Second Books, 2007.

Ottaviani, Jim, Zander Cannon, Kevin Cannon. *T-Minus: The Race to the Moon*. Alladin, 2009.

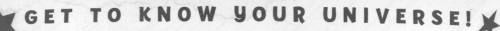

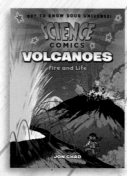